Joseph Henry Allen

# Fragments of Christian History

# FRAGMENTS

## OF

# CHRISTIAN HISTORY

*TO THE FOUNDATION OF THE HOLY
ROMAN EMPIRE*

BY

## JOSEPH HENRY ALLEN

*Lecturer on Ecclesiastical History in Harvard University*

*(Author of " Hebrew Men and Times," &c.)*

Cujus omnis religio est sine scelere ac maculâ vivere.
LACTANTIUS.

BOSTON
ROBERTS BROTHERS
1880

UNIVERSITY PRESS:
JOHN WILSON AND SON, CAMBRIDGE.

# PREFACE.

MOST of these "Fragments" have appeared, from time to time, in various journals, and I have been repeatedly asked to bring them together in a more convenient form. It certainly is not altogether such a form as I could wish, or as I might possibly attempt with a longer prospect of working time. The book is but a slender gleaning in a wide field, which has been well reaped by stronger hands.

Still, it exhibits, as fairly as I can give, a view of the subject which I have never seen properly worked out. In whatever way we regard the origin and early growth of Christianity, whether as special revelation or as historic evolution, it appears to me that the key to it is to be found, not in its speculative dogma, not in its ecclesiastical organization, not even in what strictly constitutes its religious life, but in its fundamentally ethical character. In either way of understanding it, it is first of all a gospel for the salvation of human life. And to this primary notion of it everything else has been subordinated to a degree that astonishes me more and more as I look into its original documents. A motive so intense and so profound — however crude and misinformed — as to dominate the reason and imagination for more than a thousand years, and to create a civilization which had (we may say) every great quality except that of a voice for its own interpretation, which stifled thought in the interest of morality, which reduced art after its rich classic development to a bald symbolism, and made a free science or literature impossible, — whatever else we may think of it, is certainly an amazing and unique phenomenon in human history. From Constantine to Dante that is, substantially, the fact we have to study. The Fragments that follow are designed as a contribution to the right understanding of it.

This volume is very far from claiming to be a history. Yet just as little is it a compilation. The judgments it expresses are such as have been ripening during thirty years of reasonable familiarity with most of the phases of the subject I have attempted to present; and they rest, in all cases, upon the acquaintance I have been able to make with the original sources of the history. I was so fortunate as to begin these studies within reach of the Congressional Library at Washington, which is (or was) exceptionally rich in the earlier authorities; and to continue them as part of my stated labors here, with the far ampler treasures of the University Library at command. Of course I have availed myself, where I could, of modern expositors and standard historians, — of which due acknowledgment is made in the notes. My constant authorities, however, have been the volumes of the Fathers, of the early historians, and especially of Migne's *Patrologia*, both Greek and Latin. I have endeavored to keep true to the maxim which ought to govern such an exposition: that it should include the secular as well as the religious side of events; that it should deal primarily with moral forces rather than speculative opinions or institutional forms; and that it should rest at all points directly on original authorities, wherever these are accessible.

A brief Chronological Outline has been added, not as sufficient for the uses of the student, but in order to make the bearing of allusions and events more distinct to those who are not otherwise familiar with the ground. To the student the standard historians, especially Gieseler and Neander, to the general reader Milman's histories and Greenwood's *Cathedra Petri*, to those who seek sufficient information in the briefest space the excellent text-book of Philip Smith, may be recommended to fill in the sketch which is here attempted. Better still, perhaps, would be Smith's Dictionary of Christian Biography, just completed, and covering almost the precise period included here.   But it cannot be too strongly urged that some acquaintance with Catholic authorities — as Rohrbacher, Ozanam, Montalembert — is indispensable, if not to a knowledge of the facts, at least to an apprehension of the spirit and motive, of this early time.   I may add, that this volume is, in a sense, a continuation of " Hebrew Men and Times," in which some of the earlier topics will be found presented in more detail than the present plan admits ; and that I hope to follow it by a similar review of the Mediæval and of the Modern period.

I should not do justice to my own feeling, without adding here the acknowledgment of my constant obligation to Professor F. H. Hedge, D. D., my predecessor in this lectureship, whose learning and eloquence are known to many ; whom fewer, perhaps, have known so well as one of the wisest of teachers, one of the kindest and most generous of friends.

HARVARD DIVINITY SCHOOL,
September, 1880.

# CONTENTS.


Introduction: Study of Christian History . . ix

I. The Messiah and the Christ . . . . . . . 1
II. Saint Paul . . . . . . . . . . . . . . 21
III. Christian Thought of the Second Century 47
IV. The Mind of Paganism . . . . . . . . . 71
V. The Arian Controversy . . . . . . . . 100
VI. Saint Augustine . . . . . . . . . . . 122
VII. Leo the Great . . . . . . . . . . . . 146
VIII. Monasticism as a Moral Force . . . . . 165
IX. Christianity in the East . . . . . . . . 185
X. Conversion of the Barbarians . . . . . . 204
XI. The Holy Roman Empire . . . . . . . 227
XII. The Christian Schools . . . . . . . . . 249

Chronological Outline . . . . . . . . . . 275
Index . . . . . . . . . . . . . . . . . 279

# INTRODUCTION.

## ON THE STUDY OF CHRISTIAN HISTORY.

AMONG those who accept Christianity as a revelation, in the most definite sense they are able to give that word, there are two contrary ways of regarding it. One considers it as an interpolation in human things, — a " scheme of salvation " introduced at a definite time, completely apart from anything that went before, except as the way may have been prepared for it by a series of special providences. The other considers it as a manifestation of the Divine life common to humanity, coming in the fulness of time, and as much prepared for by all that went before as a crop of fruit is ripened by the sunshine and showers of the whole season. One sees it as a communication from without; the other, as a development from within. In the illustrations I shall attempt to give of it, I shall frankly take the latter view.

As soon, however, as we begin to follow up this view, we find ourselves quite outside the limits of " ecclesiastical history " as usually defined. Our field is, in fact, as broad as civilization itself: only that we deal not so much with its external forms, its institutions and events, but with its governing and directing forces in the thought, heart, and conscience of its representative men. What we call the history of dogma is really a very curious and instructive chapter in the development of speculative thought, — that record of intellectual effort and error, opening out from Thales all the way down to Hegel or Comte. What we call ecclesiastical polity is really one of the most interesting chapters in the development of social or political institutions, — those way-marks, guides, and buttresses of the structure of civilization itself. What we call church ceremonial is really the most skilful, the most subtile, the most effective appeal to human imagination, as one of the chief governing principles of conduct, — reaching all the way from simple decoration of altar or vestment to the splendors of form, color, and vocal or instrumental harmony in a great cathedral, or the tender impressiveness of a Catholic procession. What we call hierarchical domination — resting on the terrors of eternity, and ever at war with the powers of the world — is really the form authority came to take in the struggle, by which the expanding life of humanity has been lifted so many degrees above the savage or the brute. What we call canon law is really the summing up of several centuries' effort, by rule and precedent, to construct a code of morality, and with it to create a new social system, amidst the wreck of ancient society, or in presence of the brutal disorders of barbarian invasion. We allow for the error, the false ambition, the priestly cunning, the ecclesiastical tyranny, just as we allow for the violences, the vices, and the shames that run through all the record of human affairs. They are incidents in that wider, that universal " struggle for existence," which is the appointed means whereby Divine Providence attains its ends.

Now, history shows us many well-defined and easily distinguishable types of civilization, — Egyptian, Classic Pagan, Mahometan, Indian ; and among these types the Christian civilization is to be reckoned, — as we hold, the highest and most developed hitherto. Our present business is to see, as clearly as we can, just what this is in itself. In the study of comparative religions, which is one of the boasts of our day, we should at least make sure of *one* of the things to be compared. And this will be best done, as it is done in natural history, by patient, detailed, accurate study of its facts and features. These, it is true, are found in what is somewhat intangible, — in the thoughts and lives of a great many men, scattered along through a great period of time. But, if we will think of it, the scientific method of study — that is, of comparison and judgment, as opposed to the method of heaping up mere multiplicity of facts — is the true one, as Saint Paul himself suggests, when he speaks of his new converts as olive-shoots, grafted upon a hardy stock. It is no disparagement to pine, beech, or maple, to claim that the olive has a natural history of its own.

Again, as already hinted, this history is to be studied, in the main, on its ethical or ideal side, and not merely in the record of its facts and dates. Christianity has been not merely a type, shaping men's lives unconsciously, like the type, or law of growth, of any organic product. This it has been also, in the highest, the divine, which is also the purely scientific sense. But not only this. It has been vividly conceived in the thought of its believers as the true and only solution to the great mystery of the universe. It has been adoringly received in faith, as the symbol of the holiest the heart can love or worship. It has been earnestly, humbly, obediently accepted by the conscience, as the sovereign law of life. In each one of these three ways it has been held with fanaticism and intolerance. But in each of these three ways, also, it has been held humbly, reverently, piously, valiantly, and has thus been a great power to move the world. The right place to study it is not in its errors, ignorances, bigotries, and crimes. It must be studied in its great and brave sincerities, as witnessed by its glorious martyr-roll, blood-stained, fire-scorched; by its record of heroic names, from those who bore the faith like a flag before the despotisms of Rome or the barbarisms of Germany and Scandinavia, down to the last missionary who died for it in field or hospital; in the lives of its great patient thinkers, the prayers of its saints, the glad, tender, or triumphant strains of its choruses and hymns, the fidelity of many generations of humble, trustful, victorious lives. These are what it is the historian's chief business to set forth. These are what we mean when we say it should be studied first of all on its ideal side, and not in that which is false, cruel, turbulent, and base.

Again, when we speak of a type of civilization, or a type of mental life, we mean not something that is fixed and still, as a crystallographer or a dogmatist might understand it. The life we speak of pours in a generous flood from its unknown source to its unknown future. Scientific criticism in these days does not spare anything from its rigid search. . Of course it rationalizes upon the origins of Christianity, as it does upon everything else. But, for our present purpose, we have nothing to do with any of its speculations. Our business is with the stream itself. Theology assumes for its postulate, that the origin of all life is in God, — that is, in a source that is everywhere present and always giving forth, inexhaustible, infinite, essentially one with perfect wisdom, justice, and love.

Just how these attributes of the Infinite Life were embodied for their earthly manifestation in the person of the Founder of Christianity, has been the most fruitful ground of speculation and controversy. But, anterior to all these speculations, it is well for us to have as distinct a conception as we can of that large historic life which we denominate Christian. And this, not by theoretical distinctions or abstract definitions, but by seeing it "manifest in the flesh": that is, not merely in the "one greater Man" (as Milton calls him), of whom that phrase was first used, but (as Leo the Great interprets) in all of the innumerable company who have received and have worthily shared that life.

Accordingly, the right study of Christian history consists mainly in the study of MORAL FORCES: that is, forces which bear on men on the side of character and conduct. Of itself, state it as simply as we will, this means a great deal. Conduct, says Matthew Arnold, is at least three quarters of human life; and when to this we add character which it springs from, and aspiration which makes its ideal, and the education of conscience which gives its law, we have pretty nearly mapped out the whole field of practical religion as opposed to the purely theoretic.

Now we want a phrase which denotes sharply that characteristic of religion most important to consider as affecting human life. Such a phrase, for example, is "enthusiasm of humanity," which we find in *Ecce Homo*, as best describing the religion of Jesus and his disciples. But it seems to me that the higher and broader phrase ETHICAL PASSION denotes better the quality I mean. Whatever else religion may include, at any rate it means this. A strong and victorious religious movement takes place, when the ethical passion I speak of is blended with the mode of thinking dominant at a given time. Indeed, a better definition could hardly be given of an historical religion than the coincidence of these two, originating with some crisis in human affairs. The passion itself is the essential motive force: its association with one or another form of dogma seems almost pure accident.

I do not, of course, claim that this noblest of the passions is peculiar to Christianity among the religions of the world. In its elements, it certainly is not. In degree, at least, I think it is, — certainly in that line by which, through Puritanism up to primitive Christianity, we trace our own spiritual descent. As to this, however, we need assume nothing at all. Christianity at all events has shown itself in the world primarily as a moral force. It is this quality in it that we have first of all to keep in view in the different phases of it we shall meet. Its creed, its symbols, its institutions, are what they are in the history of mankind because they are expressions of that force. They are superficial; the ethical passion they embody is fundamental.

It shows itself in many ways: with Paul, in earnest contrition and conviction of sin; with Howard, in the deep sense of evil and suffering among men; with Savonarola, in flaming wrath against hypocrisy and injustice; with mystic and monastic, in rude austerities or ecstatic fervors. It appears in the patient pondering of moral problems, with the Schoolmen; in willing and brave self-sacrifice, with the Pilgrims; in endurance of persecution, with the Martyrs; in heroism of battle, with the Covenanters; in recoil from a corrupt society, with the Anchorites; in rapturous visions of a reign of holiness, with the Saints. In all these shapes that intenser form of moral emotion which we rightly name the ethical passion may appear: its characteristic being, not merely that conscience, as against pleasure or gain, is taken for the law of life — which it has in common with the Stoics; but that conscience, so obeyed, becomes a source of enthusiasm, a ground of faith and hope, an inspiration of the will. As what Mr. Arnold calls " the lyrical cry" is not only a mark of genuine poetry, but makes the tone of true devotion, and so is the voice of religion in the way of emotional fervor, appealing to the Infinite; so the ethical passion I have named is the very heart of true religion on its manward side, and is the characteristic we have chiefly to seek and verify in the study of its history.

This suggests, again, the direction our study should take: namely, that its field chiefly lies in the lives and thought of individual men. A great deal has been said of the philosophy of history, and of the study of history as a science. But, in much of this discussion, what is after all the chief glory, interest, and value of historical study is apt to be overlooked. History studied *as science* tends to degenerate at once to anthropology; studied *as history*, its great value will be found in its appeal to imagination, its widening of the sympathy, and its education of the moral sense. Of course, we want to know all that can be given in the wide view and nice distinctions of philosophy, in the accurate terms and orderly arrangement of science. And we need not dispute whether either of them is or is not a more valuable study than history proper in itself. But, in respect of our immediate purpose, they only serve as a framework for the picture; they merely outline the conditions under which the study of history is to be had.

This is the study of human life itself, — its action and its passion ; of life on its personal, suffering, dramatic, rejoicing, heroic side ; of its sin and holiness, its error and its strength, its struggle and its grief. Nothing, in fact, is more dramatic than the life shown us in the field we enter, as soon as we pierce beyond the veil that distance of time or strangeness of dialect has thrown about it. The true way to know the men whose lives are the history we would learn, is to come as close to them as the barriers of time, distance, and language will allow ; to seek always the original sources first, at least under the briefest guidance and exposition ; never to satisfy ourselves with dissertations, abridgments, compends, or " standard historians " ; to listen to each man's words, so far as we have ability or opportunity, in the tongue he learned from his mother, and talked with his own kinsfolk, and wrote with his own pen. A single page, read in that way, brings us nearer to the man, gives us better (so to speak) the feel of his pulse, the light of his eye, and the complexion of his face, than whole chapters of commentary and paraphrase.

We have all learned, long ago, that faith is a very different thing from opinion. Yet we do not always reflect how wrongly men's historical judgments are colored by their opinions, or how shallow and poor those judgments often are, from the mere lack of power to comprehend — we might even say pardon — any very strong and sincere conviction at all. Thus of Gibbon — so masterly in grasp, so unwearied in research, so subtile in suggestion, our indispensable daily companion and guide in a large part of the field we have to investigate — the instances are rare in which he has not done wrong to the topic or the character he was treating, and let down the moral tone of a great man or a great event, such as the record fairly gives, by his strange incapacity of historic sympathy. So that, in a very large part of it, — not only in his famous chapters on early Christianity but in his treatment of each critical epoch or heroic life, — his work, indispensable for its outlines and its facts, is a masterly and very perfect model of what our study of the history ought not to be.

Again, we must be clear of that besetting sin of theologians, a controversial motive. We are not pledged, in any sense, to uphold one set of opinions, or disparage others. Our true business is to understand, if we can, the men who held them, and why they held them. The world of thought and belief has so shifted in all its bearings, that we can never be quite sure we have the mind of the early age; while the world of passion and motive remains fundamentally the same. Very good men have held in honesty of heart opinions wholly false and shocking to us. Their thin ghosts do not flit before our bar for judgment. Nay, when those men lived, they were drawn by the tragic and terrible logic of their opinions to acts in our view inconceivably hateful. In all history there is perhaps nothing quite so awful as the religious wars, the infernal tortures of Inquisition and dragonnade, the frightful persecutions of mere opinion, deliberately inflicted, for centuries, in the name of faith; so that the very phrase " act of faith," translated into Spanish, is perhaps of all human phrases ghastliest in its suggestion. I have no more the will than the power to exclude these horrors from our field, for the sake of a serener view. Humanity does well to hate the name and curse the memory of them. But our task, even for these, is to see them in their causes; to trace how they were linked in fatally with the train of opinions and events; to see how bad men could have found means to bring them to pass, and how good men could possibly have been led to consent to them as a pardonable alternative from something worse.

A very large part of our history is the record of controversies, in which we have no occasion whatever to take sides as partisans. Our business is rather to see, if we can, how each side was an element in the necessary evolution; and how a gain in mind, morals, or society is brought about, not by sudden victories of the truer opinion, but by the very obstinate conflict itself, in which each party fights toughly, whether for the gold or the silver side of the shield of truth. We have our own battles to fight; and we cannot afford to revive the passions of those ancient ones.

A word of the periods into which the history naturally falls. The main points of departure — the nodal points, so to speak, marking most visibly the coincidence of the spiritual and secular evolution — are most conveniently taken at the end of the eighth century, and at the end of the fifteenth. The three periods so given, considered in reference to the type of Christian civilization before spoken of, may be called the period of its struggle for existence, of its dominance in a definite historic form, and of its differentiation or expansion. The first extends from the origin of Christianity, through the time of its conflict with Classic paganism on one hand, and Barbaric paganism on the other, down to the founding of the Christian empire of Charlemagne. The second extends through what is called the Middle Age of European history, the period of feudal society, of the crusades, of the Holy Apostolic Church dominant under the great popes and the Holy Roman Empire dominant under the great imperial houses, down to and including the revival of art and learning, and the period of the great discoveries which initiated the broader life of the modern world. The third begins with the controversies of the Protestant Reformation, and follows its results in the liberalizing of thought, the development of speculative philosophy and scientific criticism, the vast growth of natural science (far more important to us in its effect on men's habit of thought than in its wealth of fact or its practical skill), the great movements of modern society and politics of the revolutionary period, in which we are living now.

Naturally and rightly, these last are of vastly greater consequence to us than anything in the past. Moreover, they are precisely the issues to which the great evolution of religious life in the past has conducted us. But no stage of it need be followed in the spirit of dogmatists, pedants, or archæologists. The life-stream whose course we are endeavoring to trace flows through channels, takes on forms and qualities, that enter deeply into the spirit of our own life. Not only, then, the echoes of the past are to be heard, but its footsteps traced, and its spirit felt, and its lessons heeded, on the spot where we stand, and in the moment of time when we breathe. For us, its earliest tradition is still alive. The record contained in so many ponderous volumes is not an antiquarian curiosity, like those title-deeds lately turned up in bricks and tiles of Nebuchadnezzar's time ; but is like a merchant's ledger, which lies always open to record the transactions of to-day.

The antiquarian may learn facts and dates ; but facts and dates are not history. They are at best the "raw materials," which must be "cooked" (as our friend in the story-book sagely says) before they are fit food for the human mind. It is the very business of history to turn dead facts into live truths ; to assort, co-ordinate, arrange them, find out their bearing on one another, and their relation to the life they cover, — often, it is true, as tombstones cover the forms once warm with eager life. It is not that we disparage facts. On the contrary, the mind in search of truth hungers and thirsts for them. But one must not be mistaken for the other. A hundred thousand facts will very likely go to the making of a single truth.

And for method, the simplest is the best: that is, to fix a few marked lives and dates, " as nails in a sure place." A very few, well fixed, will give us the latitude and longitude of our facts, and save them from being mislaid or lost. I once watched an artist beginning to draw a portrait. He measured with a straight stick one or two dimensions, marked them on his panel, took rapidly the bearings with his eye, made a few swift strokes ; and, almost in less time than it takes to tell, my mother's face, dim and faint, began to be shadowed out under his trained hand, which hours and days of patient skill would be needed to complete, but with features and expression already there. In some such way, if not with an artist's skill, yet with his patient accuracy, we may so outline this vast and magnificent field of our inquiry as never to lose from memory the features and expression of that life which we accept as a continual and yet unfinished revelation in the flesh of the Universal Life.

# FRAGMENTS OF CHRISTIAN HISTORY.

## I.

## THE MESSIAH AND THE CHRIST.

OUR first task, in approaching the study of Christianity as an event and a vital force in history, is to see it on the side of Judaism, out of whose soil it sprang; and to trace — at present in its purely historical or human aspect — the connection between the old religious order and the new. This is best seen in the transition, in religious history, from the name Messiah, with all that it denotes as the culminating of the old dispensation, to the name Christ, with all that it denotes as the inspiration of the new.

No revolution that we know in the affairs of mankind, especially in its spiritual history, has been so significant as that suggested in the connotation of these two titles, of which each is a literal translation of the other. One brings before us the passionate, ever-baffled, and finally most disastrous hope of a perishing people, — the narrow, intense, fierce patriotism, that had its boundaries sharply defined in the little state of Palestine; the other, a world-wide spiritual empire, seated on the deepest foundations of faith and reverence, and showing the ideal side of a manifold, rich, powerful, and proud civilization, which has as yet no ascertainable limit of duration.

While the name Messiah is at best the title of a hoped-for prince who might do for Jerusalem what the empire of the Cæsars did for Rome, — that is, establish it as the seat of enduring dominion founded on "righteousness" in the Jewish sense of that word, as the other was built upon the Roman Law, — the name Christ has come, by successive changes and enlargements of its meaning, to be the title of the spiritual or ideal leader of humanity. Nay, so instant and so marked was this transition, as soon as the name had passed from the local dialect into that Greek which was the tongue of all known thought and culture, that Paul (who did more than all other men to bring it about) already uses that name to mean, not simply the Person, however exalted and revered, but a Force purely spiritual and ideal, — " Christ the power of God and the wisdom of God."

It belongs more properly to an appreciation .of the life and work of Paul to consider this transition as it looks to the future, and opens the way to the new, large development of a religion of Humanity. It is our immediate task to consider it as it looks to the past, and connects itself with the history of a peculiar people.

That wonderful Messianic hope, which in the ways of history was the indispensable preparation for the advent of a gospel preached to every creature, emerges amidst the desperate struggle of a little colony in Judæa to defend its altar and temple from the stranger, and saves that struggle from despair. We need not go over here the story of that time which we call the Maccabæan period. It is, or should be, tolerably familiar. We can at best attempt to make reasonably clear one or two points of view, which may help us understand its bearing on the impending revolution.

Standing at the date of the gospel history, we seem to have fairly firm ground on an island in the great ocean of the past, or at least to be swinging at a tolerably sure anchorage among its restless waves. The prophecy of Malachi, with its abrupt menace of "the great and dreadful day of the Lord,"— the last headland laid down on the chart that most of us have sailed by, — is four hundred years away: about as far as from us the conquest of the Eastern Empire by the Turks, the Wars of the Roses, the break-up of feudalism in France under Louis XI., the revival of letters and arts in Italy, a few years before the discovery of America by Columbus. A few dates like these may serve to help our sluggish imagination, and show what we mean by historical perspective. Near midway, again, to where we are standing, is the glorious revolt of the Maccabees, another point in the perspective to be fixed as firmly as we may: not quite as far away as the Commonwealth in England, and the Thirty Years' War in Germany. In other words, to the contemporaries of Jesus the hero of the struggle was somewhat nearer than Oliver Cromwell is to us, and the visions of Daniel were about as near as Paradise Lost.

I am probably not mistaken in thinking that this comparison of dates startles us a little by bringing the events so close. But, in fact, they are much closer than that. If our daily walk took us past Whitehall, or a stroll into the next village to the hillside where Hampden fell, the events of that time would come incomparably nearer to our imagination. How was it, then, with the Jews of Palestine in the time of Jesus, who had no other memories, who knew no other landmarks, whose only science and only dream lay within the strict limits of the interpretation of the Scripture that embodied, confirmed, and illustrated their one only hope ? Herod's wife was great-grandchild of the hero's nephew; and Herod's handiwork was there, unfinished, before their eyes. The aged Simeon might as a child (to take the average of several learned guesses) have known the writer of Enoch, and he the writer of the visions of Daniel. Three generations might thus touch hands across the whole space that separates the Old and the New.* The chasm is apt to look abrupt and impassable, like the gorge at Niagara; still, it is not so very wide but that we may fly a cord across, and that shall carry a strand, and that a cable, and the gulf is bridged.

Looking now a little more carefully at the point of time which we have succeeded in bringing so near, we see that the stream of national, or rather race

---

* Thus I recollect as a child going to see an old man who had been an officer in the " French and Indian War" (1756–1763) ; and he, by fair possibility, might have known some one who had seen the execution of Charles I.

life, flows in three pretty well defined channels, — in fact, ever since the time of the earlier dispersion and the return of the pilgrim colony to Jerusalem, almost six hundred years ago. In Egypt that stream is widening out towards the placid lake of speculative philosophy, which we call the new platonism of Philo, — a great reservoir, which was pumped abundantly long afterwards into the sluiceways of Christian theology, to spread and dilute the river of the water of life till it could float the heavy-laden bark of St. Peter. Eastward in Babylon the stream loses itself, as it were, in wide marshes, where it breeds in course of time that monstrous growth of water-weed and tangle, with flowers interspersed of rare and curious perfume, which we call the Babylonish legend, or the later Talmud.

With either of these our subject has very little to do. The learning which interprets the schools of Jewish thought in Alexandria has been thoroughly worked up, so as to be easily accessible and (I was going to say) cheap; though it can never lose a certain charm of its own in the blandly-flowing discourse of Philo, or a very real interest to one who cares to trace the sources of Christian theology.*  The more remote and intricate study of the Eastern branch has still less present concern for us: it belongs really to the strange and curious history of modern Judaism, — a

* Though Philo is called a Jew, and uses the Jewish scriptures as the text of all his fluent expositions, his cast of thought is so entirely Platonic or Grecian, that Ewald (in a conversation I had with him some years ago) insisted that he was to be counted as no Jew at all, but a Greek, quite outside the line of Hebrew development.

side-shoot, which has grown, independent of the main trunk, into a vigorous, persistent, fantastic life of its own.

So our subject narrows down to the course of the central stream, what we may call the Palestinian life of the Jewish people. This is, from the outset down, intensely national, patriotic, local, — yet none the less intensely confident in itself, disdainful of all life or thought outside, and buoyed through great tides of disaster by an immeasurable hope. Indeed, that great miracle of patriotic valor, the achieving of a real though brief independence by the Maccabees in the face of the splendid monarchy of Syria, might almost justify any extravagance of hope.

We call that hope Messianic. In a certain vague large way it dates back to the elder prophets of Judah, Isaiah and Micah, who give not only hints, but splendid pictures and symbols, of the Lord's reign in righteousness and peace. When the flood of conquest had flowed over the state of Judah, in the long Captivity of Babylon those superb strains of prophecy had been composed,* whose only fit interpretation yet is in the gorgeous and tender harmonies of Handel's *Messiah*. But now the prophecy becomes distinct, vivid, personal. Intelligent criticism is well agreed in setting the visions of Daniel at the precise period of time we are dealing with: in fact, it narrows the date of their composition within some ten years, from 168 to

---

* Isaiah xl.–lxvi., the "Great Unknown" of the Captivity (Ewald), sometimes spoken of as the younger Isaiah. The title "Messiah" is here first given to Cyrus, as deliverer of the Jews from Babylon (xlv. 1).

178 before the Christian era. These visions, doubtless, it is easiest for us to bring before our minds as songs of patriotic hope and cheer, in the strain and stress of a conflict all but desperate, rather than expound them painfully in their detail, as they apply to the nearer past and the immediate present.

What we have definitely to do with them, for the purpose now in hand, is to see how they fixed—crystallized, as it were—that patriotic hope about the person of a Deliverer, who again was (like the "man of sorrows" of the Prophet of the Captivity) hardly to be distinguished in our criticism from Israel himself in his great agony. " I saw in the night visions, and, behold, one like a son of man came in the clouds of heaven, . . . and there was given him dominion, and glory, and a kingdom: . . . his dominion is an everlasting dominion, which shall not pass away, and his kingdom that which shall not be destroyed." And again, "The kingdom and dominion . . . shall be given *to the people of the saints of the Most High*, whose kingdom is an everlasting kingdom, and all dominions shall serve and obey Him." *

Now this promise comes close upon a description which, by the universal understanding of interpreters, points to the condition of the East among the successors of Alexander,—that is, the immediate oppressors of the Jews. There is no reason to doubt that the coming of this " Son of Man in the clouds of heaven " was passionately waited for, expected, longed for, to appear from day to day, any more than that

* Daniel vii. 13, 14, 27. Compare Stanley ("Jewish Church," Vol. III. p. 385 of Am. ed.), whose rendering is here followed.

Christ's second advent was daily expected in the Apostles' day, or has been and still is in ours. Most likely some passing triumph of Judas, or Jonathan, or Simon, the heroic brothers, brought from time to time that fervent confidence and hope to rest on them. And again, the hope deferred lay always ready to be evoked anew, and applied to whatever champion seemed at the moment likely to accomplish the unreasoning but fervid expectation. Thus, after a century and a half of disappointment, it was just as ready to centre upon Herod the Great, whom Antony and Augustus had set in secure dominion, — a painful travesty, indeed, of the great Hope, when we think who and what Herod was, a son of Edom and a tyrant; but how genuine, we see in the Herodian party in the Gospels, and in a sober argument by Epiphanius, three centuries later, in its disproof.

In point of fact, we are apt to think too much of the Messianic hope in a formal, dogmatic way, or in the way, perhaps, of learned exposition. We associate it too exclusively with the august strains of prophecy on one side, and the yet more august series of events that flowed from it on the other. We do not always stop to think how simple, how natural, how human it was, after all. In one sense it is a miracle in history, a phenomenon without any exact parallel, — the brooding tenacity, the passionate resolve, the revival from defeat, the endurance through centuries of humiliation, that characterize the Jews' faith in their coming Deliverer. And so, again, it is a thing that is and must remain without example, that a national hope has been transfigured in the person of One who, after near nineteen centuries, is still looked up to as the spiritual Chief of humanity, and whose name has been received as the symbol of what is Infinite and Divine, nay, as a name of the Infinite himself.

But look at it, again, on its nearer side, and it is not so hard to see — not only that it was altogether human in its passion and limitation, not only that in its wild frenzy it led straight to a tragedy of unexampled horror; but that in its elements it belonged quite naturally to such a time and people. In its vehement persistency, in its passionate devoutness, it is fairly matched by the four centuries' struggle in which the fighting tribe of Montenegro, under their bishop-prince, have consecrated themselves to the crusade against the Turk, — a struggle whose issues it is not long since we were watching in the telegraphic bulletins of the day. In its temper of stern patriotism — sombre, tender, unyielding, pathetically hopeless — it is like that other amazing phenomenon of our time, the life that smoulders in the ashes of thrice-desolated Poland.

We do not always think how close these great historic passions may come to our own life. There was lately living quietly among us a princess of the blood of old Lithuanian heroes — Antonia Jagiello — who, with more than the heroism of a Deborah or a Judith, led the forlorn hope at the head of her regiment on the battle-fields of Hungary. Let me copy here a picture which I find in a powerful French romance: it is of the hapless insurrection of 1863, and it is a young Pole that speaks, who visits his mother in Paris, feeling himself dead to honor ever since he

1 *

signed in prison a pledge not to persist in war against the oppressor: —

" Before me was a figure in alabaster representing a woman crouched and in chains, with the inscription, *Polonia exspectans et sperans*, ' Poland waits and hopes.' Above hung an ivory crucifix; between the crucifix and the crouching figure my portrait in medallion. Here my mother had gathered all her love, — her God, her country, and her child. How strange the position of that portrait seemed! What had that woman in chains, that crucified God, to say to him? What had he to answer them? But no, I said, this portrait is not I. It is that other, — he who had a faith, and is dead. And I thought of these things with unfathomable pity, — that hidden manna, that bread of life, held in a mother's heart."

This is all over again the picture of that passion which we have seen in the figure *Judæa Capta* seated beneath a palm; which the women of Judah had in their hearts when they wore the turreted ornament on their head, "the golden city," as a witness that they should never forget the fallen and loved Jerusalem. The Polish lady learns her son's forfeited honor, disowns him, and dies. It is exactly the old Hebrew phrase, "cut off from his people." The terrible story of Josephus tells of a temper as stern and high, among the women of Judah who fell in their country's fall. And a passion as deep, though not vindictive and fierce like that, lay doubtless in the heart of Jesus, when he said, "O Jerusalem, Jerusalem! that killest the prophets, and stonest them which are sent unto thee, how often would I have gathered thy children together, as a hen gathereth her chickens under her wings, and ye would not! Behold, your house is left unto you desolate." And again, " Daughters of Jerusalem, weep not for me, but weep for yourselves and for your children."

Intense, narrow, patriotic, human as it was, the Messianic hope was very little ideal, had very little of what we should call religious. So far as it looked at all beyond the fact of triumph and independence, it seems to have been entirely secular, even sordidly practical. It meant meat and drink, olives, corn, and vineyards, sheep, cows, and oxen, and a vigorous lording it over other people. Wherever the Jewish imagination trusts itself in images of the future, it takes very strongly to such realities as these. So much, at least, we can get from a glimpse or two at that masterpiece of fancy running riot, the Babylonish Talmud, with its monstrous banquets of behemoth and leviathan, and its vast clusters of grapes, each clamorous to be gathered before its fellow. The Messianic kingdom was to be established in " righteousness," it is true; but, so far as consciously developed, a righteousness like that of the Scribes and Pharisees, — quite sincere in its way, but wonderfully dry and thin, resembling what we think of under that name very much as lichen resembles flowers and grain.

But we need not dwell on this side of it: first, because it is sufficiently apparent in the censures of Jesus himself; and secondly, because the Jewish people never since the Captivity fairly exhibited their qualities in an independent national life. Forced in upon itself by oppression or else antagonism on every side, the petty monarchy enjoyed at best such independence as it could win from the mutual jealousies of Syria and Rome. The real history of the Messianic period is a history of almost constant struggle, often heroic, and at critical periods in the highest degree tragical.

That period, properly defined, includes about three centuries. It begins with the revolt of the Maccabees and the visions of Daniel; it ends with the brief messianic reign of Bar-kochab (or Barcochbas),* who perished in the final conquest of Jerusalem by Hadrian, and the martyrdom of Rabbi Akibah just a hundred years after the crucifixion of Jesus. Within this period — nay, in that brief space of restless spiritual agitation between the death of Herod and the fall of Jerusalem in A. D. 70—I have seen it stated that no less than fifty adventurers were more or less widely recognized as Messiahs, and were known under that claim to history. Lawless and turbulent insurgents, most of them, against Roman rule, or else the fiercest and most stubborn of military leaders when the storm of conquest and destruction fell. The hard matter-of-fact rendering given in such events as these, of a hope so fervid and ideal at the start, — a rendering of it at once sordid and fierce,— it seems necessary to bring into strong relief, if we would see it as a natural thing in human annals, and at the same time know the real background of that purely ethical and spiritual interpretation, which at length displaced it, and transfigured the Messiah to the Christ

---

* This title signifies "Son of the Star," in allusion to Balaam's prophecy (Numbers xxiv. 17).

It does not belong properly to our task to attempt a solution of that central problem of history, the origin of Christianity. Science is not content until it has traced one by one the links of sequence that guide from antecedent to result, and is sure that there is no missing link. But science does not define or assign the Cause, which it must always assume, or else ignore, — historical science as much as any. This particular antecedent of Christianity, which we find in the Messianic hope of the Jews, it is well for us to see as distinctly as we can, — how it was, in the way of historical perspective; what it was, in the way of historical imagination. When we would apply it to explain anything in the rise of Christianity, we find it, so to speak, not at the heart, but rather at the two edges of the phenomenon we are seeking to explain. We find it at every step in the gospel narrative, where it makes an element in the mental atmosphere, without which the course of that narrative would be manifestly inconsequent and incredible; and, when the scene shifts to apostolic times, we find it just fading away in all its grosser features, while it is getting transfigured into a sacred memory and an ideal truth.

The first thing we have to do, then, is to take the record of the facts, if we can, absolutely without the warp of any preconceived opinion, or any theological dogmatism. Looking at them so, it appears plain that what we may call the messianic consciousness of Jesus, which is so intense and even predominant towards the close of his ministry, was a comparatively late development in him. To put it in theological phrase, his generation as Son of God was anterior to his appointment as Messiah of the Jews. In the language we usually apply to human experience, his vocation as a moral and spiritual teacher was recognized first; and only as an after result came his strong conviction that he was the chosen Deliverer of his people, though by a way they could not understand or follow.

At first they knew him only as a village enthusiast, a Galilæan teacher, at best a Rabbi, like other interpreters of the Law, one of the school perhaps of Rabbi Hillel or Rabbi Simeon, like them setting the weightier matters of justice and mercy above the mint, anise, and cumin of current exposition. For a background to the understanding of his discourses, one should know something of the wonderful well-meaning pedantry of the rabbinical interpreters, and something too of the genuine and wholesome ethics which the better sort, Hillel at their head, had tried to engraft upon it.

But here was a new and astonishing phenomenon. Their placid moralism, their commonplaces of natural ethics, suddenly blazed out in a passionate and even haughty conviction, — flooded too with a glow of fervent trust, a wealth of human tenderness, a strain of poetic beauty, which made it all, as it were, a new revelation to his hearers, and "he taught them as one having authority." All this is indicated, plainly enough, in the austere morality, the sharp transitions, the strange and winning sweetness, the tender and bright imagery, the perfect expression of religious trust, that make the Sermon on the Mount different in kind from all other existing words, — from the calm

beatitudes of its opening to the stern and menacing
parable at its close. This we must take as the type of
the teaching of Jesus in its earlier stage, apart from
all critical questions that touch its literary form or the
sources of its doctrine. The swift flow and the vivid
personality we find in it are the very stamp, the very
person, so to speak, of the young prophet of Galilee.

But this is not the person of the Jewish Messiah,
even by the highest Christian interpretation we can
give that title. The consciousness of this special
mission was developed in the mind of Jesus later than
this, and gradually. If it had crossed his thought before, the scene of the Temptation seems to show that it
had been definitely put aside. But it lay, so to speak,
very near, and offered itself once and again. Without any doubt he had been nurtured in that fervent
patriotic hope whose peculiar home was Galilee, and
felt it as strongly as any of his countrymen. And,
again, the words of John the Baptist had greatly
quickened that restless and eager expectation in the
general mind, which began already passionately to
demand the coming of a Deliverer. Remember, too,
how near, in the mental perspective, was that day of
sudden glory which had redeemed a martyr people
from a yoke more cruel and seemingly as strong as
that of Rome; and how the name of Elias the forerunner, mysteriously hinted by Malachi, and repeated
in more vehement strain in the prophecy of Enoch,
was already current in men's mouths.

Now it was not the words of purely religious teaching in the discourse of Jesus, it was not the moral
loftiness, or the strong appeal to conscience, that

made the people's heart acknowledge its King in him, and so (as it were) flashed back the conviction upon his own. It was rather those other signs of personal power that went with his word. It was that his presence, by some unexplained force, could stir great multitudes, as the waves of the sea are moved by the wind or lifted by the moon; that his voice could soothe brooding insanity, and control the wild demoniac, and charm away the passion of despair or grief; that healing went from his touch, and sick men in his sight became conscious of new health and strength, — it was these things that so wrought on them that they "were ready to take him by force and make him a king."

Now when a man becomes aware in himself of some rare, perhaps unparalleled, personal power, — power, too, of a sort that distinctly imposes on him a special mission to his fellow-men, a task to fulfil altogether his own, and a destiny apart from theirs, — this conviction is apt to come upon him with awe and sadness and a certain terror. "Ah, Lord God!" said Jeremiah, "behold, I cannot speak, for I am a child." But the Lord said, "Say not, I am a child; for thou shalt go to all that I shall send thee, and whatsoever I command thee thou shalt speak."

This spiritual crisis, we may conceive, came to Jesus not before but during his public ministry. It is indicated by his shrinking from the observation and contact of men; by his spending whole nights apart in prayer; by the Transfiguration, in which he is forewarned of "the decease which he must accomplish at Jerusalem." Before it, his words are such as

I have spoken of,—the deep conviction of moral truth, the pure poetry of the religious life. After it, we have his vehement appeals to the Jewish people, his passionate denunciations of their timeserving and false leaders, his brooding tenderness over the near fate of Jerusalem, his whip of small cords for the traders of the temple, his apocalyptic visions of the coming terror, his vague but awful hints conveyed in parables of the Virgins and of the impending Judgment.

These all belong to what we may call the later or Messianic period of his ministry. I do not mean that in its essential spiritual elements, in its assertion of righteousness and mercy, not partiality and wrath, as the heart of the Law, this second period was at all altered from the spirit of the first; but only that its force was narrowed more and more in a single channel, towards a special end. How distinctly he may have thought of a national rescue and triumph like that of Judas the Maccabee as a possible thing, before the great shadow fell upon him in the Garden of Gethsemane, we are not, perhaps, entitled to judge. If he did think of it as possible, we may be sure it was by way of divine miracle, not of human valor. There was one hour when it would almost seem as if he accepted this conception of the Messiah's work, — when he rode into Jerusalem over palm-leaves and garments strewn in the way. There was one moment when a word from him might have raised a storm of popular passion, and possibly have secured a few days of bloody triumph, like that which, forty years afterwards, went before the final tragedy, — when the recognized Messianic war-cry, "Son of David, to the rescue!" broke out in the crowd, and "all the city was shaken, as by an earthquake," as he entered it.[*] But this most powerful appeal to the frenzy of the hour passed by him, like the rest. And it takes nothing from the serene altitude of his spirit in the hour of martyrdom, if we assume that it was won at last in answer to his passionate prayer in the agony of bloody sweat; and that the cup which he prayed might pass from him held in it the disenchantment of a glorious, unselfish, patriotic dream.

That dream — the dream of present deliverance from the alien yoke — was shared by those who had caught imperfectly his spirit, and who, with mistaken thought but loyal heart, continued to believe in him. The belief in him had grown upon them till it had altogether possessed their souls; and life itself was no longer possible to them without it. His spiritual and ethical interpretation of the great Hope had definitely resulted — for us, and for them as fast as they were able to receive it so — in emancipating it from all boundaries of race or time, and making it signify the deliverance of the soul of man from everything that is evil, and a world-wide reign of righteousness. But we know how long they clung to those narrow renderings; how persistently they looked for his visible coming in the clouds; what plain words of promise they believed had been audibly spoken to them by angels out of the sky; how passionately a remnant,

* So we may understand the expression ἐσείσθη (Matt. xxi. 10). The force of the cry *Hosanna!* ("Save now!") was suggested to me in a conversation with Rabbi Gottheil.

under the disdainful title of Ebionite or Nazarene, or
hiding, perhaps, in the disguise of the holy order
of the Essenes, clung to the very soil of Palestine
where had walked those blessed feet which they had
seen "nailed for our advantage on the bitter cross,"
and looked patiently for that vision of the Son of
Man, even from the blasted hill-sides of Judæa and
the ruined walls of Jerusalem.

But those blasted hill-sides and those ruined walls
had at length, to the great body of disciples, broken
the spell, weakened by years yet not wholly lost, by
which their eyes were holden so that they should not
know their Master. At first they had pieced out (as
it were) the outline of a life that in its earthly appearing was defeated and broken, by visions borrowed
from old seers and their interpreters. They had ad-
journed to a second advent * that perfect fulfilment
of his work which was wanting in the first. They
even clung to a doubtful prophecy that it was fore-
ordained there should be two Messiahs : the son of
Joseph must first come, to suffer defeat and death ;
and then the son of David should come to victory
and endless reign.† And upon those of their countrymen who had been won to share their faith there
came a passion of remorse at his rejection, which was
only pacified, at length, by the assurance that his
death was the one appointed Sacrifice, which at once
completed and dissolved the system of ritual expiation
that had made the corner-stone of Hebrew polity.‡

* παρουσία.  See especially First Thessalonians.
† Compare "Hebrew Men and Times," pp. 405–409.
‡ As shown in the argument of the " Epistle to the Hebrews."

But in the lapse of years, in the growth of other sympathies and duties, and the keen interests of daily life, all that was special and local in the Messianic hope must inevitably thin out and disappear. How it became transfigured in the minds of those who had not known Jesus after the flesh, till for the Messiah we have at length the Christ in history, belongs rather to a study of the life and work of the Apostle Paul, — who was a Hebrew of the Hebrews; who "for the hope of Israel" was bound in chains; but who was also the great free-thinker of the Apostolic era, and has been the real interpreter, some would say even the founder, of Christianity for the modern world.

# II.

## SAINT PAUL.

THERE is nowhere a finer challenge to the historical imagination — that is, to our power of seeing
things in a former time just as they really were —
than that offered by the very beginnings of Christianity as an organized power, as a social force.  Let us try
to take up that challenge as if the facts were all new
to us, and we had to study them for the first time.

First of all, what was the source of the indomitable
faith, the victorious moral force, which made that
little company of disciples the corner-stone of a new
order of civilization?  How was it that the incon-
spicuous gathering of about a hundred and twenty in
the upper chamber at Jerusalem had in it the seed of
a great growth, which spread its roots amidst the decay of the old order of things, and flourished most
abundantly when all that splendid structure of art
and empire was a mass of mouldering ruin ?

A full answer to this question would cover the
whole ground of the early Christian history.  Without attempting so much as that, it is enough to say
that every great political or social revolution will
have its type in the life, the character, the work, of
some one man ; and that the great moral and spiritual
force we are considering is typified, more than any-

where else, in the vehement conviction, the ardent temper, the impassioned eloquence, the organizing skill, the personal experience, and the vivid religious imagination of the Apostle Paul.

He is the man of genius and the man of power of the first Christian age. Comte calls him, frankly, the real founder of Christianity, holding the legend of Jesus to be a pale and ineffectual myth. But in Jesus himself, as already seen, there were—besides the indefinable something which resides in personality—at least two elements, one of vast personal force, and the other of great historical significance: his intense conception of purely moral truth and of religion as a life, and his equally intense conviction of his calling as Messiah of the Jews. These were the necessary antecedents of the revolution, looked at from its purely human side. But, as soon as the movement widens out beyond the narrow range of a merely personal and local influence, then the life and work of Paul come to be just as essential to any real understanding of it. To show how that indispensable service was enlisted, and how the new movement was inspired and guided by it, is what we mean by an intelligent study of his life.

The martyrdom of Stephen and the journey to Damascus mark the critical moment of Paul's conversion. The Council at Jerusalem, which is put some fifteen years later, marks the critical moment when Christianity burst the bounds of Judaism, and stood before the world as an independent faith,—in short, when the mind and influence of Paul had become predominant.

But for each of these moments there is a previous question, before it becomes intelligible : for the first, What was the bond of union among the first disciples, that held them together so tenaciously and so long ? and for the second, What was the attraction in them that drew the gentiles that way, so that it was a privilege to join their body, and there was a demand for the grave concessions (as they regarded them) which they felt bound to make ?

It is easy to answer both these questions by saying that it was all a miracle, and then to take the only record we have as simply a statement of the fact. For my part, I do not see any reason to doubt that the early Church had extraordinary powers — such as gifts of healing, insight, and fervent speech — which they would necessarily think miraculous. "Every good gift," says James, "comes from the Father of lights." Similar gifts have been asserted, with sincerity and often no doubt with truth, by various bodies of religionists in every age.

But take the account as literally as we will, that is only to cut the knot which we are trying to untie : the facts, so seen, are *ascertained*, not *understood*. We want, if we can, to see them just as they lay in the minds of the witnesses, and as we should see them if we could cross-question those witnesses. This we cannot do. We can only look at the thing in a broad way. We hold the facts, as it were, in solution in our mind, and wait for them to crystallize in such shape as shall most naturally represent them to our mind.

We listen, then, to the reports that spread abroad that the crucified Jesus had actually reappeared in the flesh; we see the eager readiness with which those reports were received and cherished; and then the lingering expectation that he might resume his public career and assert a triumphant messiahship appears to give way, almost insensibly, to a belief among his followers that he had been taken up visibly into the clouds, and would presently reappear, just as visibly, to establish his victorious reign.

I take it for granted that this belief of theirs was very precise and simple, and that there was nothing in their habit of mind which made it at all difficult for them to receive it so. As to the narratives of the Resurrection and Ascension, I do not undertake to explain them all away, or in fact to explain them at all. From the arguments of the early apologists, it is clear that they were received as precise and literal fact by the general body of believers. But no amount of testimony would be enough, to the mind of the present day, to convince men *as a new fact* that a body once really dead had been restored to life; still less, that it had been actually seen to pass into the sky "with flesh, bones, and all things appertaining to the perfection of man's nature," as the later creed declares. Such, at least, was not the view of Paul; who, indeed, asserts very earnestly the reality of the resurrection and the glorified life of Jesus in the eternal state, but with equal explicitness declares that not flesh and blood, but a "spiritual body," is that which can really inherit the kingdom of heaven.

The first element of power in the early Church was, then, a distinct and literal belief of certain facts, coupled with a very positive and confident assurance that a definite prophecy was going to be fulfilled. That such an assurance is a real power and a bond of union, however shadowy its ground may appear to us, we see in those sects of Adventists who have appeared at intervals ever since, and who, after eighteen centuries of disappointment, are probably as numerous in our day as ever. But we must conceive, if we can, how intense and vivid, beyond all modern comparison, this expectation of Christ's second coming must have been in that age, and so assume it here as the first unquestionable and all-powerful bond of union; remembering, too, that at this point we are dealing only with Jews, at the very heart of the long period of intense and heated expectation which we have called the Messianic Era.

But this is only one point. Why was it that a little inner circle of Jews, — whose leaders were "unlearned and ignorant men," more intensely Jewish, and (so to speak) more bigoted and narrow than the average of their countrymen,*— why was it that they could exert such an immense power of attraction and persuasion that in one day three thousand were added to their number, and in a few months they reckoned a community of five thousand souls, and in a few years multitudes were knocking hard for admission at their doors, and in a few generations the whole Roman empire was at their feet? Never in all history has there been the parallel case of a growth so genuine, so vast, or so powerful, out of what was at the start a purely moral movement, or a purely religious impulse.

* See Acts ii. 46, iv. 13.

2

A full answer to the question includes a great variety of things: earnest faith, strong mutual attachment, a common loyalty, skilful organization, good lives, gifts of healing and the like (which they called "powers," and which we call "miracles"), the contagious enthusiasm that often comes from isolation and from martyrdom. But the power of the *organized movement* at the start seems best explained by what we are told of the socialistic sentiment and theory of the early Church. "No man among them believed that aught which he possessed was his own, but they had all things common." That is, they did really try to put in practice, in the most literal way, those precepts of boundless and uncalculating generosity which are contained in the Sermon on the Mount.

And this, if we will look at it, was of itself a prodigious force. Its power is commonly seen not in the well educated or in the well-to-do, who in general know nothing of the socialistic sentiment and rather hold it in contempt. But look at the prodigious fanaticism it evoked in the first French Revolution; look at its terrific and obstinate strength in the Paris Commune of 1871; look at the martyrdoms willingly undergone for it in Russia at this day, where it has been enthusiastically embraced by high-born men and ladies delicately bred, who submit to persecution, confiscation, exile more bitter than death; * look at the

* "Students leave the lecture-rooms to mix with the peasants; princes leave their palaces to seek work in the factories; noble girls flee from their families to go into service as cooks and seamstresses; and, if they are disturbed in the midst of their propaganda by the police, they wander with unbroken courage to

grand, almost sublime, even if mistaken munificence with which the workingmen of England and America in these last years have borne one another's burdens, so as to win some far-off victory in the battle of capital and labor; — and then you see that the socialistic sentiment is one of the great moral forces to move human society to its foundations. Not sordid interest, but uncalculating sentiment, is what carries the day in the great crises of humanity.

The early disciples were hard-working, plain-speaking people; " not many great, not many rich, not many mighty, not many noble were called." A part of their working faith was a most generous, a most unsparing doctrine of the sharing of goods and burdens. Read the story of Ananias and Sapphira. Read what Paul says of missionary and charitable gifts. Read the Epistle of James, which in its denouncing of the vanity, wealth, and fashion that began to creep in, speaks the very heart of the first church at Jerusalem, as it echoes the very thought of those who assail most formidably a proud, rich, and dominant ecclesiasticism at this day.

A crisis came to the affairs of the church at Jerusalem, after six or eight years of unmolested growth, with the death of Stephen. He was a sort of half-Greek, a man of greater vigor, boldness, and mental breadth than the rest, and is held to have been, in a sense, the forerunner of Paul. His martyrdom shows the first sharp collision caused by the Greek or foreign element

Siberia, march defiantly to the gallows, always setting the dangerous, contagious example of triumphant martyrdom. Of what use, then, are blows, chains, the scaffold ? "

asserting itself in the Church.  Now Paul — at this time known by the Jewish name of Saul — "was consenting to his death."  He was a man of thirty, in the hot glow of a first conviction, trained austerely as a Jew of the straitest sort, and doubtless thought he ought to do something by way of testimony against these disturbers of the comfortable religious peace.

But his heart was very much larger than his creed.  How much he had been impressed in a quieter way before, by the spectacle of that close-clinging and devoted life of the Christian community, nothing is told.  But the shock of that first martyrdom — the noble head of Stephen, with a face "as it had been an angel's," battered out of human likeness by jagged stones flung from fierce and cruel hands of a mob of bigots right there on the pavement before his eyes — struck him like a blow.  That was putting the whole thing in quite another shape.  Out of sheer wilful consistency, as we may imagine, he proceeded to carry out his commission, "breathing out threatening and slaughter," and to put it in execution as far as Damascus, some hundred and fifty miles away.  And then — we know the story: the blinding flash from the sky; the voice as of the very Crucified One in his heart, in sorrow, rebuke, appeal; the three days' groping in darkness; and then the sudden, eager, glad embracing of a new life.

It is quite beside my purpose to give even a brief sketch of Paul's life, or anything like an analysis of his system of belief.  A single glance we may be permitted at his person, as described by the earliest witnesses: a man's physical frame and countenance are often the best type of the personal force he carries.

Paul, then, according to the legends, was a man little of stature — under five feet high they say, high-shouldered, beetle-browed, stooping, with head bent forward, his beard and hair at middle life of an iron-gray; his brow wide, his face thin, his eye deep and somewhat sad; the dark eye, the marked features, we may imagine of the strong Jewish type. His bodily presence was weak and his speech contemptible, — so his enemies said. That his speech was hesitating and slow, when not roused, we may believe easily enough: it was so with Demosthenes; it was so with Mahomet, who, next to Paul, has shown the most burning and effective eloquence of the Semitic race, and in whom, like Paul, that barrier of hesitating and imperfect utterance gave way on occasion to a hot flood of passionate and eager words, that stirred great tides of popular conviction. How vivid and dramatic that eloquence of Paul's could be, we see in the noble speech before Festus; how dignified, serious, and apt, in the address on Mars' Hill. But these were flashes of power, with misgivings and rebuffs between. "I was with you," he says, "in weakness, and fear, and much trembling." "Lest I should be exalted above measure, there was given me a thorn in the flesh, the messenger of Satan to buffet me." This thorn may have been (as Dr. Brown of Edinburgh thinks) a dimness of sight — probably with much pain — ever after the shock that blinded him on the road to Damascus; but perhaps we shall understand it better if we connect it with that moral conflict of flesh and spirit, which I shall speak of later, as more than all else the source of Paul's peculiar power.

We get a much more vivid notion of his interior person (so to speak) from Paul's own words, than we do of his bodily presence through doubtful tradition. I will recall a few phrases which reflect the native pride, the utter lack of vanity, the sensitiveness to affront, the eager craving for sympathy, that go along with such a temperament : — " It is a very small thing that I should be judged of you, or any man's judgment; he that judgeth me is the Lord." " We have labored night and day that we might not be chargeable to any of you while we preached ; as you know, these hands have provided for my necessities." " We both hunger and thirst, and are naked, and are buffeted, and have no certain dwelling-place ; we work with our own hands ; we are made as the filth of the earth, the offscouring of all things." And again : " We are troubled on every side, yet not distressed ; perplexed, but not in despair ; persecuted, yet not forsaken ; cast down, but not destroyed ; — servants of God in much endurance, in afflictions, in necessities, in distresses, in stripes, imprisonments, tumults, labors, watchings, fastings, — in honor and dishonor, in good report and evil report ; deceivers, and yet true ; unknown, and yet well known ; dying, and behold we live ; sorrowful, yet always rejoicing ; poor, yet making many rich ; having nothing, and yet possessing all things." The vehemence and the love of paradox, which run so well with many veins of religious experience, show strongly here.

And again, of the way of life : that had fightings

without, and fears within. "Of the Jews," he says, "five times received I forty stripes save one. Thrice I was beaten with rods. Once I was stoned. Thrice I suffered shipwreck: a night and a day I have been in the deep; in journeyings often, in perils of waters, in perils of robbers, in perils by my own countrymen; in perils by the heathen, in perils in the city, in perils in the wilderness, in perils in the sea, in perils among false brethren; in weariness and painfulness, in watchings often, in hunger and thirst, in fastings often, in cold and nakedness; and, besides all these things, which are without, what comes upon me daily, anxiety about all the churches." This, it will be remembered, is no idle complaint or appeal to pity, but an indignant retort to those enemies of his at Corinth who appear to have called him weak, irritable, and "a fool." "What do you mean, to weep and break my heart?" he says at Cæsarea; "I am ready, not only to be bound, but to die at Jerusalem." "It is for the hope of Israel," he says at Rome, "that I am bound with this chain." And to the Roman governor, "Would God that not only thou, but all that hear me to-day, were both almost and altogether such as I am, except these bonds."

In such words as these we already find hints of the jealousies and disputes which followed him five and twenty years, all the way from conversion to martyrdom. It was with much natural misgiving that the disciples admitted him of their company at all and very reluctantly that they let him speak frankly to the Gentiles in their name. Even then (as we have seen) taunting opponents would sneer at his stature, or gait, or the imperfections of his speech. Men of narrower culture and less ardent temper would set themselves against his innovations, and he must "withstand them to the face," as he did Peter and James at Antioch; failing so of his own fond dream of a communion in which diversities of gifts should be reconciled in the bond of peace, and sharing, instead, the numberless frets and irritations that beset a divided party, outwardly bound together, inwardly sundered and harassed.

The work he has painfully done at Corinth is half undone by jealous brethren, who throw out slurs against his authority or his soundness in the faith. Some officious intruder has "bewitched his foolish Galatians" with scruples he thought silenced long ago, and put him to the double task of defending his own character, and arguing all over again the first principles of his gospel. And it is a symptom at once painful and strange of those early controversies, that more than a generation after his death his memory was attacked, under a false name, by the partisans of Peter; and phrases of his writings are travestied in Antinomian discourses ascribed to the arch-heretic Simon Magus.

Doubtless there would be something to say on the other side, if we had the words of any who were near enough to say it. We too, if we were near enough, should most likely have found faults in what we dimly see now as excellences; should have shared the jealous alarm of the earlier disciples at his daring innovations on their faith; should have resented his off-hand claim of official equality and mental superiority; should have joined the rest in calling him testy, irascible, and overbearing. But these small personal traits fade in the perspective of time; and we remember only the strong, brave, ardent, tender-hearted man, whose very faults of temperament were a sort of goad in the work he had to do. We remember only that that eager and many-sided mind has done for us the necessary task of transforming the Galilæan idyll, the tragedy at Jerusalem, the narrow Messianic hope, from a local tradition to an imperishable possession of mankind.

. This is the verdict of history upon him, and it is just. But it is also made easier to us by the fact that it is through his own words we know him best. The most transparent of men unconsciously idealizes his thought and aim. In the very effort to interpret himself to others, not only what is most real, but what is best in him, comes clearest into view. So that it is to Paul's advantage, as well as ours, that he is his own interpreter.

A few words may tell us the noble and fit close of the story. Some Jewish fanatics had conspired, and sworn his death. Forty of them vowed that "they would neither eat nor drink till they had killed Paul." Rescued by the captain of the guard, he appealed to Rome. Naturally, he "had a great desire these many years" to visit the Eternal City, then the sovereign centre of mind as well as empire. A stormy passage, broken by shipwreck on the coast of Malta, brought him among a few friends there whom he had once met at Corinth : here was the little nucleus of the Roman Church. After two years there, busy and unmolested, — a prisoner, as it were, on parole, — he travelled, as the traditions say, westward into Spain, and even to the "farthest isle," by which some understand England, or even Ireland. When, some time later, Nero (as the people charged) set fire to Rome in his brutal and insolent caprice, he turned the charge upon the Christians, says Tacitus; threw them to wild beasts in the arena, or wrapped them in tarred cloth and set them afire at night to light the imperial gardens. Paul was brought more than once before the judgment. "At my first answer," he said, " no man stood with me, but all deserted me ; but the Lord stood by me and strengthened me, and I was delivered from the lion's mouth." As a Roman citizen he might not be cast to the beasts, or die a slave's death on the cross, but was beheaded with the sword. "I have fought a good fight," he said, while waiting his doom. "I have finished my course, I have kept the faith. Henceforth there is laid up for me a crown of righteousness, which the Lord, the righteous judge, shall give me at that day."*

Recognizing that the forces which guide human events are essentially moral forces, and have their source in men's conviction, passion, and will, and that events themselves are (in a sense) but the reflex, at least the outgrowth, of personal character, I have gathered thus a few scattered phrases in which Paul lets in light on his temper, motive, and acts. Per-

---

* 2 Tim. iv. 7, 8, 16, 18. I say nothing about the genuineness of the epistle, which is well known to be doubtful. But it is certainly easier to concede it to be Paul's, than to imagine it written by anybody else.

haps, with all these, we should not appreciate the strong hold he had on his friends by way of sympathy, but for those touching words in the parting at Miletus: "And when he had thus spoken, he knelt down and prayed with them all; and they all wept sore, and fell on Paul's neck, and kissed him, sorrowing most of all for the words he spoke, that they should see his face no more."*

We see, then, that the immense influence which went forth from Paul's life — perhaps the most remarkable, considered in all its effects, that ever flowed from the action of a single mind —- had its main source in the character of the man. His opinions are of secondary consequence; in fact, they belong as much to the time as to him, so far as they are merely speculative. But, so far as they grow out of his character, and express, not simply belief, but passionate conviction in him, they become most important elements of power. They are the very avenues and conductors by which, as from an electric pile, that vivid force made itself effectually felt.

A word, first, of the documents in which these opinions are found. It will be convenient to divide Paul's epistles, roughly, into three groups; assuming the Thessalonians (I. and II.) as the earliest; then the four great epistles, Romans, Corinthians (I., II.), and Galatians; lastly, the Ephesians, Philippians, and Colossians. That to the Hebrews is almost certainly not his; and the three short "pastoral" letters to Timothy and Titus are of doubtful genuineness, and of less doctrinal account.

* Acts xx. 36-38.

Strictly speaking, only the main central group is quite undisputed; but the first nine mentioned have a close connection and a like interest. They mark three stages of a well-defined system of thought, which we know best by the name of Pául. This system turns upon two points or pivots, — one of chief importance in the history of speculative doctrine, the other in the view of Christianity as a moral power in the world. I shall attempt here only a brief and imperfect exhibition of each.

I. Paul's doctrine of Christ is not only very marked and striking in itself, but it shows exactly the transition from the Messiah-doctrine of the Jews to that order of speculation which has been dominant in the Church ever since.

In trying to understand this phase of opinion, we must bear in mind that Paul had never known Jesus as a man — "after the flesh," as he phrases it. If he had, we should probably have never known anything of his Christology. He claimed to have received knowledge of his Lord direct, by revelation. Such knowledge must have been strongly colored by sentiment and imagination, especially in such a mind as Paul's, impressed as he always was by the powerful and haunting remembrance of the vision near Damascus. Whatever else we may think of Paul's opinion on this matter, we must attempt, at any rate, to conceive it as psychologically true.

We must remember, too, that he was first of all and intensely a Jew, in belief, in habit, and in education. His starting-place was not the simple and unwarped desire of speculative truth, which we might look for in a thorough-bred Greek philosopher, but an eager attachment to and apprehension of *a particular order of truth*, developed in Hebrew schools, assuming a distinct historic background, and a definite grasp upon the future. The widening out and idealizing of his earlier messianic creed we may conceive as the work and the growth of those secluded years in Tarsus, after his conversion, before Barnabas summoned him to the front at Antioch.*

1. First of all, accordingly, we have the fervent expression, in "Thessalonians," of faith in the risen and glorified Messiah, and the vivid assurance, which, if not Paul himself, at any rate his hearers must have taken as fact, to be literally and presently brought to pass : † "The Lord himself shall descend from heaven with a shout, with the voice of the archangel, and with the trump of God; and the dead in Christ shall rise first; then we that are alive and remain shall be caught up together with them in the clouds, to meet the Lord in the air: and so shall we ever be with the Lord." ‡

This second coming of Christ has about it still the vindictive temper, and the promise of a sweet revenge, · so characteristic of the elder creed : " It is a righteous thing with God to recompense tribulation to them that trouble you "; and Jesus will be " revealed from heaven, with his mighty angels, in flaming fire taking vengeance on them that know not God, . . . . who shall

* About A. D. 40–50.

† All the allusions to Christ in the first epistle, and most of those in the second, are qualified by the expression " waiting," " hope," " coming " ($\pi\alpha\rho\upsilon\sigma\acute{\iota}\alpha$), or the like.

‡ 1 Thess. iv. 16, 17.

be punished with everlasting destruction from the presence of the Lord and from the glory of his power." *
This is the first stage of Paul's thought: it is simply a vivid and expanded copy of that vision of Daniel, repeated as a promise and a solace to a longing, waiting, suffering church.

2. But this first close and impatient expectation must pass away. Incessant cares, varieties of peril, daily duties, the need of controversy, instruction, and advice, all served to put off, thin out, refine this grosser vision, and irradiate it with a purer, inner light.

In the "Corinthians" Christ is first of all a spiritual lord and chief, "head of every man," soul of a body having many members, the mystic "rock" of the old covenant, the source of doctrine and authority, in whose name believers are "washed, sanctified, justified," "by whom are all things, and we by him." Paul knows him now in person: "Have I not seen Jesus Christ our Lord?" He speaks of "visions and revelations of the Lord," which he distinguishes from anything that can be had by sight of the eye or knowledge after the flesh.

To the Galatians, again, he speaks of Christ as the Deliverer who has "redeemed us from the curse of the law" and has lifted off yokes and burdens: the disciple is "no more a servant, but a son; and, if a son, then an heir of God through Christ."

But perhaps it is in the epistle to the Romans that, after toiling through much knotty and tangled argument about the law of sin and the soul struggling in bonds of flesh, he bursts (in the magnificent eighth

* 2 Thess. i. 6–9; compare 1 Thess. ii. 14–16.

chapter) into the very noblest expression of grateful joy in Christ as a pure spiritual presence, felt in the soul, to reconcile, comfort, and uplift. It is still the risen Christ in heaven, " at the right hand of God," as in the old prophetic vision; but it is now of a purely gracious celestial force he speaks, manifesting itself in the soul's own comfort, joy, victory, strength, and peace. " I am persuaded that neither death nor life, nor angels nor principalities nor powers, nor things present nor things to come, nor height, nor depth, nor any other created thing,* shall be able to separate us from the love of God, which is in Christ Jesus our Lord.".

3. The later letters have been called "epistles of captivity." Paul writes as a " prisoner of the Lord " from Rome, in declining strength, debarred from his eager activities, very likely in clear anticipation of the inevitable end. His thought of Christ is now wholly reverent, vague, idealizing. He has given full play to the imagination, fed both by the familiar teaching of Jewish schools and by the forms of speculative philosophy that had taken so strong hold on the Jewish mind in Alexandria and elsewhere, which had come to him, doubtless, in the way of his learned education. Now, the Christ of his revering fancy retains no more the sharp outline of the messianic hope, retains but the faintest trace of human personality; he becomes a type of that Divine Energy which it was the chief study of religious speculation then to personify in some form less vague than the Infinite, less precise than a Person or a Will.

* More strictly, " any different order of creation."

Paul does not use the phraseology about the Divine Word which presently became so familiar in Christian philosophy; but the Christ of the "Philippians" and "Colossians" is a bright and vivid reflex of those emanations of half-oriental imagination: "the brightness of the Father's glory and express image of his person"; "in the form of God, though not claiming equality with God"; a pre-existent being, who "takes upon him the form of a servant"; "image of the invisible, first-born of the whole creation"; "through whom all things were created, in heaven or earth." This eager, fervent, passionate expression of reverence and homage, — cleaving still to the image of a suffering and glorified Saviour, to one who, "though he was rich, yet for our sakes became poor," and "took on him the condition of a slave," to die a slave's death on the cross,* — retaining as it does the phrases that had been the familiar utterance of Jewish hope, is the final exaltation and idealizing of that hope. It was the one thing which — by a splendid quickening vision, by a great surge, as it were, of religious enthusiasm, and warm, passionate emotion — floated the yet crude and hesitating thought of the Christian body beyond the boundaries that held it, and made possible the conquests of an aggressive faith.

II. The other point, still more important in considering Christianity as a moral power in the world, is Paul's doctrine of Sin and Justification. I should like, if I could, to get rid of all theological preposses-

---

* This is the image which more than any other impressed the imagination of the early Church, and is most dwelt on in appeals as to the character of Christ's sacrifice.

sion in regard to the meaning of those terms. Paul was, first of all, a Jew, "a Hebrew of the Hebrews." Now, whatever else the Hebrew tradition taught, it certainly did teach the worship of "a Power, not ourselves, that makes for righteousness." It certainly did teach, along with much that was narrow, perverse, grotesque, a very close and anxious obedience to a "law of righteousness." By a thousand petty symbols of ritual purification it enforced the notion of an ideal purity as an attribute of God, and as the aim of man's better life. And over against all this, conceived as it was with the impassioned vividness characteristic of the man, Paul saw — what ?

I will not speak in general terms of " a world lying in wickedness," — the familiar exaggeration of the apologists, one side all black, the other all bright. It was no such thing. The life of Agricola or Germanicus, · as afterwards of Trajan, shows that manhood and public virtue were not extinct in Rome. The stories of Eponina, of Arria, of the elder Agrippina, show that womanly honor and domestic love still remained. The correspondence of Pliny, and the later possibilities of the Antonines and of Epictetus, show that many of the graces of life, and some of its noblest virtues, survived among those who either had heard nothing of the new faith, or else deliberately preferred the old. But I will say, for specific charges, read the ᵗ first chapter of " Romans "; and, for comment, read Tacitus, read Juvenal, read Seneca, read if you will Petronius, written at the very time Paul lived " in his own hired house " at Rome.

Against that insolent riot of indulgence his ethics,

at once austere and humane, stands out in superb
relief. What he calls Sin had a very real and intense
signification to his mind; it forced a heavy burden
and challenge upon his conscience.* In what he says
of the Divine judgment of sin he does not once appeal,
except by vague allusion, to the terrors of a future
world, so strongly pronounced in the Jewish popular
imagination, and reflected so powerfully in the Apocalypse and the parables of Jesus. He speaks of *the
evil thing itself:* the source of it, in human passion
and infirmity; the law of it, that it makes man its
slave; the result of it, in wretchedness, despair, and
death.

Paul's theory of moral evil is mixed up with some
traditional belief of inheritance from Adam; with
some technical philosophy of a threefold nature, —
body, soul, and spirit; with some shadowy view of a
"spiritual body" in the resurrection, to be free from
the corruption of grosser flesh. But, apart from all
matters of mere opinion, I do not know where we
could go for an equally keen and profound sense of
*moral evil in itself.* And, go where we will, I do not
think we can find anywhere so noble, so delicate, so
elevated, so austerely sweet, a code of ethics as we
find scattered through the writings of Paul. The
defects lie on the side of social questions as they
come to us among our political liberties in a more
complex civilization; the errors are almost all from
a certain ascetic vein (not very dangerous to us), or

---

* Sin (ἁμαρτία) is conceived by Paul, in strict accord with the
realistic philosophy of the time, as an objective reality, and not
merely a phase of moral experience. See Romans vii. 17.

else from sundry odd prejudices and grossnesses of the Jewish schools.

The Pauline ethics differs from that of the Gospel in being not purely ideal or sentimental, but practical and definite. For it is to be noticed that the Christian scriptures contain, not one type of ethics, but two: one purely individual, ideal, spiritual, found in the Gospels; the other social and organic, assuming the mixed duties and relations of a somewhat complex society, found in the Epistles.* The background of the first is the simplicity of village life, or else the austere purity of Hebrew worship; the other is incessantly conscious of sharp contrasts in human condition, and of the corruption and cruelty of that profligate age. And, in Paul's exposition of it, it is matched, intentionally and intensely, point for point, against the degrading doctrine and practice of the gentile world. I am sorry that I cannot take time to illustrate this; but there is less need, since nine tenths of the best Christian teaching on the subject (it is hardly too much to say) is made up of illustration and explanation of the texts of Paul.

But, if this were all, it would not constitute, properly speaking, a moral force, any more than that average tone of exposition just spoken of. It might amount to no more than the eloquent declamation of Stoics like Seneca, weak-kneed when the special

---

* It is worth while to notice here that the exaggeration of the former type led to the various forms of Christian asceticism and solitary life, while the other made the base of ecclesiastical organization; and that they will be found represented respectively in the distinction, so sharply drawn in later years, between the regular (or monastic) and the secular clergy.

temptation came: indeed, it is believed by many, with some show of likelihood, that Seneca was a serious student and correspondent of Paul; or it might amount to no more than the gloomy and sceptic satire of Tacitus or Juvenal. What made Paul's doctrine of sin a moral power among men was *his own conviction of sin.* Here, again, I have to use a theological phrase, reluctantly, because there is no other. But the fact itself is easy to see in a study of the man. A certain nervous and morbid temperament, native in him, was prone to exaggerate whatever touched personal feeling; his strict training in the Law made him intensely conscious of whatever bore on personal conduct; a certain eagerness to assume responsibility, to make any given task his own, is seen in his hasty undertaking of the charge to crush the Galilæan heresy at a blow. But here was the one horrible thing which he could never hide or disguise: that battered head, that crushed and bleeding form of the martyr Stephen, and he standing by, eagerly " consenting to his death." That one thing, in his eyes, made him — no, showed him — " the chief of sinners "; and it is as if we saw him with his head bowed and his face hidden, when he says, " I am meanest of the apostles, and not worthy to be called an apostle, because I persecuted the church of God."

The germ of his moral power lay in this, then, that he frankly rated himself — not simply by self-condemnation and regret, but by passionate and deep contrition — among the very ones who most needed the deliverance he announced. To exhibit this point fully it would be necessary to show those symptoms

of a strange and eager craving for expiation by any
sort of religious rite, common alike in the Jewish
and Pagan world.*  The real expiation, the only expiation possible, Paul taught, — and he taught it with
conviction and with power *because he knew it*, — must
be found in a crisis of religious experience, and come
from an act of faith.  All this is wrapped about in
" Galatians " with strange subtilties of argument that
mean nothing to us.  It is joined in " Corinthians "
with technical points of anthropology, and curious
glimpses of personal experience.  It is wrought up
in " Romans " into the most intense and passionate
expression of the burden and the terror of a soul
confronted with the awful law of holiness: " O
wretched man that I am ! who shall deliver me from
the body of this death ? "  And then the peace, sudden
and sweet as a child's sleep after an agony of fright,
when once the reconciling moment has come : " The
Spirit itself beareth witness with our spirit that we
are the children of God ; and if children, then heirs, —
*heirs of God and joint heirs with Christ !* — that if we
suffer with him we may be also glorified together."

So, with all the wickedness and the bondage that
confronted him in the spectacle of the world as it
was, — the gods all dying or dead, old pagan faiths
fast fading out, political freedom perished, a frenzy
of vice and a gloom of superstition invading all the
sanctuaries of human life, — Paul was able to appeal
in the tone of absolute conviction, courage and hope.
Whatever was bitter and intolerable in the evil of
the world, he had shared it too.  Whatever of good-

* See below, pp. 98, 99.

ness men despaired of, he not only believed in, but knew as a fact in his own life: it had broken upon him as a great light out of a black cloud; and so he could change their sullen despondency into an immeasurable and glorious hope.

For the present these are the elements of power which we have to recognize in the life of Paul. I do not add to them that activity in the building up of churches, and their regulation, in which so much of his work consisted: first, because, when the conviction and the brotherhood are strong enough, they will make their own organized forms at any rate; and secondly, because that model organization of the church at Rome, which was presently to embody all of Christianity that men knew or cared about, included so many other elements of power that we hardly think of it as an apostolic work at all. To discuss the forms and the beliefs of the little religious communities which were all Paul knew, would be mere antiquarianism. It is in no antiquarian temper, but as students of those great permanent forces which did once and can again move the world, and create new systems and societies on the ruins of the old, that we should try to understand the genius, the life, and the work of the Apostle Paul.

# III.

## CHRISTIAN THOUGHT OF THE SECOND CENTURY.

WHEN we shift our view to the second Christian century, the first thing that arrests us is the wide gulf that parts us from the comparatively clear ground of the apostolic period. The interval between the last of Paul's undisputed epistles and the first of the extant apologists is something more than eighty years. It is hardly too much to say that that whole space is covered with a heavy mist, out of which, at its close, a few well-defined figures are seen emerging. Any bridge across it must be built, so to speak, "in the air." We can erect our two towers, but the cables will not meet.

Now this period of eighty years is precisely that covered by unsettled controversies respecting the authenticity, date, and authorship of the later New Testament writings, including all the Four Gospels; or illustrated by historical glimpses so dim and few that a chance notice of Tacitus and an official letter of Pliny become our most instructive documents. The gulf hides, so to speak, the very secret of Christianity itself; for, as we shall see further on, what we find in germ only in the apostolic period — in particular, the identification of the Logos with the person of Jesus —

then took root and substance and form.  This subterranean life of the first Christian age has its most touching symbol in the name which belongs to just that period, when those germs were brooding there, — "the Church of the Catacombs."  Of course we do not forget the beauty and interest of the few half-legendary accounts we have of this period, or the purely religious value of some of the writings of the so-called Apostolic Fathers.  But, for purposes of strict consecutive history, it is not too much to say that we have to jump a gulf of more than eighty years.

This statement should not be taken for more than it distinctly asserts.  Its limitation is in the phrase "strict consecutive history."  The period spoken of has even a rich literature of its own, including all the Gospels (probably), as well as several of the later Epistles, the Apocalypse, and the Apostolic Fathers. But the authorship or date of few if any of these is quite undisputed; while the events of the period are almost all in good part legendary or apocryphal.  The existence of the gulf is recognized by all historians; but its importance in the history of doctrinal development is not always sufficiently considered.

Now the existence of this gulf is not a thing to be particularly wondered at.  A very nearly parallel case occurs close by in the strange intellectual slumber which fell upon the Roman mind after the storms of the Republic had subsided to a sullen peace, and which lasted for near a century.  Virgil and Horace had both found shelter from those storms in the patronage of Augustus; Ovid was born the year that Cicero died. After these court poets passed away, only here and there a satire, or a moral essay, or a discourse of rhetoric, breaks the long silence, till comparative liberty and security brought with it the great writers of the silver age. Anecdote and legend, often apocryphal and obscure, are what make most of such history as we have of the earlier Cæsars and their age. So that the forty years during which Palestine comes into strong relief — counting from Matthew to Josephus — make a sort of oasis in a century extraordinarily barren of events or men, though in the full glare of all the imperial splendor and all the ostentatious luxury of the Rome of the Cæsars.

I do not propose to go into any of the literary controversies, or any of the curious antiquarian research, that belong to this obscure period. My business is simply with what we find in the condition of Christian thought at the end of it. For we must not, at all events, suppose that thought was idle during all those years. On the contrary, there must have been a mental movement going on, whose activity and intensity are but feebly reflected to us, — partly in a few stray expressions gathered from epistle or anecdote, but more distinctly (as hinted before) in the figures seen emerging from the mist that overhangs the gulf.

In fact, the period may be best described as one of an intense, warm, *brooding* life. It was a period of incubation, during which were evolved in dim embryo the types that shaped the theological conflicts of many an after age. Landed well on this side of it, we find



D

the Logos doctrine fully developed, — shaped, indeed, into a pretty well defined trinity in Justin and Athenagoras, who appeal to intelligent pagans (like Aurelius) to recognize it as a theism at least as good as the Greek pantheon.*  It is not of the slightest consequence whether we date this Logos doctrine from Philo, before the gospel times,† or from John, towards the end of the first century, or from Christian speculative schools, early in the second.  What we have to observe is, that it has already reached a degree of maturity to which later controversies or councils can only add a few finishing touches by way of exacter definition; and that the mission of Jesus, on its divine or providential side, has already become thoroughly identified, in a certain personal, exclusive, and dogmatic sense, with the advent of that Logos which, existing with God from the beginning, and in its own nature divine, "was made flesh" in him.  The source of this conviction is not at present under discussion;

* This is not the same as the developed trinity of the later creeds : in particular, the distinction between the Logos and the Holy Spirit is quite undefined.  The words of Justin are : " Both Him [God] and the Son who came forth from him and taught us these things, and the host of the other good angels, who follow and are made like to him, and the prophetic Spirit, we worship and adore." Athenagoras says (Chap. 10), " Who would not be astonished, to hear men called atheists, who speak of the Father God and of the Son God and of the Holy Spirit, and who declare both their power in union and their distinction in order ? . . . The Son [is] in the Father, and the Father in the Son, by unity and power of Spirit.  Mind and Reason of the Father [is] the Son of God."  This last expression should be particularly noted, as very characteristic of the thought of the age.

† See the illustrations in "Hebrew Men and Times," pp. 374, 375.

but its existence at this time, with whatever emphasis or whatever fulness my words have already implied, is the fact to be distinctly seen. The time I refer to is from about A. D. 150, the date of Justin's first Apology, to that of Athenagoras, about 175.

One other thing before we come to the sharper characteristics of Christian thought at this time. The descent of the Logos, in the person of Jesus, was for a special work of REDEMPTION, or emancipation from the dominion of Evil. This is, of course, a simple commonplace of Christian theology. But look at it a moment, attentively, and it seems to connect itself by natural evolution with two things: first, the Jewish expectation of a national deliverance, of which enough has been said before; and, second, the drift of Greek speculation, more particularly during the three hundred years previous. That vein of scepticism as to ultimate truth, which crops out in Euripides and in Socrates, took a new turn after the great speculative period of Plato and his school: it turned men's minds to moral problems, and the search for the " chief end of man," or the highest good. Naturally, this made them keenly conscious of existing evil; and the problem of philosophy more and more was the problem of escape from it, — the Epicureans by way of acquiescence, and the Stoics by way of defiance. The Epicureans preached contentment and placidity of soul. The Stoics kept asserting that evil is only in the seeming, as if they hoped by incessant repetition to convince themselves that it is so: in some of Cicero's dialogues, for instance (as the Fifth Tusculan), it is almost startling to find a rehearsal, as it were, of the early Christian creed of emancipation of the soul by martyrdom for the truth.

"The whole creation," says Paul, "groaneth and travaileth in pain together until now, waiting to be delivered." So that the interest with which the claims of Christianity were listened to from the first was something more than a speculative interest in some new theory as to the Divine nature and the law of life. So far as the gospel was true at all, it was true as a gospel of Salvation, — that is, of actual rescue from an actual calamity. That calamity was felt to be in the very conditions of life upon this earth, as men have received them. That rescue receded more and more, in men's thought, from the notion of any special deliverance, such (for example) as the Jews hoped, which did needful service as scaffolding for a time.

The thought of it became inevitably, more and more, an intense craving and yearning: as they beheld, on one side, the political bondage, the insecurity and terror, the frequent crises of great suffering, the moral corruption of society, the doom of death that overhung the world like a pall; or dreamed, on the other hand, of a possible realm of liberty and bliss. The very despair that fell on their souls, when the golden age that Virgil looked for under Augustus, or that Galilæan zealots promised in a revolt from Rome, was set against the terrible reality men saw. Their very despair made them long and ask more passionately for whatever hope might be given them in the faith which now claimed to be the one and final refuge.

We have, I say, to conceive of this, or something like it, as the process going on, during those long years of silence, in the class of minds most apt to entertain such thoughts. The bland moralisms of Seneca, the scornful satire of Juvenal, the caustic portraiture of Tacitus, the frank urbanity of Pliny, the light mockery of Lucian, need not deceive us as to what was really brooding in the mind of the age. An anecdote of Josephus, a hint in Plutarch's *Morals*, a reminiscence of Justin, is far more likely to reflect the mood of mind sure to show itself in the next great evolution of human thought, than the phrases of those haughty and cultured men. What comes into literature is not · merely, and not even so much, the emotion or opinion of the hour; but, rather, what has been brooded on in silence for one generation, before it comes into speech in the next, and then goes into the common inheritance of mankind.

That this is the right view to take of the long interval before spoken of is shown, at any rate, by the very remarkable twofold nature of the phenomenon before us, as soon as the mist is lifted, and we find ourselves in daylight again, amongst articulating men. The phenomenon, I repeat, is not single, but twofold. It is signified to us in the names of the two groups that stand most distinctly before us at the middle of the second century: one, a school already fading or becoming extinct, and known to us only through the attacks or confutations of its opponents; the other, a company of men who speak to us very earnestly the mind of the early Church, and have traced in clear outline the speculative or moral doctrine to be filled in by later times. I mean the Gnostics and the Apologists.

I shall not attempt to add another to the many expositions of the tedious and fantastic schemes known as Gnosticism. For myself, not only I can get into my mind no intelligible meaning from those "endless genealogies," as Irenæus states them, but I cannot easily imagine that any sane mind should hold them as sober matter of opinion, much less take them as the real expression of objective truth. The form these speculations took seems to me perfectly worthless as serving to interpret to our mind what the cast of opinion really was, except as an eccentric style of mere symbolism, or mere analysis. I will say a word of this presently. But, in the mean time, there are two points which it seems to me no more than fair to keep in view, if we would do justice to the men who held to the Gnostic sects; that is, if we would not think of them as mere men of straw, lay figures, decked with impossible habiliments, which we have no occasion to think of as serving any of the uses of human life.

The first point is, that Gnosticism is a genuine and legitimate outgrowth of the same general movement of thought which shaped the Christian dogma. Quite evidently, it regarded itself as the true interpretation of the Gospel, and for a generation or more disputed its title to be that interpretation on even terms with the more orthodox view. Why it eventually failed, even dishonorably failed, I shall consider presently.

Perhaps the first thing that we find hard to reconcile to our mind is the extremely early date at which it appears. The Epistles of the Testament contain many unmistakable hints and traces of it.* Within fifty years after some of those epistles were written it was already on the wane, and in thirty years more it was dead. Yet in the interval it had been a full-fledged philosophy, pretentious and superb as the New Platonism which it helped serve to introduce, and seems to caricature. Not a vestige of it remains, except in fragments and echoes in the writings of its assailants. But, if we think of it, the very fact that its germs already existed in the apostolic time is what helps explain it. It was, in a sense, the double or anti-type of Christianity, — a reflex in men's speculative thought of the same Life which the Church embodied in another way.

In the second place, it was unquestionably sincere, — not a profane mockery and travesty of the truth. It had not, apparently, the highest order of sincerity: it does not appear that any of the Gnostics held any truth so sacred that they were ready to die for it. But that lay in their conception of truth itself. Men do not die for an opinion: they die for a faith. Gnosis, after all, was "opinion," not "knowledge," much less faith. Still, it was an opinion bravely and loyally held, in spite of odium and hostility; and it persistently called itself "Christian," at a time when the Christian name was apt to invite official suspicion or popular rage. Moreover — at least in its riper forms — it had two marked features of a high order of sincerity, even if not the highest. It had a discipline of

* See, for example, Colossians i. 15, et seq., especially the expressions πᾶν τὸ πλήρωμα (i. 19), and θησαυρὸς τῆς γνώσεως (ii. 3).

its own, often scrupulously ascetic and severe ; and it cultivated the religious sentiment, in harmony doubtless with its own style of thought, with abundant seeming fervor.   It had hymns of its own, whole volumes of them, while orthodox Christians still contented themselves with Jewish Psalms.   Thus in all outward seeming — except its incoherent variety of sects — it might well appear not only Christian, which in vehement profession (at least) it was, but a full-grown, highly developed form of religion, amply entitled to hold its own with its antagonist.   Nay, its very variety of sects is something more than mere license of speculation, or an untimely birth of "free religion."   It is a testimony to something ingenuous and spontaneous in its acceptance of the Christian name.   It is at least as good an evidence of genuineness and sincerity as that unity of creed, enforced by ecclesiastical authority or social penalties, by which the Church has always vindicated its claim of truth.*

So much it seemed necessary to say, for historical justice' sake, of those outlying groups of independent thinkers, who make the strangest problem of early Christianity.   But it is also necessary to go one step further, — to say not only why Gnosticism failed as an interpreter of the new religious life, but why it has justly been under the ban of more serious believers. And this is not because of the scandals and immoralities charged against it.   Odium at least as bad lay just as heavily against the Christian body at large ;

* As an instructive commentary on the supposed unity and harmony of the first Christian age, Epiphanius gives us a list of forty-three distinct "heresies" (including the Gnostic), belonging to the period under review.

and, if that had gone down in the great persecution, it would have gone down with a black stigma on its name, which could never have been washed off. What Irenæus said, at a distance and long after, in theologic hate, may go for what it is worth. The fatal thing in Gnosticism was that *it made of religion a theory for the understanding, and not a life to the soul.* Its creed, or "gnosis," consisted in speculations about the origin of existence, the origin of evil, and the method of salvation, — by turns ascetic and antinomian, like all mere speculative creeds. Considered in themselves, these speculations may have been as good as men could invent then, — or now either, for that matter, — vain and fantastic as they appear to us. They were, in the main, a perfectly legitimate following out of a mode of thinking, which not only has the sanction of great names like Plato, but is at bottom the same from which the Logos-doctrine itself was evolved. From the brightest orthodoxy to the blackest heresy is but a step.

In a matter vague and abstract like this, it is always best to see how the same problem shows itself to a modern mind. Read, then, that chapter in "Ways of the Spirit," where an analysis is given of the methods by which men have attempted to find out God, — in other words, to trace the passage from Absolute Being to the manifold forms of actual Existence ; and notice how helpless the mind is at every step, till it seems at length easiest to say, that there is no real existence at all except pure Intellect, of which matter or sensation is but a mood of experience. Now, imagine a busy and speculative mind,

3 *

utterly void of the certitudes of science, to busy itself with that problem. I shall have to return to this
point again, when we come to the realist and nomi-
nalist discussions of the Schoolmen. So now I will
say only this. That great impassable gulf from
Infinite to Finite, which Plato made the sphere of
divine Intelligence, in which lived those eternal Ideas
that were the patterns of all material things, the
Gnostics attempted to bridge by way of symbol and
analysis, and to fill up with Æons, or "eternals,"
having such names as Thought, Man, Soul, Wisdom,
and so on, giving these bleak conceptions a certain
fantastic life, and sequence by way of emanation or
evolution.*

These phantom-existences, set by Valentinus in
pairs, male and female, thirty in all, and made to
succeed one another by some spectral process of generation, are said to be derived from the Jewish
Cabbala. Their names are the carrying out of a
notion we find in Plato's *Parmenides*, that everything
which exists in the realm of life, or fact, has its counterpart or prototype in the region of Ideas, — which
are made to have, as it were, a shadowy life of their
own. Thus, in the scheme of Valentinus : —

DEPTH (Father of All) and SILENCE (or Thought) begat
MIND (unconscious Intelligence ?) and TRUTH ; which begat
REASON (*Logos*, conscious Intelligence) and LIFE ; which begat
MAN and ECCLESIA (or Church) : i. e. the Ideal Society.†

* Words of like but inverse meaning, as if each were the other's
reflection in a mirror. Emanation begins with the highest form
of being and works downward ; Evolution with the lowest, and
works upward.

† These eight Æons make the Valentinian *Ogdoad.*

In these it will be noticed that the former of each pair is a masculine name, and the latter a feminine; so that it was impossible to speak of them except as "he" or "she." To us they are only names, like the categories of modern metaphysics; but to the Greek mind their very grammatical gender suggested veritable forms of life, and logical analysis itself became a sort of transcendental theogony.

We may put the problem of Gnosticism from another point of view, something as follows. The age of the world being generally assumed to be between five and six thousand years (more precisely, 5200), the question naturally occurs, What was there, then, before that time (or, as they would put it, before Time was)? To this the only answer can be, The Infinite. But, again, is this an infinite Void (the Unknowable), or an infinite Fulness? Infinite Fulness ($\pi\lambda\acute{\eta}\rho\omega\mu a$), replied the Gnostics; and, to fill out the conception of it, devised their wild genealogies and cosmogonies. How, through the Æons Logos and Christ, these were connected with the Christian scheme, and how, through the Inferior Wisdom (*Sophia Achamoth*) with the realm of Matter and of Evil, it belongs to a more detailed exposition to set forth.

In short, Gnosticism is a philosophy of evolution, — vague, premature, with no substance of verifiable fact or scientific method, and carried over from the realm of things to that of abstractions or mere visions and phantasms of things. Its favorite term "genesis" — or Birth by natural process as opposed to intelligent Creation — is attacked by the Apologists, exactly as its counterpart "evolution" is attacked to-day, on the ground of incompatibility with moral freedom. To illustrate this phase of it, I translate here a Gnostic hymn of Valentinus, given by Hippolytus, which one might fancy taken straight from Shelley's *Prometheus* or Goethe's *Faust :* * —

> " All things on Spirit borne I see !
> Flesh from Soul depending,
> Soul from the Air forth-going,
> From Æther Air descending,
> Fruits from the Depth o'erflowing :
> So from the Womb springs Infancy."

All these speculations seem to me neither better nor worse — though a good deal more poetic — than the efforts to solve the problem of existence which we find in more modern times. The fatal thing about them is that they were made the substance or the substitute of Religion. In calling them a philosophy of Evolution, we have said in advance how and where they failed. Schemes of evolution, taken by themselves, do not give us the specific fact of SIN. If not avowedly, at any rate by tendency and by implication, they deny the fact of moral freedom. In trying to account for Evil, they annihilate its nature as the conscience apprehends it, — the *wilful* violation of divine law.

Here was the incurable weakness of Gnosticism, its fatal flaw. What evil it recognized was in the nature of things, in Matter as opposed to Mind. That is, it was natural as opposed to moral evil; to be known by Thought, not by Conscience. Of this we

---

* The rhythmic form of the Greek may be found in Bunsen's " Christianity and Mankind," Vol. V. p. 96.

shall see more when we come to Augustine's conflict with that final form of Gnosticism known as Manichæan. At present, we have to do only with the single point of its moral impotence. Gnosticism was in its nature absolutely — nay, ridiculously — incapable of what I have before called "ethical passion." To save society in those days, to re-create the world, to inaugurate a new era of humanity — the task which Christianity did in fact achieve — was not a speculative, it was a moral problem.* It demanded courage, faith, self-sacrifice ; a willingness to go to the rack, the stake, the lions, rather than say a false word, or do an act capable of a disloyal interpretation. Such tests do not come to us in these days, and we are apt to forget that they were needed once. When Basilides said it was permitted to throw incense on a pagan chafing-dish, or mutter a prayer to Cæsar with a mental reservation, the doom of Gnosticism was sealed.

Now, side by side with the Gnostics in the field was another class of men and women whom we call Confessors, and their spokesmen we call Apologists. Those of them who died on the field are glorified in the church record as saints and martyrs. Their tragic and pathetic story is well told by Milman, and I shall not abridge it here. Such names as Ignatius and Polycarp, as Blandina and Perpetua, ought to be sufficiently familiar. But it is very interesting to notice the style of thought that runs through the

---

* It appears to me that in his very interesting exposition Maurice misses this point, which is more distinctly seen by Mansel. Maurice is a good deal of a gnostic himself, in the fervor of his speculative faith.

Christian writings of the latter half of the century. We trace in them two things : a strong ethical reaction against the speculative tendency just spoken of ; and what Mr. Maurice * has well indicated as a distinct effort *to construct a religious system*, able to hold its own before the powers of the world, — distinct, that is, from the simple motive of seeking faith and salvation in the religion itself.  The moral reaction it is fair enough to call the antithesis of Gnosticism, and the constructive tendency its counterpart.

The most obvious symptom of the first is, of course, the defence of the Christian society on moral grounds:† the claim of purer lives, and the contrast with pagan vices ; the vehement denial of unclean and criminal acts charged against Christian assemblies ; the incessant denunciations of paganism on the ground of its corrupt mythology.

Each head of the defence emphasizes some point of appeal to conscience, to the natural sense of right and wrong.  The weak side of the old society — its easy indulgence to the flesh — is pitilessly exposed ; and a certain austere sanctity of domestic morals, a purity in the relation of man and wife, a tenderness in the relation of parent and child, quite alien from heathen custom, is especially dwelt on.  The common virtues of life, as we should reckon them in any orderly and decent condition of things, are pressed in a way that shows what bitter calumnies were in

---

* "Ecclesiastical History of the First and Second Centuries."

† It is worth noting, that none of the writers of this period (I think) except Irenæus claim miraculous powers for the Church, though some assert that demons were busy on behalf of the pagans.  This does not, however, exclude wonders in some of the martyrologies.

vogue, and with what serious pains the foundations were getting laid for those grave moralities which have been the real heart of Christian civilization since. It would be tedious to go into illustration of this; but I think no one can read the Apology of Justin, the Apostolic Constitutions, the grave homilies of Clement, or even the loud tirades of Tertullian, without feeling that a new life was growing up, organized, serious, strong, and wholesome; a life which flowed broadly below political changes on one side, and theological controversies on the other; a life which was getting knit and braced, by vigilant discipline, against the time when it must abide the storm of imperial persecution, or undertake the enormous task of meeting the wild and brutal forces of the barbarian world. Either crisis would have been fatal, unless there had been, at bottom, an absolute loyalty, most assiduously cherished, in the great war of Good and Evil. However imperfect its interpretation, or its theory, yet the life of the Christian society was staked on its unhesitating faith in a Power that makes for righteousness.*

* It is hard to overstate the extreme seriousness, what some would call puritanism, of the writings referred to. A brief chapter on *Smiling*, by Clement of Alexandria (who allows it in moderation), is, I think, the only relief to the rigor of the attitude in which the Christians found themselves, in the battle of good and evil which was upon them. The same severe temper is shown in the bitter hostility of Tertullian (when a Montanist) against the novel doctrine of Hermas, of a possible repentance and pardon after baptism. (See Mossman's "Early Church," pp. 315–320.) The most serious controversy of the Church, early in the third century, was that sustained by Cyprian against the puritan exclusiveness of the Novatians.

It is important to recognize this feature first of all, because it is disguised in part by the crudeness of idea and the very simplicity of good faith with which these defences are put forth. It is hard, for instance, to conceive how Justin could have mistaken a large part of what he says for argument; or how Marcus Aurelius could have kept the philosophic patience he was so famous for, through Justin's long, irrelevant harangue (as it must certainly have seemed to him) about the Hebrew prophecies.

Again, in the face of the calm rationalism that for centuries had screened or allegorized the old Greek fables for all thinking men, the Apologists must needs, in weary iteration, one after the other, repeat the dull recital of the scandals of Olympus,—possibly, to some good popular effect, — without hinting at anything less offensive than the baldest literal understanding of them, exactly as some modern free-thinkers have treated the Old Testament.

The frankness and vigor, too, with which the noblest doctrines of natural theology are discarded,— such as the immortality of the soul, which is thrust aside to make way for the dogma of a miraculous revival of the corpse, argued out in the oddest detail, and (naturally) with the grossest ignorance of the facts adduced in illustration, — serve to prejudice a modern mind unfairly against the main argument itself. I need hardly add the vituperative calumnies of such writers as Tatian, in his clamor against Greek philosophy, or the rhetoric of Tertullian, deepening to vindictive exultation, — which is, after all, mere rhetoric, — as he contemplates the pits of eternal flame, into which the enemies of the Church shall be cast. These things have left a stain upon the memory of that age, quite plain enough in the view of the average historian; and therefore it is right that they should be mentioned here, only to put in clearer relief the testimony to the real power and sincerity of the moral life they disfigure.

The relations of the Christian community to the Roman world at this period offer a very wide topic, of which I can touch only a single point or two. It is a familiar question, Why did the Roman empire deal so much more harshly with the Christian religion than with other local faiths, which it received on easy terms into its wide pantheon? And it is a familiar answer, Because the Christian religion was in its nature uncompromising, and at bottom carried with it the destruction of Paganism itself, with the imperial system closely bound up with it. This answer, too, is illustrated by the refusal of the Christians to pay the customary official homage to Cæsar, which they held blasphemy, — refusal that in them was held constructive treason; and, still further, by the fact that the Church was from the first a form of polity as well as a system of belief, and held the germ of a new organization of society ($\pi o\lambda\iota\tau\epsilon\iota a$), which was felt to be gradually crowding out the old. All this, it is said, must have been clear to the mind of a thoughtful pagan, like Aurelius; and sufficiently accounts for the fact that he, the most scrupulously just of all the emperors of this period save one, and most gravely resolved to heal the evils of the state, was also sternest of all to put in force the laws against the Christians.

E

To this statement, however, two things should be added : that the earlier persecutions seem all — as we see in the case of Polycarp — to have been a concession to popular clamor and the temper of the mob; and that this popular hate runs a great way back, long before the least public danger could have been thought of, from an obscure and petty sect.  Thus in Paul's church at Rome were some of Nero's household; Commodus was capriciously indulgent to the Christians; the language of Trajan and Hadrian is at worst that of impatient contempt.*  I have spoken elsewhere of the persecution under Nero, — a mere cowardly turning of the popular rage against a class that lay too easily open to suspicion.  Why was that? and why were the mob so ready always with the most abominable charges against the Christians, — " Œdipodean marriages and Thyestean feasts," as Athenagoras reports ?

It is, of course, impossible to go behind the reports to investigate the charges.  There have been students of these things, who have believed that the worst of them were true, — that the sacred " mysteries " did include the tasting of blood and sensual excess.†  Possibly, in instances.  Cases of horror, frightful or disgusting, have not been unknown in religious orgies in modern times; ‡ and Christians even then were

* The term Trajan addresses to Ignatius is κακόδαιμον, which Mr. Maurice translates " poor devil."

† The specific forms of these calumnies may be found in Tertullian's *Ad Nationes* and *Apologeticus*.  For illustration of the style of criticism referred to, see the very curious volume of Daumer.

‡ Take that of the *Convulsionnaires*, for example, a century and a half ago, which sprang from a sect with such grave antecedents as the Jansenists.

not slow to throw off the charge upon heretical assemblies.  Think of the raw material that entered into their composition, — in Syria and North Africa, for example ; and that they called, avowedly, "not righteous, but sinners, to repentance."

But consider, too, how likely the religious language of Christians was to invite, or at least give color to, those charges.  If the Apocalypse, for example, or any of its imagery, was composed and current in the time of Nero, what more likely than that its vague threats of a sea of fire to engulf the guilty kingdoms of the earth should have been caught up and used to accuse the Christians of that vast conflagration in which half Rome perished ?   What more likely — at a time when the most innocent word easily took a lewd signification * — than that the Christian language about a God of love, and of greetings with a holy kiss, should have been grossly but honestly misunderstood ? What more likely than that the frank symbolism,· favorite and familiar to Christian lips, — " Except ye eat the flesh of the Son of Man, and drink his blood, ye have no life in you," — should have been quoted to justify the most horrid accusation of cannibal banquets at the table and the cup of sacrifice ?  We know how easily such stories spread, and what frenzy of hate they will engender.

It is likely, too, as implied in a hint of Suetonius, — nay, from what happened in the ferocious revolt under Hadrian it is certain, — that the popular mind made no distinction between Christian and Jew.   It was not so much, says Tacitus, the charge of the burn-

---

* Thus, in his own time, Erasmus says, it was not reckoned comely to use the verb *amo*.

ing, as of hatred against all mankind,* that embittered the persecution under Nero. And the fresh memory of the horrors in Cyprus and Palestine, more than fifty years later, which Justin alludes to as the background of his dialogue with the Jew Trypho, had its share in keeping up the frenzy of popular hate and fear which, more than any imperial policy, was the real ground of the terror that always menaced the Christian body: just as we may imagine the horrors of the Paris Commune, in 1871, not only to sharpen the vigilance of the German police against socialistic conspiracy now, but to goad the enemies of socialism with the haunting, unforgiving hate that is born of fear.

There is one other illustration of the Christian life of this period, of which a word must be said in conclusion. I have spoken of the temper that runs through most of the "Apologists," as a moral reaction against the purely speculative views of Gnosticism. Of course, that reaction ran out into crudities and excess. The hostility of Marcion against the Old Testament; the sect of " Alogi," or " Wordless " Christians, who would hear nothing of any Logos at all; the harsh asceticism of the " Encratites " or " wrestlers " against Satan, — are to be reckoned as so many " heresies," more or less allied with Gnosticism, yet of rather an ethical than speculative cast. The exaggerated, untempered, and eccentric moral phases exhibited by Tertullian, Neander explains by calling him an " anti-gnostic," — making this the extreme form the reaction took, and so accounting for what most offends in him.

* Merivale's interpretation of *odio humani generis*.

As part of the same phenomenon, too, we must reckon the blazing out of the spiritualistic fervor of Montanism in the East,* which cut adrift, like Quakerism or Methodism, from the formalities and the sober traditions of the Christian body, and claimed to be a new dispensation, under the immediate guidance of the Holy Ghost, as promised in the last discourse of Jesus, — a sort of Gnosticism reversed (as Baur explains it), finding in its dogma an account, not of the *beginning*, but the *end* of all things.

That peculiar fanaticism has reappeared, in many forms, from age to age, — always, it is probable, as a protest against some exaggeration of formality and tradition ; and the heat of it has always been absorbed, to thaw out some gathering stiffness, or to warm some pale intellectuality. The extravagant pretensions of Montanism did no particular harm. But they occasioned some scandal, and even alarm, at a time when the Church was not used to dealing with such disordered symptoms. Its language was blasphemous, perhaps, to the sober ear. It made more apparent the value and the need of the restraints it despised; and so had its share, doubtless, in strengthening the hands of authority, to the confirming of creed and ritual.

This, then, is the condition to which we are brought at the end of the second Christian century. One great phase of purely speculative development has been left behind. The growing life of Christendom has been asserted, again and again, to have its roots

* Of which Mossman's "Early Christianity" gives a very appreciative account.

in morality, and for its law the law of personal holiness, — however technically, ascetically, or imperfectly understood. There is already a lengthening calendar of saints, martyrs, and heroes, making a sacred and powerful bond of union. There is a fast-growing consciousness that Christianity is to be shaped and developed into a community, understanding itself, organic, with its own authoritative belief and law. The pressure of imperial power and of popular suspicion still holds it in check from spreading too vaguely, and melting away in fatal forms of compromise. And, for the expression of that life, we have already the group of writers and teachers I have named, whose lives are closing with the century, — Irenæus, Clement, and Tertullian, to be immediately followed by the equal or greater names of Cyprian and of Origen.

# IV.

## THE MIND OF PAGANISM.

IN our study of early Christianity, it is easiest and most common to think of Paganism simply as its antagonist, or opposite ; and to regard the process going on as one purely of conquest or conversion. It is so in the main. There was a new spirit at war with the old institutions and beliefs. The eye catches first and most readily the dramatic contrast, watches with keenest interest the fortunes of the battle. The radical difference is what we have seen something of already, in the Christian thought of the second century, and shall see more of in the sharper collisions yet to come.

But this is not the only view. It is not even, strictly speaking, the truest view. Leaven works in the lump, not by destruction, but by co-operation. Christianity was at work " like leaven," — like a new element of great power suddenly set free, not to the extinction or exclusion of those that were there before, but to the making of new compounds, in which all their former potency abides under other names. Nitrogen and hydrogen are not nearly so unlike in their own apparent properties, as in the combinations they make with the oxygen that attacks them both. To understand the Christian movement justly, however imperfectly, we must know something of the material it wrought upon. And of this, not merely its falsehood, unbelief, or moral decay; but the positive side as well, — the serious thought, the vigorous life, the genuine piety, that still had their place in the mind of Paganism.

For it is to be seen, not only that the old Pagan faiths had not died out at the coming of Christianity, as we are apt to think; but that what was best and truest in them had taken a new start, as it were, and a genuine pagan revival was to some extent keeping pace with the stronger religious growth that at length absorbed, or else suppressed it. For a time, however, not only the two movements are not antagonistic to each other; they are, in a sense, independent efforts after a similar ideal. The rapid and powerful process of organization in Christianity itself would not have been possible, unless a part of its work had been already done by its antagonist. The Providence itself that wrought in it would not have been so clear, without that spiritual and moral preparation which was going on in the pagan world.

It has been common enough to recognize two forms of this preparation. One is in the way of religious craving after some good yet unattained. "We know," says Paul, "that the whole creation groaneth and travaileth in pain together until now, waiting to be delivered." Of this I shall say a word presently. The other is in the way of philosophic speculation, which failed to interpret these longings for a higher life, but did much to shape the mould in which the victorious dogma was long after cast. Besides these is a third phase, which makes the object of our study now.

Attention has been called * to the great contrast in temper and spirit between the time of the fall of the Roman Republic and that of the culmination of the Empire two centuries later, between the time of Cicero and that of Marcus Aurelius. In the earlier time we have complete scepticism and negation. The fountain of old belief seems to have quite run dry. As to the forms of pagan ritual, once so venerable, Cicero does not see how its diviners can look one another soberly in the face. In his writings — by far the broadest and completest reflection we have of the mind of any ancient period — we find three phases, or moods, so utterly distinct as to seem out of keeping with any one era, not to say any one honest mind. In his Speeches, he is the eloquent conservative, appealing profusely for popular effect to the immortal gods, whose providence is too plain for cavil in any crisis of the state, whose judgments are sure and terrible to all who defy their law. In his Dialogues, the very existence of these gods is an open question, calmly debated in friendly philosophical discourse; while the ideal life of pious contemplation, the confident hope of immortal peace and communion of conscious spirits beyond the grave, appear to make the sure foundation and deep background of his thought. In his Letters, both these phases disappear: the friendly courtesy, the party passion, the personal mortification or resentment, love or hate, are purely on a

* Boissier, *La Religion Romaine*, from which several of the following illustrations are taken.

secular level; even the confidences of intimate friendship, or the sharpest sorrows of private life, give no one hint of anything so distant and unreal as a religious interpretation to its riddle, or a ray of that comfort of which he is so eloquent when he robes himself as a philosopher. For any personal conviction, any guidance of conduct, any stay of character, religion —if it means anything more than Roman justice or Roman pride — is an absolute blank. And, beside the best of his contemporaries, Cicero is a man of even exemplary piety.

Now immediately after the age of Cicero, in the first years of the new Empire, there are symptoms of a profound change. Not only the head of the state professes himself the patron of piety and morals, and chooses a religious title, "Augustus," by which he is to be most familiarly known to the minds of men: speaking the most serious thought of his time, Virgil dwells on the golden age which a divine providence is just opening to mankind, in images and phrases which many have thought borrowed directly from Hebrew prophets; so that his name and verse became the charm that won for the mind of Paganism a place in the widening domain of Christian culture. And as the Empire, in spite of calamity and crime, grew more broad, magnificent, and strong, the same feeling deepened into a *religion of the Empire*, all the more formidable to the Christian faith because it was genuine and sincere; not merely, as we are too apt to think, because it was cruel, degenerate, and corrupt.

This New Paganism, as we may call it, went along with an increasing moral earnestness and religious fervor. The moral feeling might be capricious, blind, and intolerant; the religious fervor might run into the wildest superstition. There was never a faith · yet that was not disgraced by its most zealous adherents. But the contrast is hardly greater between the implacable passions of the civil war and Virgil's pious hopes of peace, than that between the blank incredulity of Julius Cæsar and his age and the serene kindliness of Antoninus Pius, or the religious Meditations of Marcus Aurelius, — the noblest of Stoics on the most august of thrones.

The Stoic doctrine was the intellectual interpretation of the new pagan faith. In its speculations on the origin of things, still more in its ethical ideal, it is curiously near to some of the noblest phases of Christian theology and morals. It is not likely, though many argue still, that Seneca learned that doctrine from the Apostle Paul; but no one can read the writings of both without feeling how much is of a common spirit, if not from a common source. And what in Seneca is mere ethical glow has within a century become, in Antoninus and Aurelius, the fervor of a genuine religious life. The "reign of the Stoics," represented by such names as these, does infinitely more honor to the faith that inspired it than anything we find in the first half-century, at least, of the Christian Emperors. We may even have to come down as far as St. Louis of France to find their parallel.

How far, on the other hand, may the Christian theology and morals have been indebted to the doctrine of the Stoics? A few words will serve to show their points of likeness, and their fundamental difference.*

The Stoic cosmogony shows itself as a compromise between the conception of a pre-existent personal Creator, outside the universe which he brings into being, — the idea of earlier philosophers and of the world at large, — and the notion of Matter blindly guided by Force, the doctrine of Democritus and Epicurus. To the Stoic the universe was not *made by* God ; it *was* God, and endowed with all the attributes necessary to his conception of a Divinity, including power, intelligence, wisdom, and justice. This Divinity had from eternity a fixed and unchanging purpose, which was the *Pronoia,* or *Providentia,* — the everlasting Reason appearing in the succession of events. Such a Divinity differs from the Christian ideal chiefly in the absence of personal love and care for his offspring ; and even as to this, the *Pronoia* is almost an affectionate interest in Man, — not *men.* The fact that this Being is identified with the universe is of no account. It would be more true to say, that the universe is identified with the Divinity. The world is seen as the successive emanations and withdrawals of the Divine Reason, the eternal *Logos.* It is the systole and diastole of the Divine nature, alternately developing, through the series of the four elements, from fire — conceived as the primitive and natural form of intelligent matter — into the other three, in the order of their density, and back again to the form of fire. Thus the fundamental conception is not creation, but evolution or emanation.

* Compare " Hebrew Men and Times," pp. 352–357. For some of the following illustrations I am indebted to Prof. J. B. Greenough.

Of this animate universe, with its periodicity of creation (if we may call it so) and extinction, everything, even the soul of the Stoic sage, forms a part. Virtue is the perfect adjustment of all the desires and acts of the soul — in Christian phraseology, the submission of the will — to the universal and persistent LOGOS, the divine reason and providence. Virtue is thus, necessarily, one and indivisible. This ethical view is essentially the same with that of the more rigid Christian sects. "Whosoever shall offend in one point, he is guilty of all." All wrong-doing and all right-doing must be alike in value. On this side the razor's edge, it is all good; on that side, all evil. Growth in goodness, properly speaking, there can be none.

All the Stoic paradoxes are the logical following out of this view. A man either is, or he is not, in harmony with the divine order of the universe. If he is, he is "the wise man" (*sapiens*); if not, he is "the fool" (*stultus*). These two are all. A man cannot be approaching wisdom. He is no nearer to it with a thousand excellences (*virtutes*) than with one, — like the string of a piano, which makes a discord till it is perfectly in tune. The "wise man" is the perfect human being; * that is, perfectly adjusted to the rest of the universe of which he forms a part. The one problem of life is to make the Divine Reason paramount and supreme in the sphere of one's own conduct. "He has a truly great mind," say the Stoics, "who surrenders himself wholly to God." His

---

* "Operis sic optimus omnis est opifex, solus sic rex, solus formosus."

assurance of the right is his only and sufficient reward. To him can be no evil, and no pain : all is. reconciled in the universal Order. He alone is free, or rich, or of a sound mind; he, in truth, is the only sovereign.

Of this serious and enlightened pagan gospel a single point may be remarked. To say nothing of the wealth of doctrine gathered about the Messianic idea and the person of Jesus, Stoicism lacked the one thing which made the Christian gospel a power in the religious life of mankind. This was what we may call Paul's method of salvation, of which the cardinal points are *conviction of sin* and *salvation by faith.* This method is as true, psychologically, as it was then and is now essential to any genuine vigor of religious life in the soul. If we allow ourselves to think of Christianity as the development of a system of doctrine, we shall exactly miss its secret, — the one thing that makes its triumph intelligible or its history worth our study. Christianity as a scheme of doctrine may be doubtfully balanced against one or two pagan schemes, Stoic or Neo-Platonic, from both of which it borrowed very largely. But, as *a method of the divine life,* it had a power from another source, for lack of which Stoicism miserably failed.

We have before us, then, two features of the later Paganism, which we may call the religion of the people and the religion of the philosophers. To these we may add a third influence, working powerfully in the same general direction, and shown in the reform of the Roman Law. The period we are considering is called by Gibbon " the learned and splendid era of jurisprudence." It culminated, a little later, in the great jurists of the third century; but the expanding, softening, humanizing process, carried out in the successive Christian codes, was distinctly the fruit of the early imperial age. The crude, stiff formalism of the older code,* with its effete system of domestic tyranny,† was shaped and tempered by larger maxims of equity, and by the humaner spirit that grew up as national boundaries melted into the large system of the Roman world.

These three — piety among the people, Stoicism with the philosophers, law reform among the jurists — we must set over against the decay of faith, the moral corruption, and the political languor which are the symptoms most commonly taken note of in the pagan empire. They are not the whole of the picture. They are not, by any means, its more salient points. But, hidden as they often are in the background, they serve not only for relief to darker impressions; they are quite necessary to be taken into account, to explain the remarkable phenomenon of the extension of Christianity at the end of the second century. "We are a people of yesterday," says Tertullian, in his tempestuous challenge to the pagan world; "yet we have filled every place among you, — cities, islands, forts, towns, assemblies; your very camps, your tribes, companies, palace, senate, forum. We leave you nothing but your temples."

These words, we must remember, were written hot

* See illustrations in Gibbon, and in Maine's " Ancient Law."

† The *patria potestas.* See Troplong, *De l'Influence du Christianisme sur le Droit Civile des Romains*, p. 62.

from witnessing the martyrdoms of Carthage, not long before the persecutions of Decius, which made the signal of a war of extermination against the Christian Church. To a cooler eye, that war must have seemed likely to succeed. The persecution of Christianity by the Roman emperors, it is true, was capricious and occasional; and it occurred at long enough intervals — averaging some twenty years — to allow amply for the peaceable spread of the new religion. Christianity not as a moral force, or even as a system of dogma, but only as a quasi-political structure dangerous to the state, was the thing attacked. Moreover — to judge from the edicts of Diocletian — quiet suppression was the thing aimed at: the atrocious cruelties recorded by Eusebius were wilful acts of local governors, and the very execution of the edicts might be systematically evaded (as by Constantius Chlorus) without any rebuke from the central power. We find nothing in these centuries to compare with the virulence and ferocity with which the Reformers in France and the Netherlands were hunted down; still less, to compare with the diabolical craft and efficiency of the Spanish Inquisition. Pagan Rome showed never such wary and patient cruelty as Papal Rome. There was, however, one moment when its whole weight bore on the rising faith to crush it. If Christianity triumphed in the end, it was by virtue of a very wide sympathy and a very extensive preparation in the mind of Paganism. And the moral ground on which this rested was the same that had already put forth that independent growth of conscience and piety, just spoken of as the latest and best fruit of the ancient creed.

If we look more carefully at the case before us, we see that this later Paganism, the popular religion of the Empire, grew up along with the great political change which suddenly turned a grinding municipal tyranny into a broad imperial system embracing many states. Christian writers have always pointed to that system as the manifest opening of the way by Divine Providence to the march of the true religion. We shall see, for example, how distinctly this thought lies in the appeals to faith of Leo the Great.

It is just as true of the religious and moral conditions as it is of the political conditions. The old nature worship, formulated in the popular Italian creed, and embodied in the state religion of republican Rome, was as formal and rigid as the aristocratic code of the old law; inconceivably precise, minute, timid, and often cruel. Ovid* relates the curious myth — a grotesque parallel to the intended sacrifice of Isaac and the substitution of a ram — in which the good Numa palters with his deity, and evades the shocking demand of human sacrifice, outwitting the divinity in a play of words. "I demand," says Jupiter, "the head" — "of a leek," says the pious king; "of a live" — "fish," interposes Numa; "man," insists the god; "one hair I give you." Jupiter laughs, and Numa's point is gained.

Livy has many a story of the same grim half-humorous formalism. Thus, to foil a prophecy that the Gauls should occupy the soil of Rome, two captive Gauls, a man and a woman, are buried alive within the city limits. Some soldiers in revolt think

---

* Fasti, iii. 339–344.

to free their conscience from their military oath by killing the consuls, to whom they have sworn it. Papirius, on the eve of battle, is deceived by a false official report of a favorable omen : the sacred chickens have eaten heartily. Being told, later, that the report was false, " The peril," said he, " is with the officer who sent it ; him the gods will doubtless punish justly ; as for myself, I am bound by the report sent me in due form." Accordingly, he is victorious in the battle, while the lying officer is killed.

Political sagacity or military sense, again,.kept the old formalism in check, so that it was rarely suffered to stand in the way of policy. Its verbal juggles were oftener used to patch up some atrocious state-craft or treachery, like that by which the Roman armies escaped from the Caudine Forks, where the general held as hostage, assuming to be a Samnite citizen, insults the Roman envoy, and so brings on a new cause of war ; or else gave way to a rude rationalism, as when a commander of the fleet orders the sacred chickens that will not eat to be pitched overboard, where at any rate they must drink. But the sentiment of it lay very deep in the popular heart. It is a remarkable illustration of Roman feeling that, on the day of his triumph, Julius Cæsar, the Epicurean rationalist and the merciless destroyer, mounted on his knees the long flight of stairs that led up to the Capitol, that by this act of ostentatious humility he might avert those divine judgments supposed to be provoked by inordinate felicity.

It is not easy to see just how the Italians regarded their popular divinities. Their worship (if we may

call it so) seems often frank fetichism of the rudest
sort. Their very names, as Augustine recounts them,* 
seem as consciously make-believe as those in a fairy
story. Thus, as we should say, the babe is brought
to birth by the good fairy Light (*Lucina*); a second
(*Levana*) receives it in her arms; ministering sprites
(*Cuba, Rumina, Cunina*) take charge of the offices of
sleeping, nursing, and laying the infant in the cradle;
in due course he is given in charge of the attendant
fairies Walky, Talky, Eaty, Drinky, Outgo, Home-
come, and so on to others, whose names are about
equally ingenious and recondite, down to the sad
genius Waily (*Nænia*), lamenting at the burial.†

In all this, which the excellent Christian saint
stigmatizes as idolatry and superstition, — to say
nothing of deities that to him are simply unclean
devils, — we should probably see nothing more than
the same childish, half-reverent fancy, which crowds
the infant lore of our day with similar innocent im-
personations. Human life is beset, and the natural
world is crowded, with very real powers, utterly
mysterious to us; and what we call the old nature-
religions include, along with many a dismal superstition, some tender, trustful, grateful recognition of
a living Force, to which mere natural science is apt
to blind us. What made these simple fancies hateful
and abhorrent to the Christian mind was that they
were part of the habit and the system wrought up

* *De Civitate Dei*, vi. 9.

† Among these names are *Educa, Potina, Cuba, Abeona, Adeona,
Iterduca, Domiduca*, and many others, for which see Keller, x. 3
(Dietz's Paris ed.).

into the tremendous despotism of Rome. The paganism which included them had also its horrible and revolting side, full of violence, cruelty, and corruption ; and so they had to take their flight, along with the nymphs of mountain, wood, and wave, before the wrath and hate of an austerer faith.

The great gods of Italian worship were no doubt simply the powers of nature personified. Saturn is the seed-time, Jupiter the sky, Juno the air, Janus (Dianus) the sun-god, with his feminine partner Diana, the moon ; Mars is the mighty, Venus is spring-tide (later, beauty or love), and so on. Our associations with these names come mostly from the Greek fables, which Latin poets and mythologists imported ready made. To the popular mind, most likely, they were abstractions nearly as vague and dim as our Electricity, Gravitation, and the like,— except that they were objects of more real awe, and were regarded with the same curious formalism we have noted before. As has been said, they were divine Functions (*numina*), rather than divine Persons. As soon as the functions are dimly seen, or absorbed by a growing positivism, the divinity becomes a scarecrow or laughing-stock : thus we see how Plautus makes fun of the mythological sanctities.

This list is filled out with names that to us are absolutely no more than abstract qualities, — Honor, Manhood, Terror, Fortune, Public Safety, — which seem quite as real as the rest. But the deity, the function, or the quality, is strictly localized. Each town has its own divinity, potent there, void and impotent elsewhere. For instance, a vow having been made to "Knights' Fortune," it must be paid in another city, because no such divinity is known in Rome. If a town is to be attacked, its gods are entreated, with a profusion of compliment and promise, to forsake that place and take their abode in Rome : a long formula is preserved,* which contains the right phrases and etiquette of this "evocation." This compliment performed, the Roman conscience is free; the holy places are "made profane"; the attack, which would have been sacrilege before, becomes a pious act; if the deity refuses, the peril is his own.† Thus Juno is solemnly evoked from Veii, and for the first time becomes a great goddess of the Romans. And from its first tutelar divinity, Mars, the victorious state incorporates in its worship, one by one, the deities of all conquered towns and nations, till its pantheon includes all the gods and all the worships of the pagan world.

Such a mythology as this is far enough from the vivid and riotous fancy of the Greek. It is, in essence, bald, hard, bleak, domineering. It lay in the region of ritual and form. Its rites must be performed strictly in accordance with rule and tradition; and the way of performing them duly was the secret tradition of a sacred order. Originally, the father of the family was priest as well as autocrat in

---

* In Macrobius, *Saturn.*, iii. 9.

† Hence the importance of using the exact title which a divinity will acknowledge. There is a charm in "Open Sesame" in the tale which cannot be shared by any other grain. The true name of Rome, and that of its tutelar divinity, are said to have been kept as a mystery, lest they should become known to an enemy, who might thus disarm the city of its defence.

his own household, and the ritual was closely bound up with family dignities and aristocratic tradition.

Such formal devotion has little in it of what we call religion : nothing of pious contemplation, little if any fervor of devout emotion. Indeed, warmth of religious sentiment, the emotional side of piety, it distinctly repudiates and dreads ; as we may imagine a stiff ritualist of the last century to abhor the early fervors of Methodism. Such passions only interfere with its fixed and rigid temper. They are merely a detestable, most likely an outlandish superstition, alien and hateful to the mind of a true-born Roman.

And, again, it became the centre of a very wide and powerful organization of religious motives and ideas. Rome won to itself, in ages of conquest, a monopoly of religions, as well as a monopoly of political powers and rights. The central, the real object of Roman worship we may hold to have been Rome herself, — as England was said to be the only religion of Lord Palmerston. We may well believe it. The ancient city was closely identified with the altar, the hearth-fire, the sacred Name, which marked its peculiar wor-ship.* Nothing less than that vast impersonal but very real abstraction, the City itself, could be the object of that vivid, intense, self-devoted, and narrow loyalty which goes by the name of patriotism, and made the civic virtue of the ancient State. Rome was the object of a passionate devotion, a grateful piety, a religious pride and veneration, which made the most powerful and perhaps the holiest emotion a Roman could know.

* See Coulanges, *La Cité Antique.*

But Rome — the "mother of his soul," the great loved, revered, awful State, that put her sword in his hand to strike, and set up her eagle as a symbol for his military adoration and faith, and covered him with her shield though he were the humblest citizen in the remotest corner of the earth ; Rome, at whose name the magistrate at Philippi trembles when Paul appeals to her protection — was a haughty, tyrannical, unjust sovereign to those stifled nationalities that made up her imperial domain. Nothing in all the history of despotism is more hateful than the dealings of Rome with her conquered provinces ; no aristocracy was ever more insolent, domineering, and profligate, than the oligarchy of officials and ex-officials that made the Roman Senate in the latter days of the Republic.* To believe Cicero's eloquent and generous harangues, — himself proud of his place in that famous oligarchy, — the feelings of the provincials towards Rome could hardly have been anything but a helpless despair and hate. That divinity, to which so many millions of human victims had been sacrificed, could hardly have been, in their eyes, anything else than an omnipotent, omnipresent, and inexorable Demon. Ireland in her bloody memories of Cromwell, Poland in her struggles following the Partition, Greece under the brute despotism of Turkey, may help us understand the condition of Syria, Macedonia, Sicily, Gaul, or Spain, as provinces of the imperial Republic. The word empire (*imperium*) in that day meant simply military rule. By political tradition, these provinces were held by the law of conquest.

* See Froude's "Julius Cæsar."

The municipal law that for centuries had grown up as a system for a single city made the one type and rule for a government as wide, almost, as the civilized world. It was administered purely in the interest and in the name of that one city ; and its executive officers (*pro-consul, pro-prætor*) were simply her military commanders or civil magistrates, who had served their term at home.

The evil and iniquity of this system had been seen a hundred years before the Empire had been established in its place, — if by no others, by the great tribunes Tiberius and Caius Gracchus, who both died victims of the Roman aristocracy. A hundred years of civil war had exterminated the old parties of the Republic. The genius of Julius Cæsar and the cautious policy of Augustus had created a new system, in which all rulers, magistrates, and commanders were made subject to the one Chief of the Roman world. It is not necessary to speak of the new evils which now came in place of the old evils. In one word, political freedom was extinct. But that freedom was the very thing men hated and feared. For many generations that freedom had meant violence at home, and flagrant oppression in the provinces. Whatever else the revolution in the state accomplished, it at least set the subject states free from the irresponsible class despotism they had been suffering under so long. It was a revolution that brought them comparative prosperity and repose.

The phrase "peace of the Empire" * is the name of what they felt to be an unspeakable relief and gain.

* The *pax Romana*.

Their sovereign was no longer the hard, cruel, grasping, abstract impersonation of the City, with her far-reaching hundred hands, like those of a Hindoo idol. It was at least a Man, who could make his will prevail over the petty persecution of innumerable despots. As Paul appealed from Festus, so men throughout the Empire could appeal from their local tyrants, to Cæsar. Whatever his personal vices or crimes, at least he represented the unity of a sovereign state. To him all subjects, all states, were equal. It was no great flight of imagination to make him in men's eyes the type of a universal, impartial Providence,—"image of all," say the Christian Clementines.

In men's eyes he was more: he was, very literally and simply, a god in human form. As a god, Virgil says, sacrifice shall be offered monthly on his altar. And Velleius Paterculus, who went with Tiberius into Germany, tells in vivacious narrative how a barbarian drove his canoe across the stream, pressed through the crowds that surrounded the imperial command, gazed long and earnestly at him, and went away saying, "To-day I have seen the gods." *

We do not enter readily into the state of mind that made it easy and natural in that day to look on a man as a real divinity; that literally deified him

---

* So when Pope Alexander III., in flight from Barbarossa, landed at Montpellier, a Saracen in the crowd pressed close to his stirrup, so as to have a fair view of the Christians' god. The feeling of the barbarian in Velleius is exactly reflected in that of the Southern negroes during the civil war. "What you know 'bout Massa Linkum?" said one of them to an army officer, who was criticising some act of the government. "Him like de Lord; *him eberywhar.*"

because he was, as we should say, the incarnation of an idea. Though to us, too, the worship of Paul as Mercury, and of Barnabas as Jupiter, at Lystra, ought to make it, if not clear, at least credible. To us it is a very crude mythology; yet it certainly was one of the forces that made it possible to reconcile men's minds to a creed whose corner-stone was the Incarnation of a Deity. The notion of a "man-god" — that is, of a Divine Person in human form — was already familiar to the pagan mind. The Emperor was spoken of in language that reflects, or prefigures, with strict exactness, that applied in the later creeds to the human life of Christ. This belief in the visible presence of divinity upon earth springs no doubt from sources very different in the Christian and in the Pagan mind; but they ran closely parallel, and merged in the faith that included both. The philosophical elements that entered into the faith belong to the history of religious speculation, and we shall have more to say of them further on. Just now it is enough to say, that — however crude or impossible it may look to us — there never was a faith in a deity actually walking the earth and conversant among men more positively, sincerely, or in its way devoutly held, than this deification of the Roman Emperor among the people of the provinces.*

---

* The worship of the Emperor was forbidden in Rome, tolerated in Italy, universal in the provinces. Sixty districts or towns of Gaul, each with its separate shrine, joined in a common ritual in his service at a metropolitan temple close to the wall of Lyons (see below). The assemblies here made a sort of provincial parliament, and sent regular reports to Rome; having, however, no power of independent legislation

For it was not court flattery, — the impious adulation which craves "the thrift that follows fawning." It was the expression of gratitude for a blessing too great to have come from a merely human source, for deliverance from evils too great to be stayed by a human hand. The wreck of old political institutions had destroyed or set afloat those old local faiths that belonged to them ; and this rude but vigorous growth of a popular religion had come to take their place, and throve on their decay.

Very significantly, too, there is scarce a hint of it in the more familiar literary sources of our history. Its record is in scattered monuments and inscriptions, only brought to light and deciphered within the last few years ; just as our earliest contemporary records of · the popular Christian faith are in the monuments and inscriptions of the Catacombs. From such sources we learn that there was not only the vague popular adoration, such as Tacitus speaks of when he ascribes the working of miracles to the Emperor Vespasian. There was also an organized worship of the Emperor, with temple and ritual, and a consecrated order of priests.* Every year embassies went up from the provinces to Rome to carry him their thanksgivings or vows or expressions of religious homage. To be a member of that priesthood, or head of such an embassy, was a dignity held in reserve for men who had discharged the highest official trusts in their native district, a dignity to be recorded in inscriptions on their funeral monuments.

* The official title of this priesthood was *Flamen Romæ Divorum et Augusti.*

The religious vows were not merely the formal or official language of diplomatic speech; but plain men, of humble life, of no official station or ambition, recorded their private reverence and homage, or that of their households, — just as a pious Catholic might record his self-consecration to a patron saint, — in words of pious gratitude for the blessings devoutly ascribed to Cæsar as author and giver of daily benefits.* While each nation had its especial deity, he only, men said, was one god over all the earth.

To us, who know that succession of Cæsars mainly from the court scandal of Suetonius or the lurid tragedy of the Annals of Tacitus, there is something strange, and even pathetic, in this ascription of divine honors to such names as Tiberius, Nero, or Domitian. The habits of old faith, the terrible memories of conquest, the immense relief of comparative equity, security, and quiet, are all necessary to be kept in mind, to make it credible.†

In one way this imperial creed brought the Pagan mind into most sharp and direct collision with the Christian faith. The religion of the State became more and more identified with the worship paid personally to the Emperor; and any symbolic act of that

---

* See examples of these inscriptions in Coulanges, *Institutions Politiques de l'ancienne France.*

† That the Roman State — still a Republic in name — should have endured for fourteen years what it is charity to call the insane freaks and caprices of one sickly and weak-minded youth, Nero, is partly explained by the remorseless cruelty of the Roman temper and manners, but chiefly by the name of Cæsar, which he inherited, and by the deep horror left on men's minds from the century of the Civil War.

worship — swearing to the name of Cæsar, or casting incense in the formal ritual — became in a special way the test of political loyalty. To refuse it, under whatever pretext, was constructive treason. It was this, and not any hatred of the Christian system, or inclination to persecute it as such, that so often put the Christians under the ban of the State. Most of the Emperors, it is quite clear, would have been glad to evade any such attack on a class of safe, obedient, trusty subjects, which the Christians generally were; so the early persecutions were spasmodic, of short duration, and far apart. Even Trajan, who will not have the Christians hunted out or betrayed by informers, must submit them to the test of "worshipping my divinity." *  In short, the more sincere and the more fully developed this new state religion, the more inexorably it must needs deal with any rival creed.

It is to be noticed, also, that the antagonism spoken of comes to a head about the middle of the second century; and that from that time forth it is open war, with little truce, until the stronger faith prevails. At first sight it is strange that this war should have been declared by the wisest and most scrupulously just of all the Emperors, — by Marcus Aurelius, who is addressed by Justin as if he was almost persuaded to be a Christian, and whose ethics are as clear and austere as those of Paul. But it was because Aurelius had

---

* So I understand the phrase *supplicando diis nostris*, comparing it with *imagini tuæ supplicarent* in the letter of Pliny. The specific act of sacrifice is the one thing demanded in the edicts of Diocletian.

religiously consecrated himself to the service of the State, because he scrupulously endeavored to make himself worthy of the worship which the state religion enjoined, that he saw the more clearly how inevitable and uncompromising the conflict had come to be.

It was in his time that the worship of the Emperor came to its highest reach of sincerity and fervor. The personal virtues of the "five good Emperors," of whom he was the last, contrasted with the vices of most that went before, had carried the grateful homage rendered to Cæsar to a certain loyal and devout enthusiasm. As a picture of Napoleon might be found sixty years ago in every French peasant's cottage, as an image of the Virgin adorns the home of every humblest Catholic devotee, so the figure or bust of the good Emperor was to be found at the family altar of every pious Roman subject; and the inscriptions of veneration and homage become more fervent now than ever.*  The popular religion of the Empire had now reached its completest development.  And, if there had been an abiding principle of life in it, Christianity might have found a worthier rival, and a more doubtful encounter.

But we have not far to look for the causes of its rapid fall from this culminating point.  We need not suppose any wordy hollowness in the profession of

---

* "At this day"— that is, in the time of Constantine — "his statues stand in many houses among the household gods; he is even now regarded as a divinity; priests, fellows, and chaplains (*flamines*) are assigned him, and whatever antiquity has prescribed of religious offices."  Julius Capitolinus, Ch. 18 (in Coulanges). The Christian Emperors, down to Gratian, were regularly deified after their death, and had their due place in the Pagan pantheon.

faith made by the imperial Stoic. But his ideal of character seems exaggerated and strained, when divorced from a positive religious creed, like that which made the strength of Paul. At any rate, it left exposed some weak spots. It is significant, that the " decline and fall of the Roman Empire " begins with the reign of his successor. Aurelius himself invites criticism by his indulgent fondness for Faustina; it was even a crime against the State to leave that in the brutal hands of Commodus.

That crowned gladiator must rudely shock the pious faith that rested on his father's calm humanities. And Commodus was the pioneer in a century mostly filled with the names of military adventurers —twenty-five in all before we come to that of Diocletian (the first who was worshipped as a god in his own person) — on whose character and fortunes that faith was completely wrecked. Whatever was genuine in it was more and more rapidly absorbed in the widening conquests of Christianity, whose type of incarnation was by so many degrees more pure and august. And the final battle of the creeds, at the end of the third century, may be said to have blotted out almost the very memory that the Pagan Empire had ever so much as pretended to embody any conception of justice, mercy, or religious truth.

There is another phase of the popular religion, illustrated chiefly by funeral monuments and inscriptions, showing more of the life of the humbler classes, including slaves, respecting which a brief hint must here suffice. The cruel lot of these poor creatures was lightened by charitable societies and burial societies among themselves. The inscriptions express sometimes a pious and humble trust in terms curiously like those of the Christian monuments ; sometimes the despairing or mocking temper we might more naturally expect. The glimpse they give of family affection and kindly feeling is often very touching ; and helps us, better than almost any other thing, to understand the " good ground " in the popular heart, where the new seed had its strongest growth.

It has been necessary to speak of the long attempt to create a religion among the ruins of the old Pagan world chiefly on its formal side, — that which is shown in its modes of worship and its professions of belief. There is another side, which shows more of what we may call the heart of Paganism ; and of this a word remains to be said.

It is no lesson of antiquarian curiosity, but of the latest experience, that religious passion is quite as much to be dreaded as any other form of human passion. Perhaps, indeed, no other passion has generated so much of frenzy, cruelty, and hate. The ancient Romans did well, from their point of view, to look with dread and dislike on all excesses of religious emotion, particularly that which invaded from the East, always the hot-bed and nursery of fanaticism. When the delirious rites of Bacchus were first known in Rome, and especially their effect on female worshippers, it was with a panic of genuine terror that the Senate undertook to keep it at bay, at the cost of tortures and bloody executions.*

* Liv. xxxix. 8–18 (B. c. 185).

This was about the time of the first contact of
Rome with the East. Two centuries later, under
Augustus and Tiberius, many an Oriental superstition
was well naturalized in Rome. Isis and Serapis
were fashionable divinities. Magic, sorcery, and all
manner of religious frenzy, were chronic symptoms
of the popular mind. Virgil's *Pharmaceutria* and
Horace's *Canidia* are the familiar types of these
wild superstitions. Their home was in the East.
And with them came to Rome the crueller rites, the
self-mutilations and the bloody sacrifices, that belong
to the worship of Cybele, Dionysus, and the rest.

Now sacrifice in the earlier time, among the Greeks
and Romans, had little if any of the expiatory character afterwards given to it. There was not much, in
those days, of the feeling of remorse ; crime itself
was rather fatality than guilt ; the Furies that pursued Orestes were charmed away by no slaughter of
an innocent victim, but by a grave decision of the
real nature of his deed. There was sacrifice of human
victims — by Druids in the woods of Gaul ; by barbarians on savage coasts ; by Greeks or Romans in
moments of extreme terror ; by the Carthaginians, a
Tyrian colony, who thought to avert the ruin of their
city by slaying two hundred of their noblest children
before their Canaanitish gods.

But the ordinary act of sacrifice was simply an act
of thanksgiving, or an offering to avert some natural
calamity, not an atonement for the sin of the soul.
The father of the household, in killing the creature
destined for the daily meal, was priest as well as
provider, and set apart the due portion to the house-

hold divinity. This was simply a deliberate but rather awkward " grace before meat." " A tender lamb from the fold shall often stain the altar " which Tityrus has built to the divine benefactor (who " will always be a god " to him) that has restored his farm. This, as far as we see, was the old Greek or Roman notion. The more solemn public acts of sacrifice were acts of divination, not the atonement of national guilt — of which there might seem great need.

The meagre simplicity of ancient rites, as well as the timid scruple in their performance, and perhaps a quickened intensity of moral feeling, had something to do with the eager and passionate reception of foreign custom. The Eastern temper in such things was fervid, passionate, often delirious, sometimes brutal. How it allied itself with practice of magic, evoking of spirits, and what we should call animal magnetism — curiously like the practice of spiritists in our own day — belongs more to the latest phase of Paganism, and the extravagances of the Neo-Platonists. But the bloody sacrificial rites of the East were quite in keeping with the peculiar brutality of public temper which we find in the earlier Empire.

These rites went all the way from personal mutilations, more or less severe, to the ghastly performance of the *taurobolium*, in which the worshipper stood in a pit below a perforated platform, and was drenched from head to foot in the shower-bath of blood that gushed from the slaughtered bull above.* This horrible ritual was held to be a ransom from all guilt, and a pledge of blessedness in this life and the next.†

---

* The *criobolium* was the similar sacrifice of a ram.

† *In æternum renatus.* (See Prudentius, *Perist.*, x. 1011.)

As the worshipper, reeking and dripping with the sanguine torrent, passed out through the crowd, others pressed about him, to win some share, by a touch or stain, in the magic efficacy of that atoning rite. It is this strange custom of later Paganism, quite as much as the Levitical tradition of the Old Testament, that gives emphasis to the words written to the Hebrews: "If the blood of bulls and goats sanctifieth, how much more the blood of Christ!" and again, "It is not possible that the blood of bulls and of goats should take away sin."

We have, then, in the mind of Paganism at this epoch, the two characteristic religious ideas of the age — Incarnation and expiatory Sacrifice — distinctly conceived and plainly developed, though in forms that make them more a travesty than a counterpart of the same ideas in the Christian creed. The important thing to notice in them is, that *they are the ideas of that age.* They are not peculiar to Christianity: it would be truer to say that in origin and essence they are rather Pagan than Christian. That they had a powerful effect in shaping the Christian belief, there can be no doubt. At least, they predisposed the mind of the Roman world to accept that belief so broadly and so easily as it did. The rapid decline of Paganism in the third century, and the sudden change that shows the whole Empire Christian at the end of it, are facts to be accounted for on the common ground of history so far as may be. The triumph of the latter cannot be understood, as a human event, without an understanding of those causes, working from within, which predisposed mankind to receive it.

## V.

# THE ARIAN CONTROVERSY.

THE one period of Christian history which most fascinates the imagination at first sight, is that when the new faith came to the throne of empire· in the person of Constantine the Great.

And this first attraction is fully borne out by the real interest of the characters and events — though not in the way we might have thought at first. To the Christians, suddenly released from a great stress and dread of persecution, it would seem, no doubt, the coming of a perfect day, and the establishing of the kingdom they had prayed for, once for all. But then came the inevitable recoil and disappointment. Constantine was no saint, at best, and a very doubtful Christian; but a victorious general, a suspicious and wary politician; a man of some very great and noble qualities, indeed, but stained by one or two dark crimes. The religion he protected was no sooner in a place of security and power than smothered jealousies burst out, and religious feuds began, and the Empire rang with the noise of a controversy — often unintelligible as it was disgraceful — whose fame is hardly diminished to this day.

The Arian Controversy has these two points of interest for us. It is in itself one of the most dramatic and eventful chapters in the whole history of human opinion, turning on the adventures, character, and animosities of three or four leading actors, together with the lively passions of great multitudes of partisans; and, secondly, it fixed for a great many generations the type of the dominant belief, giving an answer to the question, What sort of a system, intellectual or religious, should come to take the place of the dying Paganism? These two make, so to speak, the pivots which sustain our interest and steady our understanding of it.

It is not hard to trace in outline the development of speculative opinion which prepared the way for this extraordinary outburst of religious rage. This, however, belongs to the history of doctrine, and need not be dwelt on here. That the opinion became a passion, and the motive of deadly controversy lasting through centuries, turned on circumstances in the history, and on principles of human conduct, not so directly obvious. First, however, a few words are needed as to the nature of the controversy itself.

The doctrine of the Divine Word (LOGOS) as manifest in the human life of Jesus had for some two centuries been the accepted key to the interpretation of the Christian Gospel. More or less vaguely, the Word was held to take the place of the human soul in him, or to be intimately united with it, so that, in virtue of it, and the Divine nature which it implied, he became the Christ.

But the term Logos itself has a double meaning. On one hand, it is identical with the Divine Wisdom, —which is, in fact, constantly used as its equivalent, both by the Greek and Latin writers; and in this sense it is simply the name of an Attribute of the Creator. On the other hand (by the habit of mind already spoken of in considering the Gnostic genealogies) it is easily, unconsciously, continually *hypostatized,*—that is, regarded as an independent Substance, or quasi-Personality; and in this sense, as a pre-existent Divine Person, is especially identified with the Christ.

It is clear that we may make either of these conceptions prominent, so as to overshadow or dwarf the other; and we shall do this according as the habit of our mind is mystical on one side, or rationalizing on the other. The mystic, reverential, imaginative mood dwells upon the Attribute, which it tends more and more to merge in absolute Divinity, in the direction of a religious Pantheism. The rational, analytic, criticising mood dwells upon the Substance, or Person (*hypostasis*),* which it tends more and more to make distinct and separate, and therefore a logically dependent and inferior being. To the first, the Logos as Divine Wisdom is necessarily coeternal with God himself, as light with the source of light. To the second, the Logos as a Divine Person is necessarily inferior to and (so to speak) younger than the Infinite, just as a son is younger than his father. To the first, Christ is the Son of God figuratively, by eternal generation; to the second, he is the Son of God literally, as the "first-born of the creation."

This radical difference of mental constitution and

* Explained by Gregory of Nyssa as bearing the same relation to the *individual* as Substance (οὐσία) to the *class.*

habit repeats itself in all the phases of the controversy that followed. The mystic tendency* appears as an exaggerated orthodoxy, later known by the names Monophysite and Monothelete, till it runs out into the peculiar fanaticism of certain Oriental sects, to whom Christ is the sole and essential Deity. The rationalistic tendency† shows itself as a harassing and incessant criticism, quite as intolerant as its adversary, not repudiating but putting its own interpretation on the accepted creed, exiled at length as Nestorianism, under which name it subsists in the East to this day. The narrow line of the church faith, between these contrary drifts of opinion, has its landmarks fixed in the decisions of the first four General (or Œcumenical) Councils. ‡

This central line of doctrine, it is almost needless to say, runs a good deal nearer to the mystic than to the rationalizing opinion. In religious controversy, it is not half so important that men should understand their creed, as it is that they should hold it in some well-defined symbol appealing strongly to the imagination. And we misunderstand both the age of Martyrdom, and the age of Controversy that immediately followed, unless we see how the fervor, nay, often the frenzy, of a passionate conviction — so nurtured by the incessant discipline of the Church when belief in it was a matter of life and death — will cling to what from outside seems a mere passion-

* Represented by the names of Sabellius, Apollinaris, and Eutyches.

† Represented by Arius, Eunomius, and Nestorius.

‡ Viz. that of Nicæa (325), Constantinople (381), Ephesus (431), and Chalcedon (451).

less abstraction. The Dutch Republic, once free from terror of the Spaniard, went straight into disputes about predestination that risked its hard-bought liberties, and cost the noble Barneveldt his head. What can be more a mere abstraction, a mere identical equation in logic, than *There is no God but God?* Yet the phrase in which it rings on the battle-field to-day hurls masses of Moslem fanatics against Russian intrenchments, and piles them dead or dying in the ditch, just as, seven hundred years ago, it hurled myriads of Saracens against the steel-clad ranks of the Crusaders. It is the symbol, not the thing, for which men oftenest stake their lives. In deliberate sober thought we choose the policy we think most wise and safe, — the theory of State-rights or the theory of the Republic one and indivisible; but in the fury of battle men think less of that than of the visible sign of it, the Stars and Stripes against the Stars and Bars!

Now it happened once in Alexandria, not far from the time we are approaching, that a certain Bishop Alexander was zealously expounding to his audience this cardinal point of Christian faith. They were lately at rest from a time of persecution, ready and hot for controversy. It was probably the exposition of the religious symbol in some such cheap religious rhetoric as most of us have heard : as that the glorious Sun in heaven represents the Father; his Light, the eternal Word; his Heat, the life-giving Spirit; and so on. But the smooth discourse was cut short by the cry of heresy. "That is the false doctrine of Sabellius!" said a voice in the crowd. Now Sabellius, most pious and unsuspecting of heretics, had preached, a few years before, a sort of "modal trinity," very much to the same effect. The voice was the voice of Arius, a presbyter, no friend of the bishop, of temper restless and litigious, an uncomfortable antagonist in a war of words. In person slender and tall, of features fine-cut and rather sharp; in manner courteous; careful and somewhat elegant in dress; ready of speech, and gifted with a certain keenness to fasten on the weak point of his adversary's statement, and follow it out in a teasing, exasperating way to some point of real or seeming contradiction; and, withal, a man who would not be silenced or put down.

It is not likely that either opponent could state his point so as to be very clear to us, or, at any rate, so as to seem at all solvable by the human mind. After many centuries, and whole libraries of dispute, it is, we may say, as far from being solved as ever. If Christ is the Son, said Arius, he must be younger than the Father, if only by a single moment out of all eternity, and so dependent on him; or, in the test-phrase of Arianism, "there was when the Son did not yet exist." * Nay, was the reply, he is the *eternal* Son of the *eternal* Father: to deny his equal eternity is to say that the Sun in heaven can exist without giving light and heat.

And so the dispute went on. It turned on a very fine point,—one, we might say, invisible to the naked eye; and there was nothing for it but the incessant

* Not, "there was *a time* when ": the Logos was non-existent only in eternity, before time was.

repetition and reiteration of the same words. The discussion is very weary to follow, and it seems to lead us nowhere. If we take the term Logos (which is masculine in Greek) to signify merely an Attribute, — conscious intelligence of the Eternal, — it is a simple and intelligible symbol to speak of it as the Son by eternal generation. If we take it to mean a Person, it seems impossible not to distinguish it, by some grade of dignity or precedence, from the Eternal One. The arguments of Arius seem the incessant sharp rattling of a logic-mill, like those windy disputes of Sophists in Plato: those of his opponents — we may look through many a hundred of the pages that record them, without finding one that any man now would care to repeat or answer.

If we would understand the importance of the Arian controversy, then, we must find it not in what is wilful, personal, dramatic in the story, — least of all in the speculative opinion on either side, what seems so absolutely apart from anything that we understand or care about to-day; but in what lies behind it and around it. It is really the great feature, the one visible feature, of the intellectual history of a time critical as any in the religious and social destinies of mankind.

Let us transport ourselves now to the time when this controversy came to a head in the Council at Nicæa (325). If we look back fifty years, we see the vast intellectual and political system of Paganism — to all outward appearance as vast and formidable as ever — just preparing to put forth all its forces in a final effort to suppress that threatening, unceasing, insidious growth of the Christian system, and on the edge of its last, most obstinate, and most cruel persecution. If we look forward fifty years, we find the same Paganism idealized in a new and arrogant system of philosophy, contending for intellectual and political revival with a speculative zeal and moral pretensions fully equal to the Christianity of the day, — a sort of eclectic or transcendental free religion, as brilliantly described in Kingsley's " Hypatia."

How was it, then, that in the middle of this century of revolution, enveloped right and left by the political forces, the philosophical systems, and the menacing fanaticisms of the older civilization, Christians had time or heart to rage so furiously together? And how was it that, in spite of a conflict which seemed to consume all its strength, Christianity came out of it in a hundred years stronger than ever, the only live organized power to stay the tides of barbarism ; at the end of five hundred years, the base and the ideal of a new Christian Empire, already rivalling the power and dignity of the old ; at the end of a thousand years, in possession of a dominion which seemed to Dante then as secure as the circles of his Hell, or the portals of his Paradise ?

There are two answers to this question, one consisting in the nature of the thing itself which was at issue between Paganism and Christianity ; the other in a comparison of the two rival Christian creeds, Arian and Athanasian.

First, it is not very hard to trace the genealogy of opinion. The laws of thought are uniform, and intellectual systems unfold naturally and easily by a method of their own.  So far as mere opinion goes, I do not see in the least why Paganism did not furnish materials of a system quite as likely to satisfy a thoughtful man of that day, as the Christianity of the first three centuries.  In fact, we see that it did so satisfy many of the very best and wisest men of the time: Tacitus, the stern historian; his friend Pliny, the courteous and accomplished Roman gentleman; Plutarch, the biographer of pagan heroes and critic of pagan morals; both the Antonines, wisest and best of statesmen; Galen, the pious and enlightened physiologist; Epictetus, most patient, shrewd, and austere of moralists.

Why should such men burden themselves with Jewish or Galilæan legends that to them must seem foolish and incredible?  Did not the caustic wisdom of Socrates, the high philosophy of Plato, the scientific breadth of Aristotle, the elevated and pure theism of Cicero, above all, the large life, the political experience, and the manifold culture of pagan antiquity, — did not these furnish materials for a religious system incomparably more broad, rich, and true than the narrow creed of Palestine?

And then, too, could not a wise eclecticism adopt and engraft upon it whatever seemed really worth retaining of the fervid religious life, the "enthusiasm of humanity," the methods of mutual help, in the Christian body?  So it seems, at least, to many enlightened and cultivated people of our own day; and so the thought must have crossed the mind of Paul, himself an enlightened and cultivated man, when he saw with a sort of amazement how God had chosen the foolish things of the world to confound the wise, and weak things to confound the mighty, and base things to bring to naught the haughty and strong.

But no. The history of opinion is one thing; the history of faith is another thing. Faith belongs to emotion, character, and will. It is capable of passion, of enthusiasm, of obstinate courage. It can disdain reason, and trample argument under foot. It cares for reason or argument only as a weapon of attack: its only weapon of defence is confidence in itself. It has its own laws of growth, which resemble more the spreading of flame than the skilful joining of architecture. It has its own methods of conquest, of which the chief is to kindle and sedulously to nurture an unreasoning devotion.

So it has been with all the great victorious faiths of history, from Elijah to Mahomet, from Paul to Garrison. What such men call reasoning is only the expression of a passionate conviction; the method of instruction such men employ is the contagion of their own ardent thought. In the great struggle against Paganism, the inheriting of that power, the secret of that method, was with the Christians, and not with their opponents. What cool and unprejudiced reason might have chosen or might have done is not to the point. I have often asked myself, in the controversies of our own day, whether reason might not have brought better and safer results than fanaticism; and the only answer I could find was, that what we call fanaticism is one of the great forces that impel mankind, while reason is not. Reason at best may serve, in some small degree, as pilot or brakeman, the flame and vapor are from quite another source.

In the second place, it is part of the method of faith, that it scorns anything that looks like compromise with its opponents. Compromise may be had after the victory is gained, but not while the fight is going on. Now Arianism was, in fact, as a system, very high-toned, nay almost extravagant, in its Christian profession. In asserting for Christ a super-angelic pre-existence all but absolute and eternal, it claimed for him as much as could be forced from the very highest expressions of reverence in the Alexandrine phraseology of Paul or John; infinitely more than could be found in the earlier and more authentic gospel. But observe. In that phrase *all but*, there lurked a flaw of heresy, of weakness, of compromise with the common enemy. Surely, in the light of simple reason, it were better to accept frankly the simple humanity of Jesus, to treat the nativity as a myth, the miracles as legends, and the resurrection as a glorious illusion; or else to say, just as frankly, that Jesus was God in the flesh, — his temptations, his sufferings, his prayers, a mere dramatic exhibition, or a mysterious by-play of his divine and human nature. At least, the first is intelligible reason, and the last is sublime faith in a glorified humanity. Either is better than that nondescript illogical compromise which is known as Arianism.

And again, it was something worse than a logical flaw. Did it not make Christ the " Son of God," after all, very much in the same way that Jupiter was the son of Saturn, and Mars of Jupiter? Did it not open the way for all the shocking possibilities, for all the blasphemous compromises, of a mongrel paganism, — nay, to all the horrible vices and corruptions that had grown out of the old worships of paganism ? If Christians too are to worship a Divinity who is after all not the Supreme God, what are they better than their enemies ? Did they, too, not worship sons of God, — Apollo, Hercules, Bacchus, and the rest ? Had not some pagan emperors — the brutal Commodus as well as the good Severus — consented in advance to such a compromise, and even admitted Jesus of Nazareth to the generous Roman pantheon ? Had not the best of all the emperors, Trajan and Aurelius, proved the impossibility of that compromise by persecuting the Christian faith ?

We need not suppose that all these thoughts came in at once, to make the feud so bitter as it proved to be. But they all lay behind, more or less consciously, to make the controversy obstinate and bitter under the successors of Constantine in a later age. For then Arianism had come to be a court party. Its perilous drift towards compromise was seen then, plainly, on the side of politics, — where it seemed somehow to flatter the self-love and fondness for power of a despotic house ; as it was seen, too, in the fact which broadly marks its destiny in history, that it kept strong hold of the speculative and subtile Greek mind, and remained an apple of discord in the East, taking many shapes and hues, one creed having (we are told) no less than twenty-seven anathemas appended to cover so many shadings of dissent ; while the central, catholic, domineering, uncompromising faith held almost undisputed ground in the West, where it became the basis of the most vast and imposing spiritual dominion ever known.

The Nicene Creed, so called, is still the authentic expression of that faith, as read in the liturgies of to-day.  It is true that the Nicene Creed was itself a sort of compromise, prepared at the summons of Constantine, whose motive was more than half political; and signed, with whatever demur, (it is stated, rather doubtfully,) by Arius himself, who presently found himself high in favor with the imperial court. · But its historical importance is very great ; and, as the central act of a most extraordinary drama, it demands a few words of mention.

We cannot do justice to the very perplexing character of Constantine, unless we think of him, with all his faults, as a man of strong, generous impulses, very much dominated at times by a vivid imagination.  It was something more than policy, it was a natural effect of the impressive, nay, appalling situation in which he found himself, — at the head of a force largely Christian marching against the rude and fierce Maxentius, who had mustered whatever there was in Rome of fanatic attachment to the old religion or fanatic hatred of the new, — that he saw, or seemed to see, a flaming cross in the sky at noon, and set that sign above the crimson banner, the *Labarum*, under which his army went, cheerful and strong, to certain victory.  A triumph in open battle against the old gods of Rome in person !  What an appeal to excited imagination on one side, to despairing frenzy on the other !

And again, when he traced the outline of his new

capital, the most felicitous choice ever made for the seat of a great Empire, he asserted, and probably believed, that he was acting by Divine guidance. "I must keep on," said he to his officers, amazed at the wide plan he traced, "till the God who goes before me stops." A man of strong imagination, lifted suddenly into a great success, comes (as Napoleon did) to look on his own acts and destiny with a certain awe: he easily thinks himself a man of destiny. Sylla believed in his star, and Cæsar in his descent from gods; and it was a like feeling, half reverent, half superstitious, that impelled Constantine, under circumstances far more impressive and strange, to set up in his new City that extraordinary symbol of empire, the statue of Apollo, or the Sun-god, with a head made in his own likeness, surrounded by gilded rays, which, said popular belief, were nails of the true cross, miraculously discovered to the emperor's mother.

It is interesting, too, and very touching, amid so much that is pitiless and stern, to see how the conqueror really wished to be the father of his people. Deserted children, who before had been sold as slaves, were adopted as the emperor's own.* It was a shameful thing, he said, that any of his people should perish of hunger, or be forced to crime by stress of actual want. It was cruel that mothers and children, brothers and sisters, husbands and wives, should be torn apart in the slave-market: let that be forbidden at any public sale.

* The first orphan asylum had been founded by Trajan, two hundred years before.

This sentiment of justice, or humanity, could not ripen into a firm policy then. At more than fifteen centuries' distance we are only groping about the problem now. It resulted in little else than making Constantinople a privileged city, which in that day meant a city of paupers and courtiers. The dry-rot of the Empire was hardly checked. The heart of society was perishing by slow decay. The old Roman valor was well-nigh extinct. The Roman state had to defend itself by legions of Goths, whom it hired, cheated of their pay, enslaved their children, and drove into a frenzy of hate, till within fifty years from the building of the splendid capital the emperor (Valens) was burned alive in the hut to which he fled from the great disaster of Adrianople (369), and the spell was forever broken by which the name of Rome had charmed and awed the barbarian world.

These calamities could not be foreseen or averted by Constantine. Yet he must have felt the slippery peril of his elevation. Some forty years before, Diocletian — whose name is linked by a cruel destiny with the persecution of Galerius, which he would have been only too glad to stay *— had tried to check the break-up of that great military empire by dividing it among four closely allied sovereigns. A tempest of disorder, following his abdication, had compelled Constantine to reduce it again under a single head. The old gods of Rome had been, so to speak, literally met and defeated in open battle under the standard of the Cross. None of the ancient sanctities adhered to the new dominion. Whatever Constantine's sincerity in

---

* See Lactantius, *De Mortibus Persecutorum*, ch. xi.

accepting the faith under whose symbol he had conquered, at least the formula of that faith must not be left to angry and endless disputes among the professors of it; and so he called together that most famous of all Church Councils which met at Nicæa to settle once for all the authentic creed (325).

Here, again, it is easiest to look upon the scene as it appeared to the imagination and human feeling of Constantine himself. When he advanced, tall and stately, in imperial robes and attended by the imperial guards, to preside in the sacred assembly, — he, the champion of the Cross, the deliverer from persecution, the restorer of peace to a stormy world, — there was no bound to the genuine homage of the throng that saluted him, as if he had been a god in human shape, or at least an angel, and "equal to an apostle." And he on his part saw them there, scarred veterans (as it were) of a long and terrible campaign, living witnesses of a martyrdom in which many of them had shared the torment, though not the palm. So bruised and mutilated, this man wanting an eye, and that an arm or leg, they seemed war-worn soldiers, who, having served out their term, were summoned once more to do battle for the faith. To one old man, whose eye had been plucked out and scarred by a firebrand, the emperor went up tenderly, and kissed with his own lips the scorched and empty socket, as if some healing virtue were in the scar; or rather, with a deep touch of human feeling, to say by that symbol how near those horrors lay to his own compassionate heart. It was wise and generous, too, as well as politic, when he took all their memorials of personal grievances and burned them unread before their eyes. "Let the God of all things judge," said he. "Respect yourselves and respect your office, as I myself would cover up any fault of yours with my official robe."

The discussion so auspiciously begun had the usual fortunes of theological debate, — "like a battle by night," says one of the old historians ; so little could either party know the ground it stood on. It lasted two months. It produced, by judicious compromise and careful definition, what is known as the "Nicene Creed," a document of some twenty lines, which was signed by the delegates, three hundred and eighteen in all. Some signed it under protest, or filed exceptions to particular phrases ; but to Constantine it was a state paper of first-rate importance, not a matter of speculative nicety, and he firmly insisted that all should sign. The test-word in it was the Greek word rendered *con-substantial ;* * and this has been the badge of orthodoxy ever since.

But the history of the Arian controversy was not ended at Nicæa, only just begun. It lasted with great violence some forty years, incessantly disturbing the peace of the state. The terms of truce were not (so to speak) officially defined before the Council of Chalcedon (451) ; the animosities of debate have not absolutely disappeared at this day. For forty years, however, it was an event in history, turning mostly on the personal fortunes, efforts, and adventures of

---

* In Greek, ὁμοούσιος (*homoousian*), i. e. "of the same essence." The Greek word ὑπόστασις (*hypostasis*), corresponding etymologically to "substance," was rendered in the Latin creed *persona*.

Athanasius, who from this time forth becomes the champion and representative of the dominant faith. He had been Alexander's delegate in the Council, — a young man then under thirty, of keen intellect, indomitable temper, and a vehement partisan, "turbulent, fiery, and imperious," his enemies said, "arrogant, revengeful, and uncapable of being quiet." His attacks on his opponents are more like shrieks than argument. "O modern Jews and disciples of Caiaphas!" he hails them. "Arians! nay, hollow Ariomaniacs, madmen! They rob God of his wisdom and his Word. They shed their cunning heresy as the cuttle-fish sheds his blackness, to benighten the ignorant and make their falsehood safe." "A heretic is a wicked thing : his heart is depraved and impious at every point."

Such are some of the amenities of this prince of controversialists. They express, it must be owned, a good deal more the heat than they do the light of his opinions. They tell how he felt, much better than what he thought. But it is these qualities, more than largeness and breadth, that give men a great place in the history of controversy. He is the one man about whom are gathered the passions of the struggle. Hostility, attack, the jealousy of rivals, or government prosecution, he met with the same defiance.

His life shows full of daring, of ready wit, of dramatic incident. As Bishop of Alexandria (where in his childhood he had played boy-bishop, as Cyrus played boy-king), he was charged with monstrous crimes, — peculation and fraud, sacrilege and murder,

— the murder of one Arsenius, whom his accusers (he says) kept hid two years to give color to their charge. One piece of evidence was the dead man's hand, used by him, they said, in magic rites. Disdaining direct reply, he led forth a man muffled in a cloak, and asked, "Does any one here know Arsenius ?" He was known to many. He uncovered the man's face: it was Arsenius himself. Lifting the cloak on either side, he showed first the right hand, then the left. "Show me where the third was cut off," said he, coolly. This was his whole defence.

Again, pushing up the Nile once in his little boat, in flight from Julian, he was nearly overtaken by armed men in pursuit. Heading boldly down stream, he soon reached them, when they hailed him : " Is Athanasius near ? " " *Close by*," said he ; and so passed on unmolested, and lay safe hid in Alexandria, while they toiled vainly towards the desert. Five times an exile, twice in Gaul or Rome, once in the deserts of Upper Egypt, once for four months hiding in his father's tomb, he was at length allowed to live eleven years in peace, till his death at the age of seventy-six (373).

But it is far from my intention to give a biography of Athanasius, or to tell the story of the time. One is pretty safe to find in Gibbon a sufficiently accurate travesty of the event : its real history is in thick volumes of narrative and controversy of the old Greek Fathers. There are only two points which I wish to present in closing.

First, in the final defeat of the Arian party, Christianity was saved from being a political or speculative sect, and saved to be a great social and reconstructive force. It is, perhaps, the misfortune of Arianism, that judgment must go against it by default. We know it mostly by report of its adversaries. But that judgment is, that it began with disputatious quibbling about words; that it did not enlist the better religious feeling; and that its strength, when it had any, lay in the alliance of the Court.

The "Catholic faith," so called, on the other hand, was very positive and explicit; unintelligible, no doubt, but dogmatic and imperative, demanding and receiving a loyalty that did not stay to reason. *Christ is very God of very God* was the challenge thrown down to all heresy and unbelief: a phrase that might not satisfy the enlightened reason, but attracted the fervent, passionate, exultant acceptance of whole populations. Its root and strength were in that unreasoning — if you will, fanatic — loyalty. Its defence, for forty years, lay in the intrepidity of a single man, — ardent, whole-souled, uncompromising, the one man then living who dared openly to defy an emperor's will.

Athanasius was not a great man; perhaps he was not a just man; but he was, in his way, a very strong man. He knew well how to appeal to men's imagination, sympathy, reverence. And the stamp he gave to the creed of his day was just what was wanted to keep the faith hot and intense, as a working force.

Again, there is a broader way in which this controversy has told on Christian history. As against his antagonists, the triumph of Athanasius was the triumph of Europe and of Rome. Rome was then the one metropolitan church of the world unrent by theological feuds, first and last a stanch defender of the faith and of its exiled champion. The dividing line between Eastern and Western Church, so sharply drawn that at this very day the Pope prefers that the infidel Turk should triumph rather than the Orthodox Russian, begins to appear in history about this time. The symbol of this division is a phrase (*filioque*) which the Roman Church long after appended to the Catholic creed, claiming that the Son is one with the Father as the source of spiritual grace.

Now the quarrel is none of ours ; we are quite neutral in the theological debate between " orthodox " and " catholic." But it is a very great matter for us — for better or worse, and (we may fairly claim) much for the better — that our civilization, on its political, religious, and social side, is the inheritance of the West, and not the East. The overwhelming defeat of the imperial army by the Goths, five years after Athanasius's death, was the signal of the fall of that avalanche of barbarian invasion which presently overwhelmed the Roman world. Under the terror of that disaster, the Empire took refuge with a chief of orthodox piety, Theodosius the Great, part of whose work was to give imperial prestige to the ecclesiastical power — in the person of the great Ambrose — which was presently going to be the salvation of the West.

More than anything else, it was just then important that the power to organize society and create the institutions of the future should be a moral power. And that was the same as saying that it should rest on a religious conviction held with unreasoning fervor, defined in a symbol positive enough to enlist like a flag the passionate loyalty of multitudes of men. A decaying civilization, a perishing social fabric, a political framework battered and just yielding before a frightful tempest of invasion, a decrepit Paganism, guilty of vices that might not be named and cruelties not to be recalled without horror, — these were on one side; and on the other, the sublime faith, held with whatever of unreason, turbulence, or feud, that Almighty God had once lived bodily among men, and that He did really in person lead them now in the fight against His enemies.

6

# VI.

## SAINT AUGUSTINE.

AUGUSTINE, called "greatest of the Fathers," was born in North Africa in 354; was Bishop of Hippo (now Bona) from the year 395; and died during the siege of this important city by the Vandals, in 430. His fame is very great in the history of religious opinion. It rests mainly on his doctrine of Predestination, and his theory of inborn Evil to be overcome only by the sovereign grace of God. But his influence belongs far more to his warm, devout, and impassioned temperament, to his eager, incessant activity in the offices of the Church, and to the transparent exhibition which he has made of himself in his Confessions, — a long and detailed account of his religious life, made throughout in the form of an act of devotion, or direct address to the Deity.

It is not easy for a modern mind to think of Augustine as so great a man, intellectually, as he is generally claimed to be, or as perhaps he really was. In particular, he seems to want the power, which a really great mind has, of making a clear, coherent statement of opinion, especially of opinion which he has outgrown and is controverting. It would, for example, be worth a good deal to us if he had left us an intelligible account of the Manichæan heresy, from the point of view of a believer, or even of a past believer in it. As to this, we are obliged to consider it more in the view suggested from its enormous, seemingly disproportionate consequence in the history of opinion — as an object of hate and terror from its origin, about a hundred years before, down even to the destruction of the Templars about nine hundred years after the time of Augustine — than in the violently refracted light thrown on it in his own writings.

And again, his cardinal doctrine of Predestination is a purely technical and unscientific account of the origin of good and evil. With all his passion for abstract discussion, it has no more real basis in the science of thought than it has in the science of things. And it must definitely pass away — in the form Augustine gave to it, and which was all he cared for in it — under the different habits of thought that come from a different mode of investigation. In fact, he had a very sincere, what we should call a holy horror of science, in the only form of it known in his day. Mathematicians and astronomers, he thought, were prying impiously into the secrets of the Most High ; and his repugnance to their line of study was only less vehement than his repugnance to sin itself.

Still further, as Mr. Lecky shows, the influence of Augustine in the development of character, in the direction of moral goodness, itself requires to be challenged, or at least to be taken with large abatement. In the direction of personal piety it needs no such abatement. Perhaps no other writings than his, except the Hebrew Psalms, have done quite so much, directly or indirectly, to lift men's minds into the temper of penitence, humility, and adoration. But piety is not all; it is not even the chief thing to be considered. Paul puts charity before it. Now charity — that human love which has no soil of human passion — is of two sorts, and works in two directions. As growing out of tenderness and sympathy, and leading to acts of mercy, Augustine was a noble example of it. To personal opponents he was generous; in the treatment of heresy he was magnanimous; in a time of great calamity he was foremost to set the example of self-sacrifice and devoted service in behalf of the suffering and needy.

But there is another working-out of charity, which consists in expanding men's notion of what goodness is, and must go along with intellectual breadth as well as pious fervor. It is not to condemn Augustine personally, to say that the very glow of his religious conviction, narrowed as it were to a focus upon a single point of faith, made the effect of it perilous, in some ways very mischievous, when the heat of it caught a mind of baser temper and less generous zeal. Hatred of sin in himself made him very tender of sinners, in whose evil he saw the reflex of his own; but it could easily turn, in other men, into a fanatic hatred of those whom their narrow judgment condemned of sin. Awe at the Divine sentence passed on human guilt, in which he figured nothing less terrible than flames of everlasting anguish, might easily come in them to justify any violence of threat and torture by which they could lessen the chances of that appalling doom. And so that one enormous, unspeakable horror, which shadows as if with a bloody pall the history of Christendom for thirteen hundred years, — tortures of flame, rack, dungeon, haunting suspicion, infamous betrayal for opinion's sake, — all could find a sort of pretext, and in one sense had a source, in the vehement, undiscriminating, unsparing temper of Augustine's war on the heretic Pelagians and the schismatic Donatists.

It is necessary to make these large qualifications at the start, because really it is hard to speak of Augustine's name and influence so as to avoid mere blank laudation.*   He was a very strongly marked man, in his way a great man.   He is generally called the greatest of the Fathers; that is, of the Christian writers of the first six or eight centuries.   Comparisons are difficult in such a case : there is no scale by which souls can be accurately weighed; though this might be allowed without ranking him very high among the great minds of the world.   But he was, unquestionably, what may be called one of the great *characters* of history; one of the very greatest moral forces in the region both of character and of events that grow from character.

Now, when we think of a man's place in history, we are very apt to think of it as of the place of a brick in a wall, or of a statue in a niche, — as if it might be taken away with no other special loss; as if some other might have occupied it without much

* As a curious testimony to this eminence, it is said that at this day the Moors near Bona (the modern Hippo) call him, in honor, " the great Roman," and in pious memory of him visit every Friday the ruins of the church where he was bishop. — Ozanam, *Civilisation au cinquième Siècle*, Vol. II. p. 2.

change in the surroundings. But, in truth, a man fills his place among human events very much as the roots of a tree fill the interstices of the soil: they either burrow a way by their own vital force, or a way is made for them, inconceivably intricate, by the seemingly chance adjustment of stones and mould. More accurately still, he fills his place like a vital organ in the body, itself a part of that living network of tissues whose fibres and cells must be reckoned by many millions, which it has helped and helps to create. So that, when we are speaking of a very great personal force, such as that of Augustine, it is not as if it were something transferable, which might have appeared, perhaps, in another century; but something that grew out of and acted back on the innumerable and intricately mingled circumstances of the time.

What, then, were those circumstances? I must sketch them very broadly: we are already entering the twilight of the Dark Ages; and any slightest glimpse we have of them shows that we are standing at the boundary-line of two historic periods. The life we are considering spans that line at midway, and serves as our easiest transition from one period to the other.

The year 395 was one of those inexplicable times of panic, when prophecies fly about in the air, and a superstitious fear exaggerates the real terror of coming events. It was just three hundred and sixty-five years, as men reckoned, since the crucifixion of Christ. Thus the religion had endured for one prophetic cycle. A crisis had come in its destinies. Some great change was impending: its enemies said, to bring it to a sudden end, and restore the old system of things; its friends said, to open before it a new era of strength, perhaps to bring visibly the triumphant coming of the Messiah, and his victorious reign.*

Various things happened just then, as always happen at such a time, to deepen the terror, to confirm the hushed and eager expectation. That year the great Theodosius died; and with him, says Gibbon, died the genius of ancient Rome. Now first the permanent line of separation was drawn between the Eastern and Western Empire, parted between his two incapable sons. Within a month after his death, in the dead of winter, vast hordes of barbarians, no longer held back by the dread of his name, poured across the frozen Danube to threaten Italy and Greece: poured like a tide-wave, driven on by a great storm of wilder invasion behind, — in front the Goths, after them the terrible and hardly human Huns.

As that low thunder began to be heard along the North, the spell of an unearthly horror seemed to seize on men's minds, Pagan and Christian alike. Six years before, the emperor had decreed by edict the overthrow of Paganism; and at a blow, or rather by a hundred blows wildly struck at once throughout the empire, temple and altar and consecrated image and secret shrine went down. The work was done by swarms of monks, who issued from the monasteries of East and West, with eager, triumphant, iconoclastic zeal. To quote the words of Gibbon, "In almost every province of the Roman world an army of fanatics, without authority and without discipline, invaded the

* See *De Civitate Dei*, xviii. 54.

peaceful inhabitants; and the ruin of the fairest structures of antiquity still displays the ravages of *those* barbarians, who alone had time and inclination to execute such laborious destruction."

Now it was not, to either party in this wild crusade, the mere destruction of temple, grove, altar, or sacred image. Still less was it to them what it is to us, the mere destruction of Greek and Roman art. To the Pagan mind the old gods were tutelar divinities of land and city: their downfall left their walls naked to the invader. To the Christian mind these gods were Demons of awful and as yet unknown power. They had been worsted, so far, in the life-and-death struggle with a still mightier power, fervently believed to be the very presence of Almighty God himself. But suppose one shade of doubt as to this; or suppose that in his dark decree God chose to leave his people for a season naked to their enemies! Who could tell what vengeance, what terror, the " demons " they had fought against might yet have it in their power to inflict ? *

Besides, had not *they*, too, been brought up to revere before all earthly things the majesty of Rome ? Was not that very imperial majesty itself sundered before their eyes ? Were not rumors of peril such as had not been dreamed of for near eight centuries, so invincible had seemed the Eternal City, even now echoing in their ears ? They could not look forward, as we from a long, safe distance can look back, to see how the storm should sweep over and water the earth, making it bring forth a more generous growth ; and

* See *De Civitate Dei*, xx. 13 (compare ii. 10, x. 21).

how its lightnings should strike down or scorch away, first of all, noxious things, that while they stayed made any better world impossible. They were in the gloom of its blackness, and the mutterings of its thunder were close upon them. In a few years more, Rome was taken and sacked by Alaric (410). The spell of her great name was broken. Her desolation, to use the language of the time, was as the desolation of Babylon the great, and of Nineveh, which Jehovah had cursed of old. In men's imagination, the fall of Rome seemed almost the very dissolution of the globe.

History can only give us the incidents of the scene, not the passion and the terror that belong to it.* The record of a time is truly read in the minds of those living at the time: not in the events, which must be gathered and put together afterwards; but in the atmosphere, which can alone make the picture of them real. This atmosphere we find, more than anywhere else, in the writings of Augustine; and it is to him we must turn, in brief, to get such interpretation as we may of the thought of the time. That thought we shall find, for our present uses, in the three aspects under which his writings have now to be considered.

I. His public life, as Bishop of Hippo in Africa, began in that year of panic and dread, 395, and lasted thirty-five years, till his death in 430. Ten years before, at the age of thirty-one, was his conversion, — an event of such note that it is commemorated in the Roman calendar to this day. It may be worth while

* All that can be gleaned from the meagre annals of the time will be found in Hodgkin's " Italy and her Invaders " (Oxford, 1880).

here to give his own tender and dramatic account of it. He had listened to the preaching of Ambrose, and had been pondering with a friend the writings of Paul in much agitation of mind; and was strolling in the garden, when he heard a voice saying, *Tolle, lege; tolle, lege:* "Take, read; take, read." At first he thought it was spoken in some children's game; but suddenly it struck him that the voice must be an angel's. "So, checking my tears, I rose, judging it to be nothing else but a command to read the first words of the book I should find on opening. For I had heard of thy servant Antony, that coming in while the gospel was read he took it as a warning to himself, *Go sell all that thou hast and give to the poor, and come follow me;* and by that word was at once turned to thee. Eagerly then I returned to where my friend sat, where I had left the volume when I came away. I took it, opened it, and read silently the words my eye first rested on: *Let us walk honestly, as in the day; not in rioting and drunkenness, not in lewdness and debauchery, not in strife and jealousy; but put on the Lord Jesus Christ, and make not provision for the flesh to satisfy its lusts.* I read no more, and had no need of more; for instantly, at the end of this sentence, a calm light, as it were, entered my heart, and all the darkness of doubt passed away."

Nothing is said here of any change of opinion, or of the solution of any intellectual doubt that may ever have troubled him. As far as such a thing could be, it was a purely moral conversion, a change of sentiment, emotion, and will. Remorse for boyish faults, such as stealing a neighbor's pears, or for

loose living in his youth, made only a part of it, —
most likely, only a small part of it. It was rather
a recoil against the whole theory of life by which he
had been living hitherto. Especially, it was closely
connected, in his own mind, with that marked intellectual change which consisted in renouncing the
Manichæan philosophy, and accepting with great intensity of conviction Paul's own doctrine of good
and evil.*

Just what this Manichæan opinion was, what was
its strange fascination to the most cultivated thought
of that time, and what made it the great bugbear of
true believers for a thousand years together, it is not
easy to state to a modern mind. Augustine's own
statement of it, as I have said before, is turbid, con-
fused, and unintelligible. But it must have some
meaning *to us*, if we could only get at it, seeing that
it makes so large and imposing a figure in the history
of opinion.

Its essential principle is commonly explained as
simple Dualism, in some such way as this. The
Universe consists of two vast realms — infinities, we
might call them — which are polar opposites: Light
and Darkness. Where they come in contact, there is
interminable strife. The darkness aspires to the light,
hungers for it, engulfs, or (it is Augustine's word) de-
vours a portion of it; and from their contact is produced the visible world, including the nature of man.

---

* " In turmoil of mind (*æstuans*) I asked, *Whence is Evil?* What
were the agonies of my laboring heart! what groans, O my God!
And there were thine ears, when I knew it not. And when in silence I made bold to ask, loud was the cry appealing to thy mercy,
dumb the anguish of my soul." — *Conf.*, vii. 7.

In him, again, the soul represents (or is born of) light, and the body darkness.  So man is the subject of a divided empire; and the conflict, for all we see, must be eternal.

Now this may pass very well for a sort of poetry, telling in symbols the story of that strife which we see going on in the world about us, and are conscious of, more or less, within us.  But it is not easy to see why Augustine should have hated it so, when once he had left it behind; why the Church should have feared it so, that the first blood shed for heresy,* and the most ferocious of Crusades,† should have been on the charge of this deadly misbelief.  At first sight it does not seem so very different from Paul's own doctrine of the war of flesh and spirit; it looks like quite the same thing, in other terminology, with the Church doctrine of Satan as the adversary of God, which was, in fact, derived from the same Oriental source.  For the Persian Mani — who had been seized and flayed alive (according to the common story) a hundred years before by the king of Persia — had only set in more exaggerated and poetic strain the old Zoroastrian scheme of Good and Evil, engrafting on it some wild mythology of creation, and a scheme of redemption, which is only a strange phantasmagory, coupled with some Gnostic tradition of a Christ.‡  I do not know how, seen merely from the outside, we could easily tell the difference between

---

* Of the Priscillianists in Spain, A. D. 385.

† That against the Albigenses, 1208–1229.

‡ The completest statement of the Manichæan doctrine that I have seen is in Mosheim's " Commentaries " on the First Three Centuries.

Augustine's earlier and later theoretic view, as touching the conflict of good and evil in human nature.

We must look at it, therefore, in another way, from the point of view of religious experience. According to the Manichæan view, the source of Evil is physical; it exists in *the nature of things*. Man is subject to it because he is part of the system of things. The conflict is fought out, as it were, by vast impersonal forces, which he can have no hand in guiding. And so the system becomes one of Fatalism, — fatalism of that most hopeless and unrelenting sort which makes a man's soul (as it were) a mere shifting focus, where the rays of light and darkness meet, and his destiny is the plaything of their caprice. In other words, its view is speculative and physical, not ethical. It is of the conflict of Light and Darkness simply, not of Right and Wrong. "I had rather," says Augustine, of his own Manichæan days, "that thine unchanging Substance erred of necessity, than my own inconstant nature by will; and that Sin befell by immutable law from heaven, that so man should be free of its guilt, while in proud corruption of flesh and blood."

And thus the modern counterpart of Manichæism — if we would understand it from the corresponding thing in our own experience — is to be found in that scientific fatalism which is one of the threatening forms of modern thought, which we are well used to in the speculations of certain pessimists and evolutionists. I am anxious not to add to the rancor of any prejudice that may happen to exist. Evolution is the accepted dominant philosophy of the day. I accept it too, so far as I am entitled to exercise private judgment on so large a matter; desiring in all humility to know whatever there is true in it, and seeming to find in it the explanation of more dark facts in life than is found in any other system. But the instant it takes the form of fatalism as to the good or ill in human character, of helpless scepticism as to the course of human destiny, or despair of social progress, I surmise that there is something wrong, and that man's mind is capable of something better.

The insidious temptation to that way of thinking we ought to be aware of in ourselves, if we would judge the thought of Augustine and his contemporaries. We should see it not historically alone, as it touched them, but in thoughts, images, and influences that reach us too. The gloomy imagination of Shelley was strangely impressed by watching an Alpine glacier that seemed "crawling" from its bleak lair to swallow, like some monstrous dragon, the fertile valley and the smiling life below; and he thought of it as a symbol of the Fate which irresistibly overrides and crushes human hope.

Astronomers tell us the day is coming when all this globe will be blasted, empty, frozen, incapable of life; and to some this suggests a certain chilling despair as to the value and end of human effort. To others again it seems, after all these ages of costly and toilsome progress, as if civilization itself were going to be the prey of those appalling wars that have followed one another like thunder-shocks in these last five and twenty years, and still threaten; or of the vices and miseries that like a cancer eat at its very heart. And, if a serious and devout thinker, like Carlyle or Ruskin, can be tempted now to this intellectual despair, how was it in that day, when the one only fabric of society, polity, and art men knew seemed crumbling on one hand from interior decay, and threatened on the other by the irresistible avalanche of savage hordes ? The wild strange heresy of the Manichees was as it were the echo in their soul of that knell of doom which seemed clanging from all things around, in the downfall of a perishing world.

·Now it is not the warped judgment of a churchman; it is the judgment of Comte in his masterly outline of mediæval history, it is the judgment of that cool positivist, John Morley, in his apologetic essay on Voltaire, that civilization was narrowly saved, at this crisis of its fate, by the organized, valiant, aggressive faith of Christendom. How its conflict was carried on, and how its victory was gained, belongs to the study of the next four centuries, ending with the Christian Empire of Charlemagne. Just now, we are standing at the moment of time which determined what the nature of that struggle should be. And this decision was precisely contained in the nature of that change which passed upon the mind of Augustine in the hour of his conversion.

It is hardly too much to say that that revolt of his moral nature against the doctrine of the Manichees had in it the germ and the key of that great spiritual evolution. For the very point of it was that *it shifted the ground of conflict.* The source of Evil, it showed him, is not in the physical world; it is in the moral world. The battle-ground is not the nature of things; it is the nature of man. The conflict of good and evil is to be fought out in the soul. It is not as if man's salvation were staked on some great game played by invisible combatants in the wide field of the universe, — a game in which he has no hand and cannot see the moves. It is narrowed down to the field of his own mind; and, whatever outside forces are engaged in it, they are first of all, so to speak, personified in his own reason, conscience, passion, and will. Just where and just because 'he is most intensely conscious of his own personality, there and therefore comes the great alternative of right or wrong, of life or death.

Now it is in the very conviction of sin itself that one first has the true idea of good; just as it is *when we would do good* (as Paul says) that evil is present too. For the two are counterparts; so that not only we cannot know one without the other, but we cannot know either of them in any other way than through that struggle against the other. Nay, more. We cannot really know anything about God, of any consequence for us to know, except as the power *within us* "that makes for righteousness" in the struggle; that "works in us both to will and to do." The physical nature and conditions (so to speak) of Infinite Good — what we call the Divine Attributes — are as impossible for us to define as those of Infinite Evil. And so in the very struggle itself we have an assurance, the only assurance we can have, that the great spiritual forces of the Universe itself are on our side; in short, that our salvation (which means our "safety" in it) is the direct gift of Almighty God himself.

This we may take to be the real sense of the Pauline or Augustinian doctrine of justification by faith, as seen in the light of personal experience, and especially as against the Manichæan heresy. Augustine stakes his position in that controversy on the point of moral freedom. To him it is a shocking thing to say that anything is originally and essentially evil.* Evil is a corruption of some native good; a ruin, a fall, not a destiny from the beginning. To attain the higher life is not a conquest of something alien; it is winning back our birthright. This conviction lay at the heart of Augustine's creed. To conceive it, further, as a force in history, we must think of it not as a mere form of philosophic speculation with him, but as a vivid, intense, fiery conviction, such as he conceived it in the moment of conversion, and such as, in the heated warfare of opinion, he has stamped the impression of it on the Christian mind.

II. I have dwelt thus out of seeming proportion on Augustine's relation to the Manichæan controversy, both because it is the most obscure in itself, and because it gives the exact point of view from which to consider the two other chief intellectual tasks of his life. Of these the first was his controversy with Pelagius, — the great unending debate of Destiny and Moral Freedom.

In one sense this controversy is impotent and futile, turning on a question that necessarily remains unsolved and unsolvable, the shuttlecock of metaphysics

* See the "Dialogue with Faustus."

since thought began.   At whatever point we start, —
divine foreknowledge, destiny, natural law, evolution,
— strict logic brings us straight to one or another
form of necessity.   Regarded scientifically, moral liberty is not even thinkable.   On the other hand, no
sooner do we come to the facts of life, — action, conduct, the judgment of motives, responsibility for results, personal appeal, — than we take for granted at
every step that moral freedom which our theory denies.   Accept whatever theory you will of antecedent
and result, with its logical consequences, and' you
are a fatalist at once, helpless sport of destiny.   Try
to state to yourself any theory you will of human
action, and apply it to men's character and conduct,
the instant you say *I will* or *I ought*, you have come
upon other ground.   You have admitted in terms that
fact of human life which is all your opponent really
contends for, however irreconcilable to your own his
way of stating it.   Life incessantly re-creates the faith
which science as incessantly denies.

All this is very simple and elementary business.
Leaving now the platitudes of metaphysics, let us attempt to see the great debate as it enters here upon
the field of history.   It is very interesting to watch
the combatants : Augustine, with the hot blood of his
native Barbary coast, a small, thin man, nervous,
fiery, intense, goaded by memories of his own sins of
the blood, haunted by the thought of a Hand that had
been held out to snatch him from destruction, humbly
sensitive of his own helplessness in that crisis, and
clinging like Paul to the thought of a Divine Power
he must always lean on for strength, himself only the

meanest instrument of an Almighty Will; Pelagius, with the clear, cool head of his native Britain, large of frame, slow of speech, grave, honest, weighty, his self-mastery trained by strife of wind and ocean-wave, of firm, resolute will, clear conscience, cheerful courage, and masculine understanding.* The two had kind thoughts and respect for one another, for they had met in personal debate;† but the controversy their names represent lay as much in their radical difference of temperament as in the difference of theory they started with.

It is of no use now to take up their arguments. As it must always be in the field of action, vehement conviction had the better of sober common-sense, and Pelagius went back to the calmer life of his native North. Was that a thing to regret? At least it was inevitable. The men who make the deepest mark on history are the men who feel with a deep and intense conviction that they are instruments of a higher Power, their own will governed by a vast Force behind them, impersonal and uncontrollable. This seems to be the case even in direct ratio to their weight of personality and vehemence of resolution: with Paul, Augustine, Luther; with William of Orange, Cromwell, Napoleon, — the men of God, or else the men of Destiny.

And perhaps it was better so. Here I will quote the historian Michelet. "To reduce Christianity," he says, "to a mere philosophy, were to strike it with

---

* To complete the parallel, later belief added that the two great antagonists were born in the same year.

† See Augustine's letter to Pelagius (Ep. 146).

death, and to rob it of the future.  What would the dry rationalism of the Pelagians have availed when the German invasion came ?  Not that proud theory of liberty needed then to be preached to the conquerors of the Empire, but the dependence of man, the almightiness of God.  To temper that fierce barbarism, all the religious and poetic fervor of Christianity was none too intense.  The Roman world felt by instinct that it must seek its own refuge in the ample bosom of Religion.  That was its hope, its only asylum, when the Empire that had called itself eternal was passing away in its turn, with the nations it had subdued. . . . The mystic doctrine triumphed.  As the barbarians came, the controversy ceased ; the schools were closed and still.  It was faith, simplicity, patience, the world needed then."

The partisan applause of Augustine because his doctrine triumphed, and the theological odium into which his opponent fell, are both alike discreditable to the occasion and the man.  But — as afterwards in the sharp warfare in which the Protestant Reformation was plunged — it was a time of crisis and peril.  At such a time men must look well to the keenness of their weapons, and not spare blows in the thick of the fight.  It was well that that doctrine triumphed which was likeliest to enlist men's passions on the side of religion and virtue.  But Augustine, any more than Calvin, cannot claim our full verdict for all his acts.  Of the two the first had far the more generous, the tenderer, the broader nature ; and of the two his theological scheme more thoroughly and deeply made part of his own religious experience.   He felt that, in a sense, every-thing was at stake in the debate; and this is his claim for pardon, that his vehemence in controversy stirred up hate against his opponents, and they even charged him with using the arm of the law against them, and exciting the persecution under which they suffered.   At least, the moderate and gentle temper he began with gave way, and his name is unhappily used to justify the vindictive, unreasoning malice that has spurred on the hunting of heresy to this day.

III.   Of the very great bulk of Augustine's writings the largest part consists of exhortations, discussions, expositions, that filled up the spaces of his routine work during his five and thirty years of office.   One famous treatise stands out in strong relief from the mass; and for breadth of mind, largeness of view, orderliness of argument, or mastery of style, his fame rests chiefly on this, — " The City of God."

The book abounds in arguments that would seem childish now.   Its notion of sacred history is formal, uncritical, and dogmatic.   Its sketch of early events is at once tediously minute and curiously incomplete. Its reasoning on natural things shows all the igno-rance and incompetency of an unscientific age.   Its expositions of Scripture are impossible to accept, its personal testimonies of miracles and wonders impos-sible to believe.*   In other words, it has just the intellectual defects, the bigotries, ignorances, and superstitions, of the human mind at that day.

But it is not necessary to dwell on these.   They

* See in particular the very curious and detailed account of these miracles in Book xxii., chap. 8.

are faults on the surface, sometimes running down into the substance, of a great and noble work, — the one really great work that the human mind produced, we may say, for four or five centuries, at least within the limits of the Western Empire. Its substance I cannot dwell on; of its temper and occasion a few words remain now to be said.

The title of the book shows the splendid conception that lay in the mind of Augustine, — a conception which we may call the final culminating and idealizing of the old Messianic hope. It set up, as it were, a magnificent standard of faith, right on the spot and at the time that must see the great battle of Christ and Antichrist fought out.

The time of its composition was between the fall of Rome under Alaric the Goth and the more furious invasion of the Vandal Genseric. At that moment of chief horror and despair, when the bravest were appalled at a disaster that so appealed to men's imagination, when even believers began to ask whether Christianity had not proved impotent to the task of holding the defences Paganism had maintained so long,* Augustine threw down this sublime challenge to their faith.

His tone is proud, confident, uncompromising, triumphant in advance. It is attack, and not defence. He puts point-blank the contrast of the "Two Cities" as he calls them: the City of this World, the abode of superstition, cruelty, violence, conquest, lust, greediness, hate, — all illustrated in the record of pagan Rome; the City of God, with its marvellous

---

* See the Introduction, and compare Book xx., chap. 13.

chronicle of prophecy and miracle, the saints and heroes of its glorious calendar, its constant assurance and proof of superhuman aid, its magnificent promise of future ages that shall be its own, illustrated from the sacred records of Hebrew faith. The two are elaborately contrasted in their origin, their progress, and their end, in the second and larger division of the work ; the former part having already shown, in even superfluous detail, how helpless Paganism had been to secure blessing and safety to its adherents in this world, and how empty was its promise for the world to come.

The phrase itself *City of God* carries a suggestion of the compact, highly organized municipalities of Italy or Greece, and their capacity to call out and sustain the most strenuous and devoted patriotism. The ancient City stood for natural justice, armed and codified, for a common welfare, and for protection against assault. Its justice, perhaps, was class-privilege. For liberty it had only "liberties." But it was at once the highest political conception men knew then, the most sacred and revered type of authority they could comprehend. And, in making it the key to his argument, Augustine has given, as it were, the Roman counterpart of that " Kingdom of Heaven " which the Jews looked for in their Messiah's reign.

He offers, however, no such promise of a kingdom upon earth. This "kingdom of heaven is within." The " City " is purely ideal, spiritual, heavenly. The miseries of the good and bad, so far as human eye can see, will continue alike and equal through the present life to the end of time ; the visible separation will be hereafter.  The blessedness of the righteous on earth is peace ; the wretchedness of hell itself is interior conflict, even if there were no everlasting flame.*  In this fundamental thought of the "City of God" we have, again, the complement of that thought illustrated in Augustine's reaction against Manichæism, which shifts the conflict of good and evil to the world within, and stakes all in life that is worth living for on the soul itself.  This point of contrast with Manichæism is urged in several places in the "City of God."  The blessing promised to good men is not that they escape the anguish or the terror, but that they are victorious over it.

If we can look back now a few years, to the time of our own great national struggle, to those seasons of disaster and defeat when to large numbers, brave and fearful alike, the struggle itself seemed bootless and hopeless ; and if we can remember the enormous advantage then of our faith in an ideal Republic, one and indissoluble, — that sublime ideal of political justice and popular right which made the nation's victory and strength; then, I think, we may conceive something of what it was, as the world plunged into those long dark ages of barbarism and strife, to have that one flag kept proudly flying above that one impregnable fortress of the City of God !

The ages that followed, when the Church was at length victorious in its new empire, do not fulfil the promise of that grand dream, any more than our new

---

* See the exquisite chapters, Book xix., ch. 13, 14 ; also the brief but profound one, xix. 28 ; together with the noble and sweet cadence with which the work concludes.

Republic fulfils the hope of those who fought to save it, and gave their lives freely in that hope. But we can see at least that one great danger is past. We know now better than we knew then the evil and fatal nature of that which threatened the national life. So it was when men could look back afterwards, and see the strong lines in which Augustine had traced the contrast between two orders of society. And, in the appalling miseries and divisions that tormented the world for several centuries, it is not likely that one brave man, or one frightened woman, ever once looked back regretfully for the protection that could have been given by an Empire which had so proved itself abominable and accursed.

## VII

## LEO THE GREAT.

TO deal intelligently with an epoch like that of Leo the Great (440–461), it is especially necessary to bear in mind the aggressive, militant, antagonistic position of the Church in human history. Our theory of Christianity may be a theory of development; but the facts we have to deal with are the incidents of a long, obstinate, often deadly struggle. That struggle takes mainly three directions, — against Paganism, against Barbarism, and against corruptions engendered in the Church itself. At present, we are concerned only with the first.

Now, to make any conflict effective, the first condition of all is that the force shall be a disciplined force, and shall act with absolute singleness of purpose, in absolute obedience to a single will. The smooth theories of a time of peace will not suit a period of war. Christianity as " free religion " would have perished in a single generation. If we consent to see that it was in any sense at that time a saving power in the world ; if it was, in fact, the genius and spirit that carried society without wreck through many generations of confusion and disaster, — we shall be content to see the conditions on which that work could be done then. And of these the first of all was that the Christian Church should be united, organized, loyal, absolutely confident of itself, and thoroughly understanding the work it had to do.

Now, if we only remember that the last great battle fought by Rome — that in which, with Goths for allies, she succeeded in crippling the army of the Huns, in a fight that cost, it is said, three hundred thousand lives — was in the year 451; that the next year the hordes of Attila, with recovered strength, hovered like a flight of vultures above the plains of Italy; that three years later Genseric with his Vandals swept Rome almost clean of its vast treasures of gold, silver, and bronze, and precious works of art; that these things happened in the very middle of Leo's rule, while, within twenty-five years after his death, the spectral sovereignty of Rome itself came to an end, and the barbarian was lord of the Western Empire, — we shall see distinctly that we have come to the death-agony of the ancient State. And, as this great agony was coming on, the East was racked and vexed by the bitterest of theological debates, only suspended at Chalcedon in 451; while in the West, and at Alexandria, the intellectual centre of the empire, there was a revival of classic Paganism which threatened the very life of Christianity itself.

I cannot speak at length of the causes, only mention some of the symptoms, of the extraordinary pagan revival which followed for a generation or two the edict of Theodosius closing the temples, and forbidding the public worship of the gods. The last pagan writer of vigorous Latin prose, Ammianus, ends his

story with a vivid account of the desperate battle
about Adrianople (378), in which the Goths broke
once and for all the spell of the Roman name.  Three
years later, Paganism was nominally abolished by imperial edict.  But five and twenty years after that,
while Alaric was training his Goths in Italy, Claudian could celebrate alike, with easy courtliness, in
purely pagan fashion, the exploits of the brave Stili-
cho, and the holidays of Honorius who murdered him,
or recite in smooth epigram the miracles and mysteries of the Christian record ; while at Alexandria
Hypatia lent the charm of her beauty and eloquence
to the new Platonism that glorified the old gods of
Greece with transcendental finery, till she was torn
to pieces by a mob of monks (415).

The pagan games, with circumstances of barbarity
and horror of which I shall have more to say at another time, were still celebrated in circus and amphitheatre.  A certain insolent fashion of ignoring the
new creed, with the growing power built upon it, had
taken hold of the popular mind, and was still dominant in literature and art.  And, for the last strange
proof how vital and tough were the roots of old superstition, when Alaric appeared before the gates of
Rome, Etruscan soothsayers were sent for, to see if by
their incantations they could yet save the city ; and
promised that they would do it, (we are told,) but at
the cost of human sacrifice, and of rites so horrid that
the people refused them at the hour of their greatest
terror.  Even Pope Innocent the First, then in Rome,
had consented, it is said, that this last appeal to the
pagan magic should be made.

Now, at the time of this siege, the Empire had been nominally Christian for about a hundred years. How long the spirit and belief of Paganism remained after this, it is of course impossible to say. The last great work of Augustine's life was to argue in his "City of God" against this very reaction, when it seemed as if the new religion had failed to hold the ground conquered under the ancient gods of Rome. What he so argued against was but a helpless and despairing cry. The old wreck, swarming as it was with many evil forms of life, was soon swept disastrously away. As a clear-eyed man like Leo could see, even then, there was only one power that could take its place.

To the common eye the struggle might look doubtful, even yet. Paganism had lost its hold on men's reason. On their conscience it never had any very firm hold at all. But it held strong grasp on two great springs of human action, their imagination and their fear. We have just seen to what acts the terror of the siege had nearly led. And, for the imagination, it had taken full possession of the forms of literature and art. Except for a few rude hymns feeling their way to the common heart in a simple popular rhythm, except for a few rude shapes and symbols of Christian imagery, there was nothing to fill the great void left by the perishing of ancient art. For centuries yet, Christian poets clung helplessly, as it were, to

> " The fair humanities of old religion,
>     The power, the beauty, and the majesty
>     That had their haunts in dale, or piny mountain,
>     Or forest by slow stream, or pebbly spring,
>     Or chasms and watery depths."

After seven centuries of implacable monastic rule, Dante has still a half-belief in Charon and Pluto; and when the revival of letters came, a little later, the old deities sprang, as it were, from the soil of the new culture, and flourished in a sort of pallid life down almost to our day. But that life had run in all the veins of the ancient world, where each state had its own divinity, and every formal act was a religious symbol; where the head of the State was a god visible in the flesh, and the very places of public amusement were temples of Mars and Venus, the divinities of violence and lust. So that it was still, in the middle of the fifth century, a hand-to-hand struggle in which the Church was engaged, if not with Paganism itself, in its cruel older forms, at least with those compromises of its spirit found under the names of Priscillianist and Manichæan, against which Leo waged an unsleeping and untiring war.

Again, we must look from his point of view, not ours, at the controversies that divided and disgraced the Christians of the East. It was not controversy between the friends and opponents of the orthodox belief. Each party eagerly and honestly claimed his own to be the true exposition of the Nicene faith. Thus Apollinaris, fervently maintaining the doctrine of his friend Athanasius, who had sojourned with him in some of his travels, fell into the heresy that Christ's body was of heavenly, and not of human substance. Macedonius, taking the creed too literally in its limitation as well as its assertion, was charged with subordinating the Spirit to the Father and the Son; to meet which the Council at Constantinople expanded that clause a little (in 381). Nestorius, holding strongly to Christ's human nature, saw blasphemy in the phrase "Mother of God" applied to Mary; saying that Jesus was divine not intrinsically, but was made so by the indwelling Deity.* And in the storm of controversy that burst out on this, hardly stayed by the decree at Ephesus (431), Eutyches, an Alexandrian monk of seventy, went so far, in his hot orthodoxy, as to say that the divine nature in him quite absorbed the human.

·To us these disputes are battles in the thinnest of air; but then they were matters very literally of life and death. Nestorius, who had himself been a hard, high-handed ecclesiastic, was banished to the confines of Persia, where living a long life of exile he left a sect that bears his name down to our day. The party of Eutyches took violent possession of the synod at Ephesus (449), the "robber-synod," where they carried their point not by acclamation only, but by blows; so that their chief opponent was literally beaten and trampled to death, and the Roman delegates sent by Leo to maintain the primacy of Rome barely fled with their lives.

Such was the state of things, so far as touched his own immediate work, with which Leo had to deal. It presents two sides of a conflict which we find incessantly present in his writings. Now Leo was not,

* The terms by which he signified the operation of the Divine nature in him were "indwelling" ($\dot{\epsilon}\nu o\acute{\iota}\kappa\eta\sigma\iota s$), "assumption" or "adoption" ($\dot{a}\nu\acute{a}\lambda\eta\psi\iota s$), "inworking" ($\dot{\epsilon}\nu\acute{\epsilon}\rho\gamma\epsilon\iota a$), "inhumanizing" ($\dot{\epsilon}\nu a\nu\theta\rho\acute{\omega}\pi\eta\sigma\iota s$), i. e. abiding in humanity.

in any sort, a pietist, a sentimentalist, a recluse. He
was first of all a Roman statesman, with the clear
sagacity, the resolute will, the firm and inexorable
temper when a point must be carried, the wary vigilance, the unswerving persistency, that had made the
Romans masters of the world. He had this advantage over them, besides, that his policy dealt with convictions, not with armies and state powers, so that
his clear intelligence had free range to act, moving
in the intangible region of ideas, where no friction
is ; while he was in full command of the intellectual
sympathies and the moral conviction which are always the deepest moving forces of the time. One
does not read a page of his writings without seeing
how complete his convictions is, and how perfect his
command of those springs of power.

Then he was a man of absolute courage, — not simply that easy "courage of his convictions" which
enables or compels one who has any strong conviction at all to give it expression somehow without disguise, but that personal physical courage as well, which
with a man dealing in theories and policies is much
more rare. This absolute courage it was which made
him meet without blenching, squarely as an equal,
the terrible Attila, when sent to intercede with him
for the trembling inhabitants of Rome, and, by what
seemed then a miracle, but was indeed only the miracle of mind over brute force, won from him the
terms by which he left Italy unharmed ; then, two
years later, gained from the relentless Genseric such
conditions as still left security of life, when the city
for the second time was at the mercy of the barba-

rian. Perfect courage joined with dignity of office never, perhaps, won a nobler victory. I copy here the words of no eulogist, but of a clear and somewhat severe critic of the growth of papal power.

" The emperor, the court, the wealthy, and the noble had fled at the approach of danger ; the intrepid Bishop, strong in faith and hope and love, alone remained at the post of honor and of peril ; and, when the satiated foe had retired and left the city emptied of all its wealth and substance, and almost reduced to a wilderness of deserted habitations, there remained none to advise or to cheer the famishing remnant but the undaunted Bishop and his gallant clergy. These had never quitted their posts ; these had faced the foe, and averted the extremity of ruin ; and their example alone kept alive the spark of life among the despairing multitude that still clung to their desolate homes. It is in this spontaneous chieftainship that we recognize one of the most effective elements of the subsequent political greatness of the Roman bishops. The decaying mass of civil institutions became as manure at the root of the papacy. Papal Rome drew nourishment from dissolution, courage from despair. In desperate emergencies like that we have just adverted to, no one will look into or scrutinize too closely the claims and titles of the deliverer ; in such times the duties of civil and spiritual government are thrust into the hands best able to execute them ; both duties are impelled into the same channel, and flow on naturally and amicably together. To Leo it was due that Rome was not converted into a heap of smouldering ashes ; and, if natural justice were to decide the question between the Church and the State, without doubt the Pope was the rightful governor of Rome, for without him there would have been no Rome to govern." *

It is a mark of the real greatness of Leo, that these striking and dramatic events do not appear to have even ruffled the surface of his mind. They are mere incidents in the discharge of his duty, perhaps distractions from what he felt to be his true work. It is a mark of his wisdom, too. In his judgment of the relative importance of things, he was wiser in his own day than we should probably be in our judgment now. It was of more moment to the world, just as it was of more account to him, that the invisible foundation should be made sure, than that this or that should be the working-out of any political event.

The work to be done was to build up a new Rome on the ruins of the old. And, for this new structure, his one task was to care for the foundations. These were laid in men's loyalty and belief and hope, and must be constructed patiently alike in the storm or calm of outward events. You look through his entire correspondence, page by page; and you find not an allusion to events that even at this distance shed such a powerful and lurid glare on the history of the time. On the other hand, his letters † are full of the official detail of his work as spiritual Head of the Christian world, which he fully believed himself to be. On this one point there is never a word of concession, never an instant of hesitation. We have no business, just now, with his arguments, only with his convictions. Whether Peter was chief of the apostles

* Greenwood's *Cathedra Petri*, Vol. I. pp. 426, 467.
† Of which about one hundred and eighty are preserved.

in any official sense; whether he ever came to Rome and lived as bishop of the church there; whether his primacy, if he had it, descended to his successors,— all these questions, of fruitful controversy once, are nothing to the point. What we see is, that the Church at Rome — partly by its metropolitan rank, partly by the transfer of the court to Constantinople, partly by the distractions of Italy, partly by the steadily aggressive policy of its abler heads — had come to have a dignity and authority that gradually supplanted those of every other; and that, in the great ruin that had overtaken the Roman state, men came to lean more on its visible and compacted strength. We also see, or seem to see, that this power, so disciplined and firm, was the one thing capable of saving to the world its old treasures of thought and its traditions of social order. What is now our best judgment of the time was then its inspiration and its faith, and gave it courage to abide the bursting of the storm that was close upon it.

The strong heart of Leo held absolutely to that conviction, whether as statesman or as Christian believer is of little concern to us. In his singleness of purpose, he probably could not have drawn any nice line between his policy and his creed. His arguments will not count for much with us. It is hardly too much to say that he does not stoop to argument. His tone is of assertion, instruction, authority, command. Several of his letters are treatises of some length on disputed points: the famous one to Flavian, which guided the decisions of the Council at Chalcedon (451), would make a pamphlet of about twenty pages. Nowhere in any of them does he hint that an opponent is to be met as an equal, on the fair level of debate. The assumed grounds of his opinion he is willing to explain; but the opinion itself you must take, whether you accept the argument or not.

In that particular debate, Eutyches had appealed to Leo, and had gained at first his cordial support. But when the point came to be better known, above all, when the robber-synod at Ephesus showed in what a temper it was held, then Leo was perfectly uncompromising and distinct. He demanded at first that the Council should be held in Italy; and, when that could not be had, wrote his letter of instructions, taking at once the tone not of debater but of judge. His dictum has been the test phrase of orthodoxy ever since : that both natures, divine and human, were blended, in their completeness, in the one Person who was thus perfect God and perfect man; and his little treatise, in this letter, is to this day as authentic and clear a statement as has been made, or perhaps can be made, of what, by the very terms of it, is absolute and unintelligible mystery.* We may think as we will of the proposition. We may find in it, if we will, an important metaphysical truth, where we fail to see a dogmatic one. But at least we may recognize its value as a symbol, or watchword, in the crisis that was fast coming on. It is interesting to remember that the decision at Chalcedon was in the

* Its terms are, *Salvâ igitur proprietate utriusque naturæ* [*et substantiæ*], *et in unam coëunte personam* (in the Greek, εἰς ἓν πρόσωπον συνιούσης).—Leo I., *Ep.* xxviii. This is (I think) the first use of the term πρόσωπον, corresponding to the Latin *persona*, and is apparently a concession to Leo's influence and authority.

very year of the great battle of Châlons,* which broke the power of the Huns, and saved Europe from the fate of Asia ; and that, of these two events, Leo, the greatest man of the time, seems utterly and calmly careless of the one, while his whole heart is full, and all his passion roused, by the subtile point of transcendental theology determined in the other.

The permanent and real work of Leo's life was to found a new Rome on the ruins of the old. At this distance of time, it is easy for us to see how far greater was the splendor, and vaster the sway, of the spiritual empire that followed him, than of the political dominion that went before. But, in that age of ruin, it is very striking to see how distinctly it was already prefigured to his mind. We must assume that he, as a native Roman, had in his heart all the proud and passionate loyalty which for so many ages had made Rome's unbroken faith in her imperial destiny. And perhaps it was in part the obstinate resolve that that faith should not be defeated, which made him so clear-eyed as to the coming glories of the Eternal City. It is best to hear his expression of it in his own words, which I copy from a sermon delivered on the memorial day of St. Peter and St. Paul.

"These are the men, O Rome, through whom the gospel of Christ hath shone upon thee. These are thy holy fathers and thy true shepherds, who have set thee in heavenly kingdoms far more gloriously than those who laid the first foundations of thy walls. These are

* Or rather, of Troyes, some fifty miles farther south. See Hodgkin's " Italy and her Invaders," Vol. II. p. 138.

they who have advanced thee to such glory that, as a
holy nation, a chosen people, a priestly and royal state,
thou shouldst hold a broader sway in faith of God than
in dominion of the earth.  Whatever the victories that
have borne forward thy right of empire by land and sea,
yet less the toil of war has yielded thee than the peace
of Christ.  For the good, just, and almighty God, who
never denied his mercy to human kind, and always, by
his abundant benefits, has instructed all men in the
knowledge of himself, by a more secret counsel and a
deeper love took pity on the willing blindness of wan-
derers and their proneness to evil, by sending his Word,
equal and co-eternal with himself.  And, that the fruit
of this unspeakable grace might be shed through all the
earth, he with divine foresight prepared the Roman
realm, whose growth was carried to limits that bor-
dered upon the universe of all nations on every side.
But this city, knowing not the Author of her greatness,
while queen of almost every nation, was slave to the
errors of every people, and seemed to herself to have
attained great faith, because she had spurned no falsehood.  And so, the more strictly she was held in bonds
by Satan, so much the more marvellously she is set free
by Christ."

· These words we read, not as the complacent homily
by which it is so easy to glorify a victory already
won, but as the strong faith that is itself the pledge
of victory in advance.  It was in part an educated
belief with Leo, and in part the clear pointing of the
time.  No blame to him, if it was also in part his
secular and patriotic creed.  To a Roman it was the
right thing that Rome should be ·sovereign of the
earth.  To a pious and strong-hearted Roman of that

age, the one thing needful at once and possible was, that in her continued empire Rome should be a spiritual sovereign, and not a temporal one. Rome, said Jornandes, no longer held the world by arms, but by men's imaginations.

This faith, this resolute purpose of Leo, it cannot be denied that he carried into effect by diplomacy and state-craft, as well as preached it for a religious creed. In judging this, again, it is best to see the situation as it really was. Leo was shrewd, wary, persistent, determined, watchful of opportunity, after the manner of statesmen. A large part of his policy must be judged by the ethics of statesmanship, rather than by the humbler private moralities. In this, however, two things may be claimed for him : that the motive of his game was nobler, and the stake he played for higher, than that of the mere statesman; and that, while his policy was often stern and overbearing, it was never treacherous or cruel. As for personal ambition, or selfish designs, as that phrase is commonly understood, it does not appear that a shadow of such a motive passed upon his mind, or a shadow of such a suspicion ever rested upon his name. Assuming the one end and aim of his policy which he kept in view, all the acts of it were the natural, straightforward, resolute carrying out of it. That he meant to assert the spiritual sovereignty of Rome, and the official supremacy of the post he held, explains itself. That, with his high temper, he would have yielded to it in another man's hands the simple homage he claimed for it in his own, one may possibly doubt. But, standing where he did, and seeing what he did, he believed in it with all his heart; and it was well for the world that he did so believe in it.

Thus he was on the watch from the first for an occasion to put his theory into force. The occasion was quickly found : a strong man, in fact, never has to wait long for it. Two hundred years before, under Tertullian and Cyprian, the churches in Africa had been, in strength and eloquence, the worthy pioneers of Latin Christianity. Later still, under Augustine, their fame had far surpassed that of Rome, in everything except the accident of their provincial situation. But they had been torn and rent by the schism of the Donatists. Augustine himself had spent a great part of his strength in incessant controversy; and he was now fifteen years dead, and Vandal buccaneers lording it over the whole Barbary coast. The church at Rome, and Leo, its vigorous head, made the natural court of appeal for the afflicted province; and so the first stone was laid of that strong confederation which afterwards grew to be the Catholic Empire of the West.

Again, the opportunity came, half by accident, that led to official correspondence with the eastern coasts of the Adriatic, — an opportunity which Leo was not slow to improve. He always assumes his authority, never defends it; advises, urges, instructs, and in fact exercises on the soil of Greece the jurisdiction which the feebler Patriarch of Constantinople, leaning on court influence, and jealous of a claim he had no strength to enforce, found daily slipping from his hand. This advantage Leo pushed, as we have seen, to the extent of directing, almost (it would seem) of dictating, the counsels at Chalcedon. He failed, however, in the one point of securing the formal admission by the East of the claims of Rome. The Council was careful to declare — in its celebrated twenty-eighth canon, which he was equally careful to disown — that Constantinople, the metropolis and official capital of Christendom, held equal rank. And to that declaration the East still adheres to-day.

The critical test, however, of Leo's theory was in Gaul. That firmly allied with Rome, the West at least was secure. Now the churches of Southern Gaul were about as old as that of Rome; claimed, indeed, to have been founded by Paul himself.* They had been famous and strong from the very earliest time. Their martyr record was of the noblest; their Irenæus, in the second century, of far more weight than any Roman name; their St. Martin, in the fourth, the purest and bravest of all who had carried the faith into the barbarous West. Besides, that country was earliest of all, under the old Roman dominion, to feel conscious of the germs of a new nationality. "Eldest daughter of Rome" the flatteries of Catholic pontiffs have delighted in calling her; but a daughter that long and often has contested vigorously the mother's will.

Hilary of Arles, for some ecclesiastical offence, had displaced one of his bishops, Celidonius, who promptly appealed to Rome. Leo, as promptly, without waiting to inquire, but eager to assert his jurisdiction, restored Celidonius to his place. Hilary, of

---

* One of the principal ones, at Trèves, by the widow's son of Nain, who had been miraculously raised, a second time, by the laying on of Peter's staff.

ruder temper than Leo and at least as resolute, gray-haired but vigorous, at once took his staff, and went upon foot, in midwinter,* all the way to Rome. He was sure that Leo did not understand the merits of the case. He would not be put off, he said, with the smooth compliments that greeted him, and pushed his plea so hotly that Leo arrested him for contempt, and put him under guard. He broke bounds, however, and went back the way he came, noway ready to submit, — deprived, meanwhile, of a large part of the region he presided in. Still Leo's victory might have hung doubtful, but that he prudently obtained a decree from the worthless Valentinian III. (445), who ruled in a sort of phantom sovereignty at Ravenna, declaring not only the subjection of Gaul and of every other province to the Pope at Rome, but that "to all men, whatever the authority of the Apostolic See has ordained, or does, or shall ordain, shall be as law." †

Those which I have recited were the most notable occasions on which Leo asserted and maintained the spiritual authority of Rome. They were the critical acts of his sovereignty; and they have sketched, in vigorous outline, the pretensions of the Pontificate, which have been continually reasserted, in precisely the same direction and general terms, down to our day. Nothing on earth has been so consistent or persistent as this ecclesiastical policy of Rome. What-

---

* On this journey we may assume that he departed from his usual winter custom of going barefoot.

† See the terms of the Decree in Greenwood's *Cathedra Petri*, Vol. I. pp. 353, 354.

ever we may think about it now, it had its uses and
necessities once; and we shall see them the more
plainly as we get deeper into the shadow of barbarian
times, and then into the twilight of Feudalism. Just
now, it is our business to see only how they lay in
the mind and shaped the policy of one strong, resolute, and sagacious man.

Even that, however, dealing as it did with great
things, would not have been what it was in the history of human events, except for the incessant, untiring vigilance in little things. How little these
were, yet how important in his eyes, — the ordering
of a festival, the discipline of a churchman, the ex-
plaining of a phrase, the reiteration of a counsel or a
command, — one can see only in the details of his
homilies and his correspondence. In these, we watch
as it were the process by which that enormous fabric
of ecclesiastical power was woven, thread by thread,
till it seemed to wrap inseparably, like the membrane
of a living body, every limb and interior organ of the
great structure of mediæval civilization.

We see the process; but we see it only in one corner of its working, and for one moment of time. The
same thing was going on incessantly, untiringly, over
many a thousand miles, for many a hundred years,
still following the form and pattern that had been
traced by that strong hand, still appealing to and
guided by the very maxims and phrases that we have
heard from that resolute voice. The unity of counsel
in multiplicity of operations, which we call Catholi-
cism, — apparently as strong to-day, in its own sphere,
as a thousand years ago, and as able to send its ser-

vants to their post in hamlet or forest as then, as little afraid as then of sword or fire or torture or starvation, that great wonder of human history, the discipline of a vast population, like an army loyal to one flag and obedient to one word of command, — has been the task of many ages and many men. In the fifteen centuries of its existence it has produced enormous good and enormous evil. But it is justice to the name of Leo to say that the ideal good, without the inseparable evil, was what lay in his heart and made his strength; and to recognize him as the one man, in that day of terror and despair, who was wise enough and strong enough to do its necessary task.

# VIII.

## MONASTICISM AS A MORAL FORCE.

IT is hard for us to estimate fairly the value of a thing so utterly alien from the modern mind as the monastic spirit, with the ascetic practices and the religious forms that grew out of it. To judge it out of hand is easy enough from the modern point of view, which puts in relief its corruptions and absurdities, and contrasts it with what we know as the helpful and saving forces of society now. It is also easy to recount the services of the monastic orders, for several centuries, in the shelter of the weak, the preservation of letters, the building up of intelligent and free industry. What is not so easy is to appreciate the strength and fervor of the monastic passion · itself, as a moral force, and its value as a factor in history.

A series of careful studies, or else of brilliant and impressive pictures, by such writers as Guizot, Montalembert, and Charles Kingsley, aids very much to bring this matter within the range of our modern sympathy and understanding. For my present purpose, however, I must avoid all these attractive fields of illustration. I must also avoid for the most part that great, strange field of Eastern asceticism, with the exhibition it offers, sometimes tender and pathetic, often wild and repulsive, of cenobitic and eremitic life in the region that gave it birth.  My object is simply to see how it entered as an element into the larger life that was unfolding towards the West.

As early as the time of Athanasius and Augustine, monasticism had already powerfully affected the imagination of Western Europe, and led the way to some emulation of its fantastic austerities there.*  It was not, however, till early in the sixth century that it was definitely embodied and organized as a social force by St. Benedict, whose death, in 543, left his monastery of Monte Casino the acknowledged type and head of the Western monastic life.  At this date, then, it is to be recognized as a distinct and powerful element in the new civilization.

My view of the subject, accordingly, will be by way of retrospect, and very simple.  I wish to speak of Monasticism purely as a moral force, — the motive it sprang from, and the way in which it acted on men, mainly through their imagination and moral sympathy.

First of all, we must go back a little, and remember that Christianity very early showed itself as a hostile and aggressive force, in sharp antagonism to the beliefs and customs prevailing in the world.  This antagonistic attitude implies several things : deep conviction both of personal guilt and of existing evil, as in Paul ; a motive widely apart from philosophic

---

* The monastery of St. Honoratus, founded about 400, in the island of Lerins (or *St. Honoré*), off the southern coast of France, was the chief head-quarters of early Western monasticism.

speculation, as shown in the controversy against the Gnostics; a symbol of faith accepted with absolute loyalty, to fight under as a banner, as with the creed of Athanasius; a definite appointing of the field of conflict in the individual conscience or conviction, as with Augustine; a powerful visible organization, acting as one, like an army, under its official head, which post of authority had been claimed and maintained by Leo. Each of these has already been separately considered.

But, for its greatest efficiency, a fighting force needs one other thing. It needs its outposts, its skirmishers, its corps of desperate fighters; men absolutely reckless of all fears, and bound by no interests or hopes except such as identify them with the strength and life of the army itself; volunteers, who make its advance guard in battle and its forlorn hope at a crisis; a body of reserve, to whom life itself is a thing utterly indifferent in comparison with the honor of the service, and all other affection thin and cold except that which makes it their one pride to fight under the flag, and their joy to die for it. From Marathon down to Plevna, it is safe to say that no army has been great, and no military dominion strong, that could not count on the absolute devotion of such a reserve force, — a body to which danger itself has an irresistible fascination, whose one master-passion is warrior zeal, whose hot desire is for the fiery delight of combat.

To say, then, that the Church was victorious in the war it undertook, is to say that it had at its command such a body of enthusiasts, a body of absolute loyalty

and fanatic zeal; whose zeal, indeed, might outrun
prudence and turn to frenzy, yet for that very reason
could be counted on when the battle would be hopeless without just that aid, — the sharp edge of attack,
the obstinate heroism of defence.  In fact, the Church
had two such bodies of reserve : one for the time of
persecution in the conflict against Paganism, — the
Martyrs ; one for the time of organized conquest
that followed, in the conflict against Barbarism, —
the Monastics.  It is necessary to say a word on the
motive common to them both.

We must not forget — at the earlier stage, especially, of the conflict we are considering — that Christianity presents itself to us in the form of a moral
reaction, or protest, against the gross inhumanities
and corruptions of Pagan society.  This reaction would
be mild with some natures, violent with others.  So
much we may easily understand.  But what it was,
precisely, that it reacted against, requires some knowledge of obscure authorities and some hardihood of
speech to show.  We cannot always, it may be, trust
the eager invective of Christian apologists like Tertullian ; though where he refers to plain and well-known
fact, we have no right to deny his witness.  But we
have a right to judge the Pagan world out of its own
mouth ; and then there are testimonies written between the lines of classic authors — such testimonies,
for instance, as the frescos at Pompeii — which help
us to an understanding of the darker facts.  In Horace we have, mainly, an easy epicureanism, smooth
and fair, and only beginning to be withered at the
core ; in Juvenal, a stoicism no longer humane, but

bitter and austere; in Petronius, who was Nero's friend, a cynicism nakedly revolting.

These, however, are only hints of Roman manners, and perhaps may be overcharged: it would be easy to make a picture just as black of a Christian capital to-day. But there are two points of public morality at that period, which we can quite understand, and which to the most placid temper now are full of horror: its brutal cruelty, and its beastly shamelessness. · Unless we do know these, we cannot understand the violence, even fury, of the recoil against them. We look at the statue of the dying gladiator, " butchered to make a Roman holiday," and we cannot well avoid a thrill of human pity. What have we to say, then, that the wise and merciful Trajan, for whose salvation Gregory prayed, remembering his patient kindness to a widow suppliant, made the amphitheatre reek with the blood of ten thousand such, to grace one holiday? Wild beasts, we are told, were often lacking in the vast numbers needed to glut the Roman thirst for blood; but human victims, captives of war, were never wanting.

This is but an item of the charge. It is hard for us to understand or forgive the brutality of a Spanish ⁙ bull-fight, where dainty ladies applaud, or give the signal for the blow. The Roman mob — men and women, noble and base — looked on with the same eager lust of blood, when the wild bull gored or the famished tiger tore the delicate side of some modest trembling Christian girl, set naked in the pit before that gazing multitude, or else tangled in transparent nets. Three times Blandina was thus exposed at

Vienna, in Gaul, till a barbarian in mercy pierced her breast with a sword. Perpetua and Felicitas, in Carthage, were allowed out of pure horror to wrap themselves in mantles, before the gladiator finally despatched them with his "stroke of grace." These were mere girls, maidens or young wives, on the edge of womanhood, innocent, beautiful.

Religious frenzy, perhaps, made these horrors possible. But the blood-spoilt crowd of the amphitheatre needed no such motive of a heated fanaticism. To satisfy the lust of the eye, a drama representing the death of Hercules on Mount Œta was not complete without a robust captive bound and burned on the funeral pile, whose yells and writhings might counterfeit those death-agonies. "We have seen it," says Tertullian. And, with still beastlier ferocity, in the masks and mummeries of the Roman stage, the mutilations, rapes, and debaucheries, that stain the corrupt mythology of Greece, were with a horrible realism presented nakedly before the public eye.*

These hints will probably be enough to show what, in some of its more shocking forms, it was that the martyr church had to protest against. Nothing, it is plain, except the martyr spirit, in its most vehement and (if you will) fanatic form would have borne the battle or gained the victory. I say nothing and I know nothing about the frequency of these spectacles. It is enough to know that they were possible, and that

* The better known authorities for these statements are Suetonius, Martial, and Tertullian. Other authorities and details will be found in Ozanam's *Civilisation au Quatrième Siècle.* See also Renan's recent "English Conferences."

they are what the world was forever delivered from in the triumph of Christianity.* Along with the vivid picture given of these horrors in his " Antichrist," Renan tells us of the contagion of the martyr spirit, — how eagerly not only hardy fanatics, but modest matron and maiden, pressed toward the consummation of that awful sacrifice, just as volunteers press to the most hazardous post in battle or siege; and how the flame of that great passion burned away all lesser thoughts of affection, duty, and shame.

Or take the following, from one of the earlier martyrologies. "My father," says Perpetua, "came from the city, wasted with anxiety, to prevent me; and he said, 'Have pity, my daughter, on my gray hairs; have pity on thy father, if he is worthy the name of father.' And so saying, he kissed my hands in his fondness, and threw himself at my feet, calling me in his tears no longer *daughter*, but *lady*. And I was grieved for the gray hairs of my father, because he only, of all our family, did not rejoice in my martyrdom. It is difficult for us to take in the hardness of this young mother, at once to her father and her babe. It is more shocking still to think that to them the fiery or bloody death was an escape from ignominy which to them was far more dreadful. Eusebius tells of a mother who esteemed it a happy chance to drown herself with her three daughters, rather than trust the mercy of their jailer; and there is hardly a plea on

---

* Doubtless the Spanish bull-fights are almost as brutal, and the *autos da fé* of the Inquisition were, as a form of human sacrifice, still more cruel. Still, these last appealed only to the pity and terror of beholders, not to their beastlier passions.

record more piteous in its suggestion, than where Augustine argues that, by brutal treatment in their prison, Christian maidens had not lost their honor in the sight of God.

The extraordinary romance of St. Thekla, which we may count as the earliest Christian novel, is quite possibly founded upon fact. She is a young lady of high birth, who innocently and unconsciously — perhaps without the writer's consciousness either — falls (as we should say) in love with the Apostle Paul. Cast off by her mother because she will not accept the husband provided for her, she travels from place to place as a Christian missionary, is exposed in the theatre to lions, who fight with each other instead, till both are killed; the people then take sudden pity on her; and thus, miraculously saved, she finds refuge in a hermitage, where she lives a long life of pious solitude. Thus a single life serves as link between the martyr age and the age of monastic asceticism; and the same spirit is the inspiration of both.

In their most strongly marked features, however, it must be said that they belong to two different periods. The martyr age expired when Christianity came to the throne with Constantine; asceticism was most fervent, and its haunts most crowded, in the time immediately following. One, in fact, blends insensibly into the other. The eager, perhaps frantic temper, trained through whole generations up to the heat of martyr zeal, was not content to repose in the tame quiet of a religious peace. The solitude, the austerity, the self-inflicted torment, the denial of human kindness, which might have been a refuge or a compromise at a time of real danger, became the accepted way of working to that exalted temper.

What had been the passionate phase of a reaction against pagan brutality, was now an intolerant and hot protest against the love of ease and the lingering sensuality that Paganism left behind. This intolerant protest had flashed out once or twice before, in the hot anger and contempt felt towards those who had "lapsed" under the storm of persecution, whom it was held infamous, with whatever penance, to take back to the bosom of the faithful; and so had arisen the Novatian schism and the schism of the Donatists,* and the fury of the Circumcellions, who rushed in a mad way upon their death, courting martyrdom, — disorders whose tradition vexed the Church for more than three centuries. The same temper, now that Christianity was in the ascendant, showed itself in the many forms of ascetic and monastic life.

It is not necessary to dwell here on the tempting features of anecdote and adventure which illustrate that way of life. Two points only we have to consider: its power as a motive in the mind of the ascetics themselves; and its power as a moral force among men, through imagination, sympathy, or emulation.

As to the former, I do not think we are content with any theory of motives to account for asceticism, outside the moral quality of asceticism itself, and its strange fascination to an order of feeling always powerful in human nature. It is easy, but it is delusive, to say that men deliberately set themselves by austerities and penance to win for themselves peculiar

---

* Well called by Mr. Hodgkin "the Cameronians of Africa."

glories or joys in paradise.  Possibly they may give
that for their own account of it, so deceiving themselves.  But no profit-and-loss calculation like that
ever inspired that passion, of whose insanest extreme
we have so wonderful a picture in Tennyson's " St.
Simeon Stylites " : —

> " Bethink thee, Lord! while thou and all the saints
> Enjoy themselves in heaven, and men on earth
> House in the shade of comfortable roofs,
> Sit with their wives by fires, eat wholesome food,
> And wear warm clothes, and even beasts have stalls, —
> I, 'tween the spring and downfall of the light,
> Bow down one thousand and two hundred times,
> To Christ, the Virgin Mother, and the saints;
> Or in the night, after a little sleep,
> I wake: the chill stars sparkle; I am wet
> With drenching dews, or stiff in the crackling frost;
> I wear an undressed goat-skin on my back;
> A grazing iron collar grinds my neck;
> And in my weak lean arms I lift the cross,
> And strive and wrestle with thee till I die.
> O mercy, mercy! wash away my sin! "

In these strange outbursts, which echo the very
passion and fervor of ascetic life, we find something
far deeper than the balanced reckoning of chances between paradise and hell.  We find, in the first place,
a conviction of moral unworthiness morbidly intense;
and in the next place, the flame of a peculiar passion,
that feeds on everything as fuel that it can lay hold
upon.

Of the first, the intense conviction of sin, it may
perhaps be said to be, in one or another form, the
source of all the moral power existing and operative
among men.  It is not worth while to analyze it here,

where it simply takes on an extravagant, fantastic,
unfamiliar form. It becomes to us simply a morbid
phenomenon, one manifestation of a force known to
us in many other calmer and (it may be) more instructive ways.

Only, a word should be said of the root from which
it grew, in a notion of the essential iniquity of all
pleasures of sense, — an intense recoil from the extreme sensualism of ancient life. "In me," says
Paul, "that is, in my flesh, dwelleth no good thing." *
The ascetic life, says Sozomen, is "no compromise
between virtue and vice." This opinion of the radi-
cally evil nature of matter, and in especial the matter
of which our bodies are composed, must be presumed
in all our knowledge of the subject.

By a certain morbid logic, too, sensations repulsive ·
to the sense were thought a fit penance, and directly
pleasing to God. Thus, to take a few instances,
chiefly from the admiring Greek historians : — St.
Anthony would scarce suffer clean water to touch his
feet or hands. St. Arsenius would change the water he
used in weaving rushes but once a year. St. Hilarion
built himself a hut too small to let him stand upright or
lie at length. St. Hallas touched no bread for seventy
years, contenting himself with roots and herbs. St.

* This is oddly illustrated in the following formula of confession : " I confess all the sins of my body, — of my skin, of my flesh,
of my bones and sinews, of my veins and cartilages, of my tongue
and lips, of my jaws, teeth, and hair, of my marrow, and any other
part whatsoever, whether it be soft or hard, wet or dry." No peti-
tion is more frequent, in some of the older rituals, than that God
would be pleased to accept our leanness and mortification of the
flesh.

Senoch walled himself to the neck in a narrow circuit, too small to let him move or sit, and lived there for years. St. Wulfilaich was hardly persuaded to quit the pillar elevation in the north of Gaul, where he stood barefoot, summer and winter, till his nails dropped off with the bitter cold.*  Some wore heavy crosses, chains, or iron bands ; some had no covering but their long, unwashed, and shaggy hair, living in dens the life of beasts.  The brawny St. Moses, to tire down his sinful muscular strength, stood praying every night for six years, without sleep.  St. Stephen kept on weaving baskets, while the surgeons were amputating a limb.  These idle heroisms are the voice of the ascetic conscience, morbidly acute ; but they are also, like the training of our athletes, a test of what may be done in battle or endured in the siege.

Of what may be called the ascetic passion, however, something remains to be added.  It is a very shallow theory of life, to say that the main motive, with most men, is the pursuit of happiness, — at least in any sense in which happiness can be defined to the understanding, or chosen by the judgment.  It is hardly an exaggeration, on the other hand, to say that many persons set their hearts on misery, and pursue it with an obstinacy that we might call insane.  I do not think, for example, that the ascetic passion of a hermit or a monk is different at bottom or harder to understand — except for such moral quality as may be in it — than the pining, wretched, eager self-denial of

* These practices, said his unflattering adviser, may be fit for the great saints and holy men of the East ; but a poor ignorant barbarian like you should not aspire to such high things.

a rich miser, the very type that takes its name from "misery." And those argue weakly with human nature as it is, who appeal first to men's desire of comfort and selfish ease. Hardihood and adventure, the joy of conflict, defiance of danger, generous self-abandonment, are each and all more powerful motives in real life, — not perhaps for weak characters, but at any rate for strong ones. The six hundred who rode "into the jaws of death," facing loaded cannon, do not show it any more plainly than those other hundreds who went the other day to risk their lives in pestilential cities at the South; not more plainly than the father or mother, of average conscience and self-denial, who submits with never a thought to the innumerable privations which define the commonest conditions of duty or (it may be) of indulgence to the child.

And so the habit of self-denial grows, till one·may come to feel — who has not known such ? — as if the very sensation of pleasure itself were a sin. Occasionally we know of lives that are literally made a sacrifice, not so much to a mere notion of duty, however morbidly scrupulous, as to a mood of mind in which austerity itself, and self-torment, have come to take the place of duty: not that they are chosen freely as being right, but have grown into a moral necessity, and so make the men their slaves.

Look at the heart of any such man, and you find that the sacrifice, far from being a price weighed out and duly paid, has come, by the mere cultivation of a sense of duty, to be *a delight in itself*, as truly as the enthusiasm of adventure or the contempt of danger. It is, indeed, the very business of religious discipline to guide and train what may so come to be a mighty master passion. And we should not fail, through any shallow theory of pleasure, to see how prodigious a force the Church enlisted, when it gave to what we have called the ascetic passion recognition and a sphere. The time would soon come when that great force would be needed, no longer for defence or idle contemplation, but for active service.

That time came, indeed, in a very dramatic way. In the flush of his temporary triumph over Alaric, Honorius had renewed at Rome, in 404, the old splendor of the public games; and, Christian as he was, and against the warm protest of men's better feeling, brought his show to a climax by a combat of gladiators, a spectacle forbidden long before by Christian law. When the sport was at its height, the monk Telemachus, who had come (it is said) all the way from Egypt to do it, threw himself into the arena, between the swords of the combatants, and was crushed under a shower of stones from the angry mob, — "the only monk," says Gibbon, "who died a martyr in the cause of humanity." This brave act put a final stop to the brutal sport.

But Gibbon's comment is not true. Whole generations of Christian monks lived, and a great many of them died, in cruel martyrdom, in working out that long task by which the barbarian world — less corrupt, no doubt, than the old Pagan society, but almost inconceivable in its ferocity — was brought into the pale of Christian civilization. Some features and conditions of that task we shall have to consider at another time. At present we have to do only with the way in which this great moral power was trained and equipped to undertake it.

One feature of it, however, I must mention here. It is the spectacle that offers itself to our imagination, as the face of the world slowly changes, from its comparatively orderly and familiar look in the classic age, to what it had become when the barbarian hordes gave it the wild and strange complexion it wore so long. We see the process at a great distance ; and, so seen, the features of one age melt insensibly into ·those of another, so that it is no hard thing to us to call the change an unmixed good. But in the time of it, as we must not forget, there were infinite details of literally unspeakable horror, — details which you find hints of in Gibbon's foot-notes, or can read at more length in the half-barbaric authorities he cites, Jornandes, Liutprand, Paulus Diaconus, and Gregory of Tours. Now, when that three centuries' storm settled down upon the Western world, innumerable outposts were already held by religious zealots, whom an ascetic fervor had scattered through Italy and Gaul, and along the confines of Germany, some in solitary hermitages, some in bands and brotherhoods, many with a faith burning in them, and a yearning for the souls of those wild barbarians, in whom they saw — as Salvian did — more hopeful subjects of Christ than in the corrupt and degenerate population they had turned their backs upon.

Some of their religious retreats were the refuge of cowards, — so it was charged ; of men who had cast off all love of their country, who had lost the sense of honor and public duty, who dared not look the times in the face.* Most likely. Among those who simply sought religious solitude or religious fellowship in those retreats, it would be hard to draw the line between pure cowardice and genuine despair of the perishing world they forsook,— despair that would settle upon many a mind, doubtless, as if the end of all things were really at hand, and the only remaining duty were to make one's peace with God, as on a death-bed.

But not so with those who undertook such tasks as the time made possible. Many, probably most of those who are worthily recorded as the saints — that is, the moral heroes — of that evil time, were men trained in monastic discipline, hardened to service by the interior conflicts which that discipline implied.

And we have not to forget, either, the immense effect of these austerities, of the strange humanity and tenderness often joined with them, of the strange vision and the new ideal of sanctity, offered before the eyes and powerfully affecting the imagination of the rude, cruel, unsophisticated invaders. The more familiar accounts of St. Martin in France and St. Severinus in South Germany illustrate vividly this moral reaction.

In general, Catholic writers do completer justice than we do to this unfamiliar but most noble phase of religious heroism. It is hard for a Protestant to forget the strong repugnance which monastic life called out in the time of its degeneracy. But we

---

* The ground taken by Valens (about 375), in his conscription of monks for civil or military duty.

are not concerned here with those later scandals and controversies. We have only to see and understand a very genuine exhibition of moral power among men to whom that way was the best they knew, and at a time when no better service could possibly be given to the world. Some of these lives commend themselves easily to our judgment : as of Cassiodorus, the minister and secretary of Theodoric ; and of Fortunatus, a genuine man of letters, whose verses, inscribed to that gentle recluse queen Radegonda, or to his friend Gregory of Tours, make the closing pages in the great body of classic Latin poetry.* But hundreds and thousands of them passed away unknown, and only added each its drop or its rill to the vast stream which was widening into the new civilization.

Of others, again, it must be said that their asceticism was sheer idle pretence, and slid into intoxication and madness. The perils of that way of life became quite plain, even at this time ; and they needed a discipline very sharp and severe to keep them in some sort of check. The discipline which prevailed in Europe for many generations, vigorous and wholesome, was that of St. Benedict, established during the prosperous rule of the Goth Theodoric. The anecdotes of his life we need not dwell on : how as a child of twelve, with the connivance of his maid, he ran away and hid in a cave from his vicious schoolfellows, till he was given up for dead ; how, to deliver himself once for all from "the demon of the flesh," he stripped and rolled among thorns till his skin was lacerated from head to foot ; how, as head of his monastery, he ruled his

* See below, "The Christian Schools."

monks so sharply that they turned against him and tried to poison him in a bowl of wine; how his fame for sanctity grew, till he was obliged to flee again to the rocky retreat of Monte Casino, where his most famous of monastic houses continues an object of pilgrimage to this day.*

Here he established his firm code of discipline on the three-fold vow, not to be taken till after due probation and the severest tests of resolution, of Poverty, Chastity, and Obedience. The first meant simple and absolute community of goods: the religious house might and afterwards did revel in enormous wealth; but the individual monk owned nothing. We shall compare this presently with the later Mendicant Orders, so that here we have only to notice the pledge it gave of absolute devotion to the common interest, and the enormous associated strength of the brotherhood. The vow of Chastity at once forbade all family ties, and put upon the conscience the task through life of keeping up the ascetic discipline

---

* There is an odd story of the occasion of this retreat. A bevy of gay girls from Rome — whom no doubt the grim ascetics took to be emissaries of the Devil — went out "for a lark" one day to visit and perhaps cheer their dull abode; and tried, with all coquetries and blandishments, to coax them back to the city, and to carnal ways. In horror at what might possibly come of it, Benedict made all haste to the rudest spot he could find among the rugged spurs of the hills.

It was on a like occasion that an aged monk was observed to look very earnestly at the sauciest and most fascinating of the group; and when his companions asked him why, replied, "Because it is revealed to me that she shall judge us all." Within a short time, in fact, she became a penitent, and passed her life in the austerest sanctity. For Benedict's miracles, see Migne's *Patrologia,* cxlix. 965.

which had originated that mode of life. We shall see its immense consequences hereafter, when under Hildebrand the monastic spirit gained complete rule in the Church, and engaged in its sharpest-fought battle against human nature.

For the present, then, I have but a word to say of the vow of Obedience. It was in this that the Western or Benedictine discipline differed most widely from the ascetic life of the East, which (in its degeneracy at least) aimed only at piety and maceration; and it was in this that it rendered its essential service to the modern world. For obedience, in the rigidly practical rule of Benedict, meant steady, genuine, useful work. *"Laborare est orare"* became the monkish chime. Seven hours of manual labor were required daily, besides study in the afternoon. The old and feeble, who could do nothing else, were set to copy manuscripts; and so saved to the world not only a host of religious works, but whole libraries of ancient classics. The toil of the Benedictines has become a proverb of literary industry. They had abundant leisure for it. One monk is said to have spent a lifetime illuminating a single letter. Immense results came of this organized industry. It rescued labor itself from the degradation of its old servile memories, made it intelligent, skilful, and free, as well as a religious duty. There were no such estates in Europe, nowhere so thrifty farming or so tasteful gardening, as the monasteries had to show. It was the monks who were clearers of the forest, drainers of the marsh, frontiersmen, pioneers of civilization, founders of more than half the towns of

France. They steadily recruited, through times of inconceivable peril, those armies of missionary-martyrs,
by which the barbarian world was tamed and trained
to a rude civilization.

The evils of monastic life are plain to see : its
enormous seeming waste of moral force, shed like
showers on the bare sand of the desert ; the wild and
ignorant fanaticism or religious madness it often ran
into ; its hardening of the heart in the selfish seeking for salvation, so that the natural affections and
humanities were crushed, and the monks became in
due time the fit and merciless agents of the Inquisition ; the temptation to indulge indolence, hypocrisy, and spiritual pride, with secret and abominable
vices demanding periodical reform. The memory of
such things makes us content that we shall never
know it any more. Still, it would not have had its
opportunity of evil, but for the immense service it
rendered at a critical period, when old things were
passing away, and new foundations must be laid in
the absolute courage, the denial of self-interest, the
strenuous virtue, the loyal obedience, which make the
ideal of that way of life ; when not science, strength,
and skill, but poverty, hardship, and self-denial were
the power that overcame the world.

# IX.

## CHRISTIANITY IN THE EAST.

THE main stream of Christian civilization, as it affects the great events of history and as it interests us in particular, follows a westward course, and is bounded for a thousand years within the limits that contain the Catholic Empire of the Middle Age. The separation of East and West was slowly coming about for at least three centuries, before it became definite and final in the controversies of the ninth century; and the parting of the Christian world into two jealous and hostile fragments (879) lasted through many a peril that assailed them both alike, till one was swallowed up in the conquests of the Turk, and the other rent by the great Protestant schism, with its innumerable sects.

There is something of pathos in calling to mind that the most obstinate motive of a separation involving such tremendous historical consequences was the persistence of the West in holding that the Holy Ghost proceeds not from the Father only, but also from the Son, — to us a pure piece of unintelligible metaphysics, or else the statement of a very simple moral fact; and that, on the very eve of the ferocious assault in which Constantinople fell, when terms of union had been with difficulty negotiated at Florence to secure a Christian league against the infidel (1438), these terms were repudiated by the fanatic sectaries of the East, who chose the risk of Ottoman slavery rather than accept the hated symbol of Western heresy.

But we have to deal at present not with these critical events of history so much as with certain characteristics that mark the contrast of the two; and with one or two phases of the Oriental Church that show the position it holds in Christian history.

The contrast I speak of is exactly indicated, first, by the division-line between the two languages, Greek and Latin, in which the symbols of faith were respectively set forth. Greek lends itself easily to metaphysical discussions and nice logical distinctions, which Latin could but imperfectly follow, at least till it was tortured to metaphysical uses by the Schoolmen. The Greeks complained that the language of their formulæ could not be adequately rendered in another tongue.*  It is clear that, if the meaning of the Christian symbol, much more the salvation that comes of actual belief, turns on the hair-breadth dis-

---

* Thus the word *hypostasis* (to take a very familiar case), which is used to express the distinctions in the Trinity, corresponds etymologically to the Latin *substantia*, "substance"; but this word means exactly what the theologians did not wish to say, and so they chose the word *persona* instead (literally *mask*), which we very inadequately render "person," — really meaning the part, or character, acted in a play, as in our phrase *dramatis personæ*. Thus the metaphysical terms οὐσία (*essentia*), ὑπόστασις (*substantia*), and πρόσωπον (*persona*) are more or less interchangeable, and give rise to endless discussion. According to Gregory of Nyssa, what οὐσία is to the class, that ὑπόστασις is to the individual. We find this discussion going on, brisk as ever, in Peter Lombard (about 1170).

tinctions which can hardly be stated in words, and are untranslatable at best, there is absolutely no end of controversy. Leo the Great did wisely to cut the knot by laying down his own hard-and-fast definition, which contented the West then, and does so to this day; while the East wrecked itself helplessly on the successive sharp points that turned up in the crooked channel of dispute, till it seemed to drift helplessly on a sea of metaphysics.

Again, the West had a vigorous independent life of its own, — political, municipal, ecclesiastical, — of which Leo had the genius to seize the full advantage; while church life in the East was absolutely over-shadowed by the imperial despotism, under which, as in the shelter of a great forest, it throve with a certain pining, sickly, and distorted life of its own. Not that passion was wanting to it, or a certain fanatic, even ferocious courage: the religious riots of Constantinople, Antioch, and Alexandria were bloody and fierce as the old struggles of the Roman forum. But they were the disorderly, irresponsible action of a mob, that might be crushed at any moment, and periodically was, by the imperial military police, and could never develop any disciplined courage of its own. Indeed, how continually pressing, how closely haunting, the imperial despotism was, it is hard for us to conceive, unless we remember that it inherited the cruel and despotic traditions of a Cæsar or a Diocletian; and that it left its methods of merciless exaction to be adopted and followed up in the unspeakable inflictions of Oriental tyranny to-day. Ecclesiastical rule was as minute, as tyrannous, as irritating here, as ever it was in the West; but, awed by the nearness of the Court, and dazzled by the paraphernalia of Empire, it never had the free hand, even if it had the wise and willing heart, to effect any one of the great tasks of civilization.

What it could do, however, it did. The courage and the devotedness of purpose were never wanting. Long lines of saints show that the ecclesiastic spirit, with its merits and its faults, was quite as fervent as in the West. It had, in fact, a quality of its own, which commands a genuine admiration. Looking at its better side, we seem to see in it a sweetness of piety, a gentleness of temper, a single-hearted moral fervor, a purely religious courage, a capacity of warm and long-abiding friendship, an absence of personal ambition, which are not to be sure wanting, but are less prominent traits, in the restless and energetic Latin Church.*

These qualities answer well to the more dependent position just spoken of; and may be held, justly, to have characterized the churches of Syria, Greece, and Egypt to this day, — where they subsist, insulated, helpless, non-resistant, disarmed, under the scornful tolerance of the Mussulman. To these we may add a certain simplicity of living often running into ascetic poverty, a clinging family life, a quickness of social sympathy, which seem to be their inheritance from an earlier phase of Christian life than was transmitted to the West, and which correspond with the primitive and easy ecclesiastical code that permits, even

* In fact, we are hardly conscious of them there, until we come to the later and greater period of the Religious Orders.

if it does not require, the marriage of the humbler clergy.

These general traits it is well to bear in mind, in studying the somewhat depressed and monotonous life of Eastern Christendom. While they show its good side, they help to remind us, also, of the feeble executive force it has always shown, the often humiliating attitude in the presence of authority, and the ignorant, gross, imbecile condition in which we find its lower clergy at this day in Russia, as well as in Greece or Turkey. The political condition of the East, too, from the first Gothic invasion down, has shown little else than a succession of despotisms, and violent conquests, and wide-spread miseries, never once relieved by a show of genuine popular courage, or a vigorous national life. The Byzantine Empire, down to its fall in 1453, has always been a synonyme for indolent luxury, gaudy but meretricious splendor, pampered despotism, political degeneracy, and moral decay. Only a few broad features require our consideration now.

As belonging to our present purpose, there are three phases of this languid history, which may detain our eye. These are, the period immediately following the first Arian controversy; the reign of Justinian; and the Image-Controversy, with the attending circumstances that confirmed the separation of East and West, — this last preceded and followed by the vast catastrophe of the Mahometan invasion.

I. The fervor, the sweetness, and the purely religious intrepidity which I have spoken of as characterizing the Eastern Church, are seen nowhere to so great advantage as in the group of eminent and saintly men who adorn its calendar towards the end of the fourth century. There are many other names hardly less worthy ; but, for purposes of illustration, it is enough to mention four, who make a group together.

Basil the Great, of Cæsarea (329–379), eminently deserves to lead the list. High-minded, cultivated, self-denying, charitable, austere, bold before the face of power,* writer of the sweetest homilies on Creation, Paradise, and the discipline of Providence, he is the great organizer of eastern monastic life.† Next is his friend Gregory of Nazianzus (330–391), the eloquent ascetic, the personal antagonist of Julian, the vigorous champion of orthodoxy at the capital (where he raised it from a despised sect to a great popular enthusiasm), the contented exile when court intrigues drove him from the city to the harder penance of writing odes and hymns.‡ Third is Gregory of Nyssa (331–395), younger brother of Basil, a theologian and commentator, a hard, clear, and serious thinker, a student of Greek philosophy, whose treasures he would gather for Christian uses, called " father of fathers " by an admiring council, the reconciler of divided churches, the thoughtful, gentle-minded Platonist, liberal and serene among sharp party conflicts. Last and most eminent of all is the bright name of John Chrysostom

---

* Witness, especially, his intrepid correspondence with his old schoolfellow, the Emperor Julian.

† Whose rules he lays down in replies to 313 Queries.

‡ Luke's genealogy, for instance, in hexameters, and Matthew's in iambics ; besides the appalling chapters of Chronicles and Numbers, and a drama on the death of Christ.

(347–407), preacher of the "golden lips," held by many to be the greatest of all religious orators of any age, who would have been made Bishop of Antioch at twenty-three but for his generous support of Basil; who as Patriarch of Constantinople joined absolute simplicity and charity of living with steady defiance of court power and an electric eloquence that rings in his pages vivid and alive to-day; who in perfect serenity and sweetness of soul blessed God for his rod of chastisement, while he lay dying on the road under the barbarous cruelty that dragged him in age and infirmities into banishment.

In this group of brilliant and saintly names we notice, first, that they are all near friends, and two of them brothers; and next, their short career, the oldest living only to sixty-three, while the one who passed into history as "great" died at fifty. They all represent the very best of those qualities which seem the family traits, so to speak, of Eastern Christianity. It would be hard to find, in the writings of either of them, a trace of sectarian rancor, or personal vindictiveness, or spiritual pride, or dogmatic bigotry, or selfish ambition, or vanity of letters. All were humble-minded and devout, ascetic in their training, austere judges of themselves, utterly submissive to the Divine will they worshipped. The strongest impression one gets from their writings is their absolute lack of self-reference or self-assertion, and the entire good faith with which they not only assume that the ascetic life is the true moral ideal, but make its rule the law of conscience for themselves — the rule of personal purity and rigid self-denial.

But for a certain simplicity of courage, and a child-like fearlessness, we might possibly miss in them the more masculine virtues we look for in the religious character. When Basil was threatened with confiscation, imprisonment, and death, his reply was, "Not one of these things touches me. He who has no goods cannot suffer any loss. He who is God's guest cannot be an exile anywhere. For martyrdom I am unworthy; but death is only a friend to me, to bring me sooner to God."

All were lovers of nature, and lovers of what was beautiful in Greek art and letters. Their writings have all become Christian classics, and have had their share in preserving the marvellous vitality of the Greek tongue: a vitality so great, that it has not only been kept alive in the debased Romaic; but in our own day Schliemann, as he tells us, has moved a village audience in Ithaca to tears by reciting out of Homer the meeting of Ulysses and Penelope, while Xenophon and Demosthenes are used as reading books in Athenian public schools to-day. That the classic Greek is still so nearly the language of the people as to be almost intelligible, easily mastered by a few weeks' study, and rather gaining upon the modern in current employ, is greatly due to its uses as a sacred tongue, and to those writers whose orations and commentaries have further consecrated it to that use.

We notice, too, that this era of oratorical splendor and religious fame immediately follows the great controversy, and that it belongs wholly to the defenders of what was then called Orthodoxy. This fact has a certain value in the history of polemics as a phase of human thought. It shows, not that their speculation was more true, or their reasoning more honest, but that they chose the side which best expressed the warmth of devoted, unreasoning, and loyal faith.

II. The nearly forty years' reign of Justinian (527–565) is very famous in history for two things;—victory over the Vandals by Belisarius and over the Goths by Narses, which seemed likely to make the Empire whole again by reconquest of the West; and the codifying of Roman Law, which became a most important element in the later civilization. Besides these were certain marked merits of administration. Justinian, says Sismondi, first made economy a science, and systematically encouraged industry. The silk-worm was brought by travelling monks from India; trade was carried as far as China. The magnificent dome of Santa Sophia testifies to this day how the piety and splendor of the capital were cared for in the imperial policy.

Justinian himself has only the accidental glory of these achievements. His greatest general died under his unjust and cruel jealousy; and his chief merit is perhaps the steady and generous support he gave to the great jurists who labored on the Code. He was himself an ascetic, a scholastic, and a pedant, " neither beloved in his life," says Gibbon, " nor regretted at his death"; busying himself with theological disputes, in which he showed neither a schoolman's subtilty nor a statesman's skill; ruled by the strange, fascinating adventuress Theodora, whose name is shaded with the blackest ignominy or else the blackest calumny, who upheld her half-way heresy in the face of his ostentatious orthodoxy, and left her memory to the mercy of bigots who never pardon or forget.

The brief revival which this reign offers of imperial magnificence is darkened by its almost unparalleled calamities. War against the barbarian means extermination, or, at its mildest, devastation. The Vandal Gelimer surrendered, when he saw a morsel of half-burnt dough snatched from between his nephew's very teeth by a Moorish boy, — a type of the ruin that spread through Italy and Africa. A glaring comet amid these disasters seemed the scourge of God hung visibly in the sky. An earthquake destroyed, it is said, two hundred thousand lives in a single city. A dreadful pestilence (bred, say the annalists, from the bodies of reptiles left by a great inundation of the Tiber) raged more than fifty years, leaving hardly a spot or man untouched. At Justinian's death, it has been reckoned, the population of the Empire had been diminished (since Augustus, probably,) by a hundred million lives.

The decision at Chalcedon (451) had settled the standard of orthodoxy for the West, but had only heated the jealousies between Antioch and Alexandria. The partisans of a single nature in Christ never failed to make points, or split them, that would make against the accepted creed ; and numberless shades of the " Monophysite heresy " prevailed, till these flickering contests paled in the glare of Saracen invasion. A compromise — the famous *Henoticon* — carefully framed (482) to exclude the sharper lines of division, had not long satisfied either party, since each had to sacrifice the prominence of its favorite dogma. Justinian, in his desire to propitiate the more heretical sect, published a "confession," which went as far as this: "Whosoever does not confess that our Lord Jesus Christ, crucified in the flesh, is true God and Lord of glory, and one of the Holy Trinity, let such a one be anathema"; and declared the body of Christ incorruptible. They, on their part, admitted that, while there is in Christ but one nature, yet that nature is twofold : their test phrase was, that " God was crucified."

These, with some obscure matters charged as heresy against the Origenists, were the delicate differences to be arranged at another Council in Constantinople (553), which willingly enough accepted the very words of the Emperor's confession. But after his death dissensions went on widening, with admixture of strange travesties here and there, that seemed to make a fourth divinity of Mary "Mother of God," till all were swept away in a common ruin by the implacable storm of Islamism. The last attempt to reconcile them was in the compromise (suggested 633) that, though there were two *natures* in Christ, yet there was only a single *will*. This seemed to satisfy for a time, but was brought to an end by the sixth great Council (680), which established as orthodox the doctrine of two wills. The Monotheletes, including the Emperor himself, who had proposed the compromise, were now denounced, and " peace," says Gieseler, drily, " was thus restored to the Church."

This pitiful story seems fairly enough the logical outcome of the attempt to stake man's faith on accuracy of belief. Assuming that it is to be so, the natural inference surely is, that no degree of accuracy can be excessive, and no difference of belief too small to justify intolerant debate. To absolute sceptical indifference, the distinction of two natures and two wills is not more insignificant than the act of casting incense on a pagan chafing-dish,— the test which had determined many an heroic martyr-death. One, however, is a point of speculative opinion; the other, however slight, an act of free choice. One deals with logic merely; the other with the conscience, where the foundation of moral life is. One is dogmatic orthodoxy, the other is spiritual integrity. The orthodox postulate, that rightness of belief is essential to salvation, could not have been more perfectly carried out to its logical absurdity, than in these incessant, unintelligible, disastrous controversies, that cost the Eastern Church its last chance of vigorous life.

III. The third phase of Eastern Christianity to be recalled here is the extraordinary outburst of fanaticism called the Image Controversy, lasting more than a hundred years, and shaking the Empire to its centre. This need not detain us long. It broke out something more than a hundred years after the furious assault on Arabian tribal idolatry led by Mahomet. The attack on Christian images began, in fact, with the intolerant Mussulman fanaticism itself, which expelled all "idols" from the churches where it had power through its rapid conquests in the East, especially in Syria, to the despair of Christian and the vindictive delight of Jew.

The Emperor Leo III. (the Isaurian) was the first

"Iconoclast" of the Empire (718–741). He was a man of military vigor, political good sense, and resolute courage, one of the ablest and best of Byzantine emperors. Image-worship had run to a violent superstition, which worshipped statues of saints and miraculous pictures, — such as that of the Virgin Mary at Sozopolis, whose hand flowed with balsam, as well as the visible symbol of the Cross, at which no one scrupled. Images were taken from the churches by command of Leo, and a council called by his successor (754) echoed in its Acts the imperial will, holding it especially profane that she who was "literally and truly Mother of God, higher than the whole creation, visible or invisible," should be represented by "'a figure out of any sort of wood, or colors laid on by a workman's hand."

It is unnecessary to tell the furious resistance to such decrees, amounting to rebellion and civil war; or how the fanaticism was fed by companies of monks, and traded on by interested churchmen. By an odd and childlike superstition, not only prayers were said and offerings made to painted images, and lighted candles set before them; but the sacred bread, "the body of the Lord," was put in their hands, as children feed their dolls, and the color scraped from them was mixed in the cup of communion. Some councils or synods were found to sanction the custom of image-worship. Imperial edicts against it were passed in vain. Silent toleration and persecuting rigor were tried in turn; till, under a second Theodora (842), full sanction of Church and State was given to the custom, and a yearly festival was established to celebrate its final triumph. What quaint, abject, homely forms the superstition took, is told us by all visitors to Oriental churches at the present day. The dispute was finally settled by the curious compromise which permitted pictures (or colored medallions), but not images, while the Latin Church admits them both, — another rift of the breach between East and West that went on widening hopelessly. Since this separation,* the Eastern Church drifts out of the main channels of history, and floats, in a certain idle and sheltered way, in such shallows and coves as the floods of fanaticism or conquest may have spared. Its history will not detain us any longer.

To us the strange thing, the real tragedy in all these disorders, — so puerile and futile the cause of them appears to us, — is that they were the serious and real interests of Eastern Christians, while the storm was gathering in the South that soon swept them to horrible destruction. We cannot watch with their eyes the advancing tempest, or know how it looked to them, because their eyes were holden, not to see things as they were. An infatuation of security possessed them, I suppose, in the august name and traditions of the Empire, till the sweep of Mahometan fanaticism had grown irresistible. For, in the year 609, the Arab camel-driver Mahomet, in a brooding, fitful way that we might take for mania, had begun to talk of himself as a prophet of the One

---

* This was made final in 879, at a council in Constantinople, which rejected, — 1. The Roman assertion of supremacy; 2. The claim that Bulgaria lay within the see of Rome; 3. The addition of the phrase *filioque* to the Western creed. ·

God. In 622 he fled for his life from Mecca, and began to gather a force personally devoted to him. In ten years more he died, just on the edge of an enterprise that blazed out suddenly, like a conflagration. Syria, Egypt, Persia, were by 650 held by the Moslem sword, and along the confines of the Empire the Crescent bore hard against the Cross.

I am not to repeat, in ever so rapid outline, the story of those conquests, or discuss again the character and career of the Arabian prophet. We have only to look, very briefly, at the moral causes at work in the sudden catastrophe. By common opinion, Mahomet is regarded now as more reformer than impostor, as a fanatic if ever there was one, partially (perhaps) insane. At least the frenzy that we call madness is often the most effective appeal to Oriental races, and it was strong in him at times. Still, it was not only vehement passion, often on the edge of insanity. However distorted, it never quite lost the glow of religious feeling and moral passion it started with. He is said to have picked up very early in life some crude notion of Christian doctrine from certain Ebionitish sects, heretical and zealously monotheist; while his most indignant scorn was called out by some monkish travesties of the trinity, already alluded to. His career began with a furious attack on the idols of the Arab Kaabah, and this iconoclastic zeal he never abandoned. Indeed, among his followers it is as hot and intolerant to-day as it was in the first onslaught inspired by his voice.

A word of the field where this new fanaticism took root, and the material on which it fed. To the most religious races on earth Arabia itself is a holy land. There is Mount Sinai, its rugged summit scorched by the visible presence of Jehovah ; the rock, where at the stroke of Moses water gushed out for his fainting people ; the well Zemzem, which the angel showed to Hagar when Ishmael, father of the desert tribes, was dying of thirst ; the black stone of Mecca, chief visible object of adoration to the faithful, which they say fell from heaven. The Arab, we are told, claims a license to plunder all other tribes of men, in retaliation for Abraham's casting off of Ishmael. Whatever the ground of it, the license is one all travellers feel to-day.

On them, again, God has bestowed four peculiar gifts : turbans for diadems, tents for walls and houses, swords for intrenchments, and poems for laws. In their worship they allow no images or pictures : " Thank God," say they, " we have originals." The same enormous conceit glorifies their Sacred Book. No mortal man, they think, unless inspired, could wield the vast fabric of their language, swollen with unnumbered synonymes, having eighty names for honey, two hundred for a serpent, a thousand for a sword. Mahomet had never learned to read or write ; yet the revelations he gave out from time to time are held unrivalled by all poets or orators of that tongue : " the greatest of miracles, equally stupendous with the act of raising the dead, alone enough to convince the world of its divine original."

No other creed has so worked up into a fanatic passion the obscure feeling which lies at the heart of most men, that their lives are ordered by a Destiny wholly out of their control. The Moslem faith teaches that the day and hour of each man's death is written down in the book of fate. No power can avert or alter that. His freedom is only to choose the worthiest way to die. Those who fall in battle would have perished all the same, about their business or in bed at home; but basely so, most gloriously now. It is their great privilege to have fallen so; already they are in the joys of paradise. Thus fatalism is not the helpless spell upon the will it might be in a feebler race, but a passion of absolute daring. "Islam," *Submission;* "Kismet," *It is so decreed,* — are the watchwords both of that fierce courage in battle and that helpless stupor in defeat or misery, alike characteristic of the Moslem temper.

Both the strength and the impotence of Islamism consist in its having drawn off all the moral forces of the nature into that one channel, of a blind religious frenzy; in its absolute scorn of all civilized arts, its absolute surrender to the sensual delights of civilized luxury. The conqueror Omar (637) lay on the stone steps where beggars slept; the staff he leaned on was his bow; all his equipage, as he rode his one camel to the shrine at Jerusalem was a sack of wheat, a basket of dates, a wooden platter, and a water-skin. When Mustapha, ten and a half centuries later (1683), lay in his camp before Vienna, it was with pavilions of green silk and all the luxuries that could be gathered by an enormous army train, till this insolent array was swept back by the splendid chivalry of Sobieski, and Europe was saved. From that hour the formidable wave of Mahometan conquest has ebbed, steadily or fitfully, till the power which Luther thought likely to bring the reign of Antichrist is hardly propped from falling by Christian alliances. England and Russia, not Arabia or Turkey, control the destinies of the East.

But, in its first fury, it had nearly extinguished the degenerate Christian Empire. Twice Constantinople was beset by an Arab fleet, — in 668 and 716; and twice it was saved by the timely and terrible defence of the unquenchable Greek fire, — floods of blazing petroleum mixed with sulphur poured over the surface of the waves. Meanwhile the invasion spread westward, through Egypt; through the distracted states of North Africa, where it crushed at once Greek and Vandal, and both the rival parties in the Church; into the Gothic kingdom of Spain, where it won almost the whole Peninsula, but was pushed back by a religious passion equal to its own, and driven out at length by Ferdinand and Isabella; across the Pyrenees into France, where at Tours, in 732, the light horse of Abdelrahman broke all day long against the steel-clad line of Charles Martel, like surf against a belt of ice. The Arab host, when night fell, "folded their tents and silently stole away."

This set the western limit of Saracen invasion. "For," says the chronicler, "as the hammer breaks and bruises iron and steel and all other metals, so did Charles bruise and break in battle all these foes and strange nations." The Arabs, as ever submissive to their destiny, call that fatal field "the martyrs' pavement"; and to this day, say they, the sound is heard which the angels of heaven make in so holy a place, to call the faithful unto prayer.

And thus the flood, which at one time looked irresistible, was beaten back, both in East and West. The great Saracen Empire, which once threatened to envelop the whole of Christendom, still touches it at both ends of its broken crescent, reaching nearly half way round the Mediterranean. As far as the strength of merely religious passion goes, that power was well matched against its antagonist, and was perhaps even its superior. But the bleak monotheism of Islam, its sombre fatalism, its fanatical pride, its ferocious cruelty, its gorgeous and fitful luxury, never were allied — except for one brief holiday of splendor at Cordova — with the great intellectual forces, never with the sober and resolute temper and the moral will, which make religion deep and real, and are alone competent to the world's best work.

Mahometanism broods upon its departed glories. It keeps alive, as its one root of strength, its blind and intolerant fanaticism. It is the creed of perhaps the most recklessly daring fighters in the world. In winning the inferior races, and training them to a fervent worship of its own and a certain low level of culture, it has shown an aptness, skill, and zeal quite in advance of any Christian missions. But science it treats with ignorant scorn. The arts of modern life it takes at second hand, choosing always those of mere luxury or else mere destruction. And so it has no hold upon the future, only the memory of a bloody and stormy past.

# X.

## CONVERSION OF THE BARBARIANS.

ONE of the most familiar of religious images is
that which figures the Christian movement as
a Warfare. The body of believers is likened to an
Army — in the temper of its service, the aim of its
movement, the symbol of its loyalty, in its discipline,
drill, and organization. A favorite Christian phrase
has always been "the Church militant"; and many
illustrations have already shown what meaning, and
how much, lies in that phrase: that it means, not
simply that the religious life is a warfare to us indi-
vidually, which in one view it always is; but that, in
its largest sense, it is a movement of conflict and antagonism, against very definite foes, and to certain
definite ends. This image we must still keep in view
a little longer.

How in its nobler sense that warfare was carried on
for some centuries, and by what sort of men, we have
seen already. We have now to consider it, in its
largest sense hitherto, as an invasion and a conquest.
We are to think of it as a Campaign, intricate in its
plan, wide in its field of operations, long in the carrying out, conducted by wary and skilful strategy, and
brought to its close with a diplomacy equally adroit
and able. No other terms than these will fitly express

the intricate character, the mingled motives, the variety of agents, the acts sometimes heroic and then again quite questionable, by which that campaign was carried through.

Indeed, these only express it feebly. For the field includes all Western Europe, — that is, the entire front of the advancing civilization. The time it covers is three centuries. Its strategy is the steady policy of the Church of Rome, administered by a long succession of able and zealous pontiffs. Its agents are not only that great host of devoted servants, numbering many thousands, of whose discipline and zeal we have seen something already in the monastic orders; they include also barbarian chiefs and petty sovereigns, whose policies, feuds, and even crimes are, with the heat of fresh conversion, put at the service of the Church. It is of this vast campaign that I am to attempt, not a history, or outline, or even sketch, but only to hint the nature of the forces that guided, impelled, and fought it.

The three centuries just spoken of may be most conveniently regarded as extending from the time of Leo the Great, about 450, to the death of St. Boniface, Apostle of the Germans, in 755. Just midway stands the remarkable and imposing figure of Gregory the Great, — sometimes called the last of the Fathers, and the real dividing-mark between the ancient and middle age, — who died in 604. He may be held to have first distinctly conceived this great work from the point of view just indicated, and, more than any other man, to have given it the impulse and the stamp of his powerful moral nature. At his noble personal character we may glance briefly by and by. At present, we have simply to fix this period of time as a whole as definitely as may be, — its beginning, middle, and end. Its beginning corresponds nearly with the fall of the Western Empire; its end is a little before the refounding of that Empire in the person of Charlemagne.

Recall now those words of Leo, in which he recites the glory God had bestowed on Rome in making it the seat of military empire, as a preparation for the greater glory that would belong to it as head of a spiritual dominion broad as the earth itself. Those words may serve as a key to the movement we are about to consider, the Christian conquest of the barbarian nations.

But it may be worth while to reflect a moment on the amazing realization of them which we have before our eyes at the end of more than fourteen centuries. Imperial Rome never had at its command so vast a number of subjects, nor such absolute devotion, nor such diplomatic skill, nor such willing obedience, nor such wealth of voluntary gifts, nor such hold on the imagination and reverence of men, as Papal Rome, stripped of the last vestige of temporal power, has to-day. What no mere secular government can do, *it can command men to be martyrs.* Its word is a spell of authority as much in the heart of Africa or on the Pacific coast as in the chambers of the Vatican. It can by a whisper raise or quell a religious frenzy in Paris, Vienna, San Francisco, or Quebec. It can block the wheels of the strongest military power that ever existed on earth, and does it to-day. It claims to hold, alone, the key to the great social problem, the despair of moralists and statesmen, and with it to control the next great step of human evolution.

We may deny that claim; we may hate, dread, or defy the authority which still asserts itself in so many ways. The one thing we cannot do is to despise it. And among all matters of historical inquiry the one that seems best worth our understanding, if we can, is the course of events that laid the foundations of that power so deep and strong. Some of the conditions of its exercise we shall have to consider when we come to speak of the mediæval Empire-Church. Just now we deal only with the period of its foundation.

The military empire of Rome was about five hundred years * in coming to its greatest breadth and height. This was a process of conquest carried out by the patriotic valor of the Roman armies, and guided by the vigorous policy — often kept in check by the jealous dread — of the Roman Senate. Again and again conquests were undertaken reluctantly, and carried out in self-defence, exactly as they are by England in Asia and Africa to-day. In particular, Rome was obliged to resist steadily, for two or three centuries, the steady advance of barbarian tribes, in that movement which threatened to cover as with a flood the whole field of ancient civilization. She was obliged to conquer, exterminate, enslave them; to draft them in her armies; to keep them in check by military colonies; to adopt them in her political system; to humor and tolerate their religions; to give

* Counting from the invasion of the Gauls (B. C. 390) to the time of Trajan.

them whatever share and stake was possible in the wealth, art, skill, at her command. All her treasures of military skill, of population, of state-craft, had been spent in that struggle — with diminishing strength at last, and vanishing hope ; and now the end had plainly come. The Barbarian was master of the civilized world, and all its treasures were at his feet.

We need not go at any length into the vast tragedy of the Fall of Rome. It is with a single point only of its historical significance that we have to do. Just at this moment of time — the final collapse of the ancient system — the vast conception came, like a flash of genius as it were, upon such minds as Leo's, to win back all that was lost, and more, but in another way. Pagan Rome had attempted the conquest of the barbarian world, and had failed. Christian Rome should undertake *to conquer the soul of Barbarism itself*, and in God's name would do it. Such was the magnificent conception of Leo, of Gregory, of the English Winfried surnamed Boniface. Not only the thought itself was more amazing and grand than had ever dawned on the mind of general or statesman. The means by which it was carried out show a larger political grasp, a more consummate generalship, a steadier courage, a reach and subtilty of resource, a firmness of policy, to which the perishing Empire had shown no parallel.

The weapons of this warfare, too, were as original as its conception was great and new. They were, in the most literal, even tender and pathetic sense, the weapons of Christian love. The barbarian world must be won, if at all, by way of sympathy. It must be conquered through its imagination, conscience, and religious awe. The men who went out to that conquest must go animated and haunted with a great yearning for saving souls. The power with which they were clothed was the power of poverty, austerity, obedience, and self-denial.

I do not use these words at random. Volumes of the correspondence of these men have come down to us, and they show the qualities I have named on every page. They show, too, an incredible patience of detail; — such as we might vaguely imagine to be needful if we try to shape out in our minds the conditions of the task; but such as we could not definitely conceive without those innumerable strange, quaint, touching illustrations. I may attempt presently to restore a line or two of these faded memories; but first we should try to see a little more distinctly the outside aspect of the case.

There is a brief bright picture in one of Chrysostom's homilies, of the barbarian as he appeared in the market-place of Constantinople, — restless, turbulent, curious, bearded, thrusting at passers-by with the stick he carries, tossing back his shock of hair "more like a lion than a man." This is just before the great real terror of the Gothic name. St. Jerome reflects, from his convent in Bethlehem, the far-off vision of the agony at the sack of Rome by Alaric, and the haggard spectacle of vagrant, hungry, despairing troops of men and women, high-born, delicately bred, used to luxury, stripped of everything in that great desolation. "I cannot see it without tears," he says; "that power of old, and wealth unknown, have come

to such need as to lack roof, food, and clothing ; and
still the hard and cruel heart of some men is not
softened : nay, they rip up their wretched rags and
wallets, to find gold among these poor captives." *

The monk Salvian, a few years later, had watched
in Gaul or Spain the Gothic and Vandal tide, wave
upon wave, and set himself to a serious study of barbarian frankness, simplicity, courage, ferocity, or craft,
compared with the various forms of civilized vice
generated in the corruption of Pagan society; and finds
the new rude population at least as hopeful subjects
for conversion as the old, which it justly displaced.
St. Augustine about the same time recites, in phrase
that I have before cited, the judgment of God in the
overthrow of that evil world.  The dainty Sidonius
Apollinaris, writing from Toulouse (about 455), tells
jestingly of his seven-foot Gothic hosts (too big for
his hexameters), greased with rancid butter, reeking
of onion and garlic, and clad in shabby kilt and tar-
tan.†  A little later, Jornandes gives, with the vividness of an eye-witness who had felt its terror, the
sketch which all historians since have copied, of the
hardly human Huns — more brutes than men, clinging like cats to the backs of the horses they scarce
ever left, with strange flat-nosed Mongol visages and
beaded gimlet-holes (as it were) in place of eyes —
who poured on like the flood and were swept back like
the ebb, but threatened at one time to put all Europe under the yoke of Asia.

* Introduction to the Commentary on Ezekiel.
† So St. Sturmi, exploring the wilderness for Boniface, smells
the evil odor of the barbarians afar off.

These are hints of the preliminary studies, sketches of the field of operations, before the serious campaign began. Of the century of wreck and waste that followed, in the wake of Lombard and Frank invasion, we have a full-length picture, grotesque in the simplicity with which its horrors are drawn out, in the pages of the excellent and pious Gregory, Bishop of Tours, who bravely and patiently held his post in the midst of them.* A single family group, taken from his sketches and told in meagre outline, will help us more, perhaps, than any generalization of them.

Clovis,† king of the Franks, had been converted by his Burgundian bride Clotilda, and baptized by St. Remigius, who spoke to him the brave words, " Meekly bow thy neck, Sicambrian ; adore what thou hast burned, burn what thou hast adored." He was of the true faith, and impartially destroyed both Pagan Alleman and Arian Burgundian or Goth.‡ " God overthrew his enemies daily under his hand," says Gregory, " because he walked with an upright heart before him, and did that which was pleasing in

---

* These have been condensed by Augustin Thierry in his six brief and curious " Tales of the Merovingian Times."

† Barbaric, *Chlodovig;* softened in lapse of time to *Louis.*

‡ The destruction of the premature but brilliant Arian civilization of the Goths and Burgundians — assailed by the conquests of Belisarius on one side, and crushed by the brutality of the Franks on the other — is one of the obscurer tragedies of this evil time. Some features of this civilization will be found hinted at below, under the title " The Christian Schools." It is pathetic to read the warning given (in the correspondence of Cassiodorus) by the great Ostrogothic King Theodoric to the young Alaric of Toulouse, the Visigoth, to beware of the quarrel with the Franks, in which, a few years later, his kingdom perished.

his eyes." And he adds, a little further on, that, "having slain many other princes, yea, his own nearest kindred, of whom he had jealousy lest they should take the kingdom from him, he extended his power through all Gaul. And once having called together his people, he is said to have spoken thus concerning the kinsmen whom he had slain : ' Woe is me, who remain as a pilgrim among strangers, and have no kindred, who if adversity should come might give me help.' This he said," adds Gregory, quaintly, "not grieving at their death, but by craft, if perchance he might find any still remaining whom he might put to death."

His son Clotaire was of the same barbarian temper, his many murders and many wives alike the scandal of his Christian profession. One of his queens, Radegonda, whose father and brother he had killed in war, escaped with some hazard and became a consecrated nun, founding with her dower a convent of some celebrity, where with her friend, the poet Fortunatus, she found repose,— a little island of peace amidst the tumultuous inundation. The last act of Clotaire's brutality was to fasten in a hut and burn alive on some suspicion his son Chramnes, with all his family; after which, at the tomb of St. Martin, he confessed " all the acts which perchance he had done amiss, imploring with deep groans that the blessed saint would beseech the Lord's mercy for his sins, and wash out by his intercession whatever he had unreasonably done." " What a heavenly Lord is this," he said when dying with fever, " who so destroys mighty kings ! "

Of the sons of Clotaire, Gontran "the good" was held (says Sismondi) "to be a man of humane temper; for, excepting his wife's physician, whom he cut in pieces for failing to cure her, two of his brothers-in-law whom he assassinated, and another whom he treacherously slew, there is hardly any cruel act recorded of him, except it be his destroying the city of Cominges, and slaughtering all the inhabitants, men, women, and children." He was, moreover, a strong friend of the monks and clergy, founded several monasteries, and paid liberally for the expiatory rites that would give his soul repose.

A great part of the tale is taken up with the jealousies, treacheries, and ambitions of the two barbarian queens, Fredegond and Brunehild, — more famous far than the two brothers whose wives they were, — with the intrigues and murders that grew out of them. But both were zealous champions of orthodoxy. Fredegond spared no cost to purchase ransom for the souls of her hired assassins, if they should fall; and Brunehild — who was tied to a wild horse in her old age, and so torn to pieces — was a correspondent and friend of Gregory the Great, and a stanch supporter of his scheme for the conversion of the Saxons.

Such allies as these, for better or worse, the Church had found in its campaign against barbarian paganism and Arian heresy; just as half-pagan Frankish chiefs like Charles Martel sought the alliance of churchmen like Boniface against the wilder floods that still beat upon their frontier. The service was mutual, and each party was largely independent of the other. Often, indeed, the Church could only give a Christian name, without changing the thing. Thus Gregory the Great thinks it necessary to spare them the old pagan temples, only sprinkling them with holy water, and putting saints' relics in place of idols; and to adopt their old festivals, as Yule and Easter, under new associations.

Many and strange were the scandals that came of these conversions. " Here I have been baptized more than twenty times," said an old man one day, when the crowd was larger than usual, and the baptismal robes gave out, " and every time they have given me most beautiful clothes. These old rags to-day are hardly fit for a ploughboy, not to say a warrior like me." One new convert takes the opportunity to pick the priest's pocket while the water is preparing for his baptism. One proposes that a point of heresy shall be settled, not by " these long talks," but promptly, by the ordeal of boiling water. " Is it true," asks a barbarian chief, his foot already in the sacred font, " that my ancestors the noble Frisians are in hell?" " Doubtless," replies the priest; " they died without the only saving faith." "Then"—drawing back his foot — " I will not quit those brave men to join the cowards of your paradise. We will follow the ways of our fathers." And so, in comforting vision, the priest soon after beheld the defiant chief among his ancestors in the fiery pit.

It is a fair question to ask what such conversions were really worth. To this the answer is, that the first point was to bring those fierce tribes, in name at least, within the Christian pale, and *to substitute the Christian for the pagan ideal.* Everything was staked on the success with which this preliminary work was done. The hope of the world lay in those rude men; and their instructors felt it in a way which they possibly could not have explained to us so well as we can understand it for them. Take the breadth of modern thought and life, — science, enterprise, art, wealth, power, — and set it against anything that could possibly have grown from the degenerate Greek or Roman stock; and you measure in part the service that was done, when that rude vigor was grafted with the shoot of a finer life, which would in time yield such infinitely richer fruit.

Or, again, look away from the vague idealities which are apt to fill the field of history to what the Christian monks, scattered by tens of thousands all through the great wilderness of barbarism, were actually doing there: the infinite serious patience with which they went about their task; the austerities of the self-denial that trained them for it, and kept its ideal from fading in them; the hints of beastly and violent ways which they attempted to keep in check; the strange power of fascination which these very austerities exercised, to attract men to them. St. Columban establishes his post alone in the hill-country near the Rhine, because the rule of Benedict is not sufficiently austere; and the more rigid the lines he draws, the more men press to enter them.* This

* A brother who does not say *Amen* after grace must be punished with six stripes; who neglects to cross himself after blessing, twelve stripes; who does not check a cough in reciting the Psalm, or dents the sacramental cup with his teeth, six stripes; who appeals from judgment to his superior, forty days' penance on bread and water. A lay brother who gets drunk, or is sick from

earth, says Columban, is *non vita sed via*, "not a life, but a way," and to transgressors he made it very hard.

I have said before that some of those men were martyrs for humanity. St. Pretextatus, who had bravely sheltered his godson Merovig, is assassinated in his own church by Fredegond's order. St. Wandregisil keeps an angry mob at bay with pious words, and will not appeal to any arm of flesh. St. Bavon humbles himself in remorse before a slave he has once owned, and for penance compels him to shave his head, beat him with rods, and shut him up in prison. St. Germanus strips himself to the shirt to clothe a shivering beggar, and beggars himself to ransom captives. St. Sequanus goes out to live in a savage wood inhabited by more savage men. "No sooner did they see him, than from wolves they became lambs; from such as but now were a source of terror, they were thenceforth ministers of help; and what had been a resort of cruel demons and robbers became the abode of innocence and virtue." Such tales as these, with many a miracle and wonder interspersed, and enforced by many a Christian homily, and seasoned by many a· subtile theological debate, came (says Guizot) to be the mental diversion and the moral instruction of whole populations, — their Arabian Nights, their popular novel, their sermon and essay, their daily newspaper.

Yes, the hope of the world lay in those rude men. The future of humanity was staked upon such tasks

greediness, seven days' bread and water; who eats or drinks in honor of pagan idols, three years of such penance.

as those which attempted their conversion. When Gregory the Great was yet a simple monk, — so each of his biographers delights to repeat the tale, — he saw in the market-place at Rome some captive Anglo-Saxon boys, ruddy-faced, golden-haired, such as we often see in the streets, and as the Italian painters (Goethe says) take for their type of cherubs. Learning who they were, *Non Angli sed angeli* was his famous reply, — "Not Angles but angels"; and from that hour he set his heart on their conversion. Now the Saxons were rudest and fiercest of all the barbarous tribes ; and since their conquest of England, near a century and a half before, — when they overthrew the legendary realm of King Arthur, and drove back the Christian Britons to the mountains of Wales and the Western Isles, — had remained obstinately Pagan. All English histories tell the story of Augustine of Canterbury and his forty monks, sent by Gregory (597), and their conversion of the Saxon; and in Gregory's letters you may read how persistently and hopefully he followed them up, when they shrank from the terror of the unknown journey.* This was amid the very ferocity of the " Merovingian times " before described. Their protector on the way was the truculent Brunehild; and the act was one which, more than any other, marks Gregory as the head and chief in this long unbloody crusade.

Gregory is one of those men who are heroic from the steady courage and persistency of will with which

* What is so well told in so accessible a book as Green's " History of the English People," it does not seem worth while to repeat by way of narrative.

they face great disasters, and carry a great burden of duty through a hard and dangerous way. In reading his correspondence, we feel painfully that we have come upon a far lower intellectual level than we had in Leo, a hundred and fifty years before. He dwells rather pitifully on the marvels and terrors of saints' bones, and makes much of the filings of St. Paul's or St. Peter's chains, which he has enclosed in gold keys and sends as gifts of magic efficacy to barbarian lord or lady. But this childish way of thought is joined to a very manful courage and sincerity in dealing with the duties of his office. From that office he shrank back at first, as well he might; fled from the city; and yielded only when his retreat was betrayed by a miraculous light, and a white dove led the way to his pursuers. Of high rank and luxurious tastes, he cast those things absolutely away, starving himself to permanent ill health by his austerities, and enforcing such rigid monastic discipline in his own household that, when he learned once that a brother had kept (for keepsake, perhaps) three pieces of gold, he would pardon him not even on his death-bed, but cast his body with the coins upon a dunghill, saying, as Peter to Simon Magus, "Thy money perish with thee!"

These bitter rigors and self-denials were the answer made, by a conscience highly strung, to the appeal of the miseries that surrounded him in the city, thrice desolated, by violence, flood, and pestilence. But it is not the story of his fourteen years' rule (590–604), rigid, charitable, energetic, and wise, that we have to look at now; only the astonishing industry and moral energy of the man. His correspondence is immense.

His homilies, commentaries, and moral treatises, in many volumes, have earned him the title of "last of the Fathers." This great amount of work he did with a definite practical aim, with genuine humility, among the distractions of office; surrounded by what looked to him a mere chaos of wild waves, amidst which the ship he was pilot of was tossing helplessly; suffering too with illness and torments of "gout" (inflammatory rheumatism, probably), and for years able only to drag himself from bed for three hours in the day, to attend the ceremonies of his priesthood. As he grew old, he felt these pains and cares more heavily,— poisoned, perhaps, with the malaria that already began to infect the neighborhood of Rome. "Oppressed with its burden," said he, "my soul sweats blood." Yet he, more than any other one man, was the chief of that great crusade, which he directed from his sick bed; a campaign, says Ozanam, fought out by "invalids and women and slaves."

The next very eminent leader in this campaign — at the end of another century and a half — is the English Winfried, otherwise St. Boniface of Germany, who was martyred in 755. His work was a direct though distant result of Gregory's great enterprise in Saxon England. For the Saxons were at this time chief and most formidable of all the barbarous nations; and, though Christian in England, still hung like a heavy cloud all along the northeastern portion of half-civilized France, fanatic in their old paganism, till subdued by Charlemagne, with other outlying tribes, many years later, in thirty-three bloody campaigns.

I do not know where we have a higher example of
blended sweetness and courage, with a native frankness and nobleness of temper, than in the life of Boniface.    It has been asked whether his courage was not
rather of a feminine sort, considering, perhaps, the
passive serenity of his death.    But, from the time
when the first great passion seized him, at the age of
twenty-three, of giving himself to this service, till his
death at seventy-two, his life was spent by choice in
the rudest and most hazardous exposures.    While
passively obedient to meekness in his devotion to the
authority of Rome, he is plain to bluntness in rebuk-
ing to the Pope himself the disorders he found in the
Christian capital: "These carnal men, these simple
Allemans, Boians, and Franks, if they hear of such
things at Rome as we forbid, will think them lawful,
and be offended.    They hear of pagan dances, shouts,
and songs close by the church, at new-year, day or
night; and that one will not lend his neighbor tool
or fire; and that women wear amulets, garters, and
bracelets, in pagan fashion, and sell the same.    With
these carnal and ignorant people, such things are a
great hindrance to our doctrine.    If you prohibit them
at Rome, it will be a great gain to you and to us."
And he warns the Pope of grosser scandals reported
within the church.    "The pagan rites," answers Zachary, "we judge detestable and pernicious"; and he
says they must be put down.    The worse offences he
entreats Boniface "noway to believe."    This frankness
of correspondence is an honor alike to both.

It was the yearning of kindred, no less than pure
missionary zeal, that drew the Saxon Winfried from

the pleasant South of England, towards those un-
tamed Saxons of the Continent, whom he could address in his and their mother tongue.*

Now if we remember the place which this same
Saxon race has filled in history,—how it was the
steady support of the Lutheran Reform on one side and
of English Puritanism on the other; how it makes
the mass and strength of the two great empires of
Britain and Germany to-day, and of the American Republic; how its blood and its language have spread,
through its great genius for colonization, till they are
dominant over nearly a third of the earth's surface
and population,—we shall better appreciate the greatness of the work that was set on foot when Boniface
penetrated the wilds beyond the Rhine, to preach in
his native English there.

This work was distinctly understood to be the task
of civilization, and the saving of what men had then
best worth saving. We can still read the awkward
Latin of the safe-conduct given by Charles Martel to
this missionary monk, and signed with his hand and
seal. This is in 724, in the midst of the gathering
and disciplining of that confederation, with which

* The speech in which he addressed them is almost intelligible
to our English ears to-day, as preserved in this fragment of his
baptismal vows: "Forsachis tu diobolæ?—Ec forsacho diobolæ.—
End allum diobol-gelde (*fellowship*)?—Ec forsacho allum diobol-
gelde.—End allum dioboles werkum?—End ec forsacho allum
dioboles werkum end wordum: Thunaer, ende Woden, ende Sax-
note, ende allem them unholdum the hira genotas sint (*unholy
that are akin to them*).—Gelobis tu in Got almehtigan fadaer?—
Ec gelobo in Got almehtigan fadaer.—Gelobis tu in Crist, Godes
suno?—Ec gelobo in Crist, Godes suno.—Gelobis du in Halogan
Gast?—Ec gelobo in Halogan Gast." [This is a little mangled in
Migne, but restored by Ozanam.]

eight years later he met Abdelrahman on the plain of
Tours, and dammed back the flood of Saracen conquest.   The penniless unarmed monk and the powerful military chief respected one another as allies in
the defence of Christendom, — neither more indispensable than the other.   As a token of the same alliance, nearly thirty years later, Boniface anointed
with his own hand Charles's son Pepin as king of
the Franks (752), in place of the degenerate and
worthless house of Clovis, so sealing the compact of
the Monarchy and Church, and completing the first
act in the founding of the Christian Empire, which
we shall see presently as one of the essential steps of
civilization.

The service of those near thirty years was crowned
. by the founding of the monastic school at Fulda, one
of the chief fountains of German culture.*   In his
ecclesiastical residence at Mentz, on the Rhine, he
might have found rest in his old age, and his life's
work well done.   But the same great yearning drew
him towards those Low Countries where the cloud of
Paganism still hung heaviest.   " Know, my son," said
he to his successor, " that the time of my death draws
near.   Go on with the work I have begun; finish the
church at Fulda, and, when my time is come, bury me
there; prepare what is needful for my journey, and do
not forget, with my books, to send a winding-sheet."
And with these words he left him weeping.

And so he went to the rude Low Country toward

* See the curious account (copied in Kingsley's " Roman and
Teuton "), in Eigil's Life of Sturmi, of the discovery and selection
of this spot. — Migne, *Patrologia*, cv. 530.

the North, where he lived by the river-side, and baptized the converts who came to him as to John by Jordan. But one day there came, instead of the band of disciples he was looking for, a wild crew of Pagans, who "with great din and horrid array of arms burst upon the encampment of the saints." At first, his young men would resist by force. " But the holy Boniface, hearing the onset of the tumultuous crowd, fled to the refuge of spiritual defence, taking (that is) the relics of saints which he always had with him. So he checked the young men, saying, 'Do not fight, my children ; do not bear arms against our adversaries, which Holy Scripture forbids. We are taught to return not evil for evil, but even good for evil. The day long desired is come, when we are bidden from the toil and sorrow of this world to the joys of eternal blessedness. Strengthen yourselves rather in the Lord, and accept gratefully his offered mercy.' But, behold ! before his words were ended, the furious troop rushed upon them, and slew them in the blood of a happy martyrdom."

The letter of the story we may often have to question. But, without any doubt, it tells us the temper of that long campaign, in which the victory was gained, once for all, for civilization and intelligence. The barbarian world, once nominally won to the Church, would become the field of what we are to know hereafter as mediæval and modern Christianity.

But here, to make the sketch complete, we must anticipate a little the course of time. Along with the conquests of Charlemagne, — those pitiless conquests, in which (it was said) all were cut off who were "taller than the Emperor's sword,"—a sort of nominal Christianity had been carried deep into the Saxon forests, and a mongrel faith had driven back the worship of Odin and Thor. Such as it was, however, and spite of many a formidable recoil of the old superstition, it seems to have pledged those regions to alliance with the Christian monarchy of the West.

Loyalty to their creed was like loyalty to their flag. With whatever misgiving and reluctance, the rude Saxon, having once enlisted on the other side, stood stanchly by the mightier Power that had foiled his fathers' gods. The chief peril to those wavering conquests of the Church militant lay in the barbarous realm beyond. The breach might be quickly healed where it had been quickly broken; and a Scandinavian or Slavonic horde might find itself in alliance with all the passionate terrors of a lingering Paganism.

Early in the ninth century, Paschasius Radbert (whom we shall hear of again, more than once) was head of a celebrated school at Corbey. His favorite pupil was a young man, Anschar, a warm disciple of his brooding and mystical theology. In the fervid visions of his youth, Anschar had beheld the visible glory of the Lord, and had heard himself summoned by celestial voices to spend his life for the conversion of the heathen, and so to win the blessed crown of martyrdom. His heart was brave, and his will firm; but his piety often took a sombre and penitential cast, leading him to solitude and austerities, out of the line of active duty. Conceiving himself to be fore-appointed to some great enterprise, he waited for some clear call to his real work.

At twenty-four he found himself already engaged in it. From the monastic school at New Corbey on the Elbe, the Christian conquests begun by Boniface were pushed by Anschar into the remoter north. At Hamburg, where a fortress had been built among the dense forests that made the pagan frontier, and afterwards at Bremen, he had his bishopric. And here he found native helpers. Harold Hlak, an exiled Dane, had found refuge with the Emperor Louis, son of Charlemagne, adopting the Christian faith, and his return opened the way for a mission among his people. Roving Scandinavian traders, or freebooters, had been as far as Micklagard, the "great city" of the East; and there, or along the Levant, or on the British coast, or at the Frankish court, they had found the worship of the "white Christ," whose invisible might had broken the Saxon strength, and forced their old religion to hide itself among wilder mountains, in ruder forests.* The secret charm of a more powerful faith; the Roman ritual, which seemed to them the invocation of a new order of spirits; intercourse with their own Christian captives, and the sense that they were dealing with a more skilled and educated race, — all prepared them to welcome the new religion. At their request, and under convoy of a trading fleet, Anschar pursued his mission to the North.

Of the result we know not much more than that he was favored by a strong party among the Swedes; that he was partly foiled by an attack of pirates, who seized most of the royal gifts and holy vessels on the

---

* All this is told in a charming tale, "Anschar, the Apostle of the North," by Richard John King (London).

way; that he met the fierce hostility of the old Paganism, which stood savagely at bay in this its last fortress ; that his church and bishopric at Hamburg were laid waste with fire ; and that, after long wandering and peril, he died at sixty-four, grieving that his Lord had not thought him worthy of the martyr's crown.

These three, Gregory, Boniface, and Anschar, are conspicuously the heroes of that long crusade, whose glory belongs to many generations and many thousands of faithful men.  Their completed work is seen in the great fact, made clear before the end of this period, that all Western Europe, from Sicily on the south to Norway or even Iceland on the north, is allied in one spiritual empire, and embarked on the career of a common civilization.

# XI.

## THE HOLY ROMAN EMPIRE.

WE have seen in Christianity, from the beginning, something more than a system of doctrine, more than a movement of religious or reforming zeal. Its first announcement was that "the kingdom of heaven is at hand." These words were taken very literally to mean the regeneration of society, and the founding of a Divine Order on earth. Its scheme was social, and even political, quite as much as it was religious. The Church was organized for discipline and authority, quite as much as it was for piety, charity, or emotional appeal. Its success meant revolution in the state, quite as much as conversion of the soul. The Messianic hope of the reign of the chosen people passed directly over to it as a heritage, and as an element of power; and was adopted in the sense that all institutions and all authority among men are rightfully subject to the law of Christ as interpreted by the ministers of Christ.

The reign of Constantine had been in part a fulfilment of that scheme. It was the task of a Christian Emperor to make over the institutions of the Empire after the Christian model; at the very least, to make himself the official defender of the faith. We have seen how this view became idealized in Augustine's

"City of God"; and how it was expanded into the conception of a spiritual Empire, co-ordinate with the military dominion of Rome, we have heard from the lips of Leo. We have followed, for the space of more than three centuries, the conquests of that idea. We have now to see the form it takes, as the period of conquest is passed ; as the task of Christianity comes to be the shaping out of a political constitution, and the administration of secular power.

Our immediate object of study, then, is the Empire which came into being at the end of the eighth century. It is, in a very accurate sense, the goal towards which organized Christianity has been tending for about five hundred years. The great historic figures of Constantine and Charlemagne stand — as in the stately porch of St. Peter's — at the two extremities of the course. As to the series of events that fill the long interval, the task of the historian, from our point of view, is to set forth as well as he can the motive and spirit of the great Christian leaders. This is perhaps not very difficult. We see pretty clearly what was the ideal of society and life as they conceived it ; and, on the whole, we may fairly say that they kept that ideal pretty steadily in view, as the real aim of their policy and conduct.

We are not quite so clear in our view of the great social revolution now to be described. The circumstances are more perplexed. The motives are more mixed. The responsibility of power compels a new standard of judgment. Great events (such as the conflicts of the twelfth and thirteenth centuries) resulting from that revolution throw back their own light, sometimes very painfully, on the actors in it.

Still, in the main, we must follow the same rule, — to put ourselves in their place as well as we can. We must not judge that new Christian alliance of Church and Empire by the shape it actually took at any given time ; still less by the horrible abuses, the travesties, the corruptions, that came about long generations after, which are too often the only material offered for our judgment.

Nor, on the other hand, should we be misled by the purely ideal and abstract way of regarding it which we find in Dante, and in the great speculative church-men who were his teachers. All that will come before our notice in due time. But, just now, we must do it the justice of seeing it from the point of view of the men who were the living actors in it. We must take into our regard their ideal, as well as their very coarse and hard surroundings, and the equally coarse and hard temper bred by the passions of the struggle. We must see, if we can, what they thought ought to be done, what they thought could be done, and what they really tried to do.

Now we must bear in mind — besides the ideal of human society itself, which they held then, or which we hold now — that there was before their eyes a form of government actual, irresistible, invincible, and by its innumerable agents present everywhere. This was the government of Imperial Rome. We must not underrate the importance of that fact, especially the powerful charm it always held upon their imagination. "The peace of the Empire" was to them more than a phrase. For about two centuries, from Augustus to Commodus, it had been the symbol of a certain authority of law, a security of life, a frequency and easiness of intercourse, a central, controlling, and on the whole beneficent majesty, — strongly relieved against old memories of conflict everywhere, against the more dismal horror of the century's civil war in Rome, the desolation, violence, and fear men associated with outlying barbarism.* The dominion of Rome, haughty and superb, included all they knew of culture, art, splendor, civil order; all they thought of as lawful authority and power. All the sanctities which ancient life had known, such as they were, had come to be embodied in that awful and supreme dominion.

Rome had been prefigured, too, in prophecy, as last of the four great kingdoms of the earth; and so its name had to the Christian as well as the Pagan mind something of a superhuman spell. It might persecute and afflict the subjects of the Church, as under the best of emperors, Trajan and Aurelius. It might attempt to extirpate them as enemies and traitors, as under the worst of tyrants, Nero and Galerius. It might stand to them as the visible type of Antichrist, a kingdom of Satan, to be presently overthrown, as in the imagination of St. Augustine. But even then there was something about it of sanctity and awe. Martyrs of the faith testified on one side to its corruption and iniquity; but at the same moment legions

* See the very touching illustrations of this feeling given in Hodgkin's "Italy and her Invaders," Vol. II. pp. 505–508. Compare Claudian, *In Rufinum*, ii. 86–100.

of Christian soldiers — as the " thundering legion " of
Aurelius — were fighting in its defence.    Their absolute loyalty to it in idea and in theory is as strongly
marked as their absolute courage in defying its power
and enduring its torture.    We must ·bear in mind,
then, that the Empire of Rome stood to them, as it
was exhibited by Leo the Great and as it stands to
the Catholic mind to-day, the type of sovereignty, —
irresistible, august, divine.

Again, we must think of this wide and powerful
dominion as it commanded the homage and vague
awe of barbarous tribes, who knew it only at a dis-·
tance.    They were not wanting in intelligence, any
more than in courage.    Their imagination was all the
more apt to be overawed, since nothing could offer
itself for comparison with that mysterious source of
power whose effects they felt.    The weakness of barbarism before it was not lack of bravery, or lack of
men, or even lack of discipline.    It was lack of organization on a large scale.    Wherever the barbarian
came in contact with it, or heard of it by remotest
rumor, — in African waste, or Parthian wild, or German wood, — it was always and everywhere the same
Roman eagle he met, the same compact force of
small,* tough, swarthy, nervous, disciplined, indomitable men, all trained alike to obey and to die for
that distant, dim abstraction, the Eternal City.    He
met the same type of commander, — patient, resolute,
hardy : like Cæsar, snatching a shield from a common

---

* " Men of such petty size (*tantulæ staturæ*) : for our littleness is
mostly held in contempt among the Gauls, in comparison with
their own bigness." — Cæsar, B. G., ii. 30.

soldier, to fight without helm or breastplate in the van; like Hadrian, bare-headed and on foot in the hot dust of Egypt or the forests of Gaul, — and always obedient to the spell of that invincible Name.

This, I say, must have been the effect on men's imagination of those five hundred years of conquest; of those eight centuries during which no armed enemy had entered the Roman gate; of that genius for organization which created the same type of rule, obeyed the same symbol of authority, established the same code of law, wherever a Roman force got footing on the soil. The spell was all the stronger, because the source of that authority was something mysterious, vague, unseen. Or, if a barbarian embassy or captive chief came to visit the Imperial City, the great circuit of the walls and their invincible strength, the splendor, wealth, and luxury, the strange spectacle of civil order among a vast city population, could only, by report of them, deepen and confirm the spell. Thus for three centuries, while Gaul and Goth made the chief strength of Roman armies, no Gaul or Goth conceived a thought of disloyalty to the Roman name, or of substituting his own authority for that he served under. So Alaric was haunted by a voice, he said, that gave him no quiet day or night, commanding him to assault and capture Rome; * but first he led his soldiers six years up and down in Italy, as if held off by the potent charm, and when at last he had taken

* " Non somnia nobis,

Nec volucres, sed clara palam vox edita luco est:
*Rumpe omnes, Alarïce moras! hoc impiger anno,*
*Alpibus Italiæ ruptis, penetrabis ad Urbem.*"

Claudian, *De Bello Getico*, 546, 547.

the city and plundered it, within a year he was dead, and his force dispersed. So Radagaisus, with his vast host, had perished, lingering about Florence on his way to the assault of Rome. So Attila, the " scourge of God," had been deterred by the peaceable embassy of Leo, who warned him of the sudden fate of all who had offered violence to the holy city; and the barbarian had yielded, saying that he saw behind the venerable priest the apparition of an old man with a terrible countenance and threatening gesture, — which men thought was the Apostle Peter, but which we may think was the spectre of the majesty of Rome; and, a few months later, he too died, choked by his own blood. So Odoacer the Herulian giant, real sovereign of Italy, to whom St. Severinus had foretold dominion when he stooped to enter the hermit's hut, held that dominion first as the loyal officer of the last boy-tenant of the Roman throne, and then as " Patrician " by appointment of the Eastern Emperor. So Theodoric the Ostrogoth reigned thirty-three years in Italy as representing the best training that the Empire could give, and as guardian of the art and culture that the Empire had been able to hand down.

The vague awe of Rome, as something mysterious, far-off, and invincible, had thus stamped itself deep on the barbarian mind. The Empire became the symbol of superhuman, absolute, universal sovereignty, so far as that mind could conceive such a thought; for which, indeed, no other symbol could possibly occur. Accordingly — and it is one of the most curious traits of the barbarian mind — any badge of authority, any military title, the official robe or coronet bestowed by the Roman Emperor long after the Empire itself had been humiliated by disasters, dissensions, and defeats, was prized by a Gothic or Frankish chief as a dignity that no barbarian rank or mere success of arms could possibly give. To go no further back, the truculent Clovis, who did not scruple to cleave the skull of foe or kindred with his own battle-axe, took a serious and solemn delight in the title Patrician sent him by the Emperor of the East; he clothed himself with the purple robe, paraded on horseback with ring and coronet, and scattered with his own hand among the crowd gold and silver coins which he had caused to be struck, with the Emperor's image on one side, and his own name as Consul and Augustus on the other. Not that it added anything to his power. As chief of the Frank confederacy he was no doubt stronger, at any rate felt himself to be, than Anastasius on his distant throne. But the patrician rank and name gave him something that barbarism could not give, — the prestige and sanction of an authority linked with the memories and upheld by the sanctities of a thousand years.

This reverence for Roman prestige and authority became a tradition with the Frankish house, along with their fierce zeal for the orthodox faith. And it is curious to see, a few generations later, how the rude affectation of Roman dignity by the long-haired Merovingian kings, who clad themselves in royal robes and rode in state carriages drawn by oxen, ruined them with their turbulent subjects; who speedily adopted for their kings such real chiefs as Charles Martel and his shrewd, strong-handed son Pepin. So the long-haired race of "do-nothing" sovereigns passed away, and Pepin was crowned king by the hand of Boniface, with the blessing of the Pope. Meanwhile the Emperor at Constantinople had since the fall of the Western Empire held out the shadowy sceptre of authority over Italy and the West, claiming the Pope as subject. But Ravenna, his Italian capital, had been swept up in the Lombard kingdom; and Pepin, who as the Pope's ally had beaten back the Lombards, made over to the Pope the temporal rule of the territory about Rome. So the Head of the Church became an Italian prince. The celebrated "Donation" of Pepin thus founded the temporal sovereignty of the Pope (756), which lasted eleven hundred years, till it was absorbed, in 1870, into the new Kingdom of Italy.

This rapid recital is not meant for history, but to give the point of view and the point of time we have reached, at the moment of founding the Christian Empire of the West. Our business is not with the historical incidents, but with the policy, the aim, the ideal, that lay in the mind of the actors; that gave direction to one of the most momentous revolutions and shape to one of the greatest political constructions that have been brought about in human affairs.

It is one of the happiest accidents of history that associates the imposing personality of Charlemagne * with this transition, and has made the title "great"

---

* It has come to be the fashion among historians to speak of him simply by his personal name, Charles or Karl. But, as Head of the revived Empire of the West, implying not only an actual but a typical or ideal sovereignty, it seems best to retain that by which he is most easily distinguished, which Mr. Freeman would restrict to the Charlemagne of legend and romance.

a part of the very name by which he is known. The immediate circumstances that brought him to the spot where his colossal figure stands like a monument at the boundary of two ages were tragic, even somewhat pitiful, as most things look when seen too nearly. The revolution did not take place without violence and parties in the Church. Leo III. had been attacked in some street procession, dragged from his horse, thrown into prison, and nearly killed by the cruel hands that clumsily tried to blind him and cut out his tongue, and so disqualify him by personal mutilation from holding the priestly office. He had taken refuge with Charles in France; and the strong hand of Charles had set him back securely in his place.

The next year — it was Christmas, of the year 800 — Charles visited him in Rome; and, as he knelt at the high altar of St. Peter's in the vesper service, Leo put on his head the imperial crown, and the people joined in the salutation: *To Charles crowned of God Augustus, great and peace-giving Emperor of the Romans, life and victory !*. This was the first act of consecration of the "Holy Roman Empire," whose course, parallel with that of the Church, fills the central space of mediæval history, and whose stately name, veiling a thin phantom of its authority, was not abolished till after more than a thousand years, when Napoleon compelled Francis of Austria to abdicate the title, holding himself, by force of his own arm, to be the true and legitimate successor of Charlemagne.

At heart, Charles was no Roman patrician, but a German chief. He delighted in border forays and border tales. He gathered with a careful fondness the native German ballads. He lived the free life of a huntsman in the woods, when not in the stir of camp or court. He ranged incessantly from place to place in his wide ill-defined dominion, choosing for his capital not the royal town of Paris, much less Rome, but Aachen (*Aix-la-Chapelle*), near his most turbulent frontier, where he died, and where his sepulchre remains until this day. He bore with an ill grace the theatrical pomps and splendors of his office, — unless it might be to rival in public ceremonial the state of some distant sovereign whose embassy was waiting on him. Only twice in his life he put on the cumbrous robes of Roman majesty, preferring the Gallic trousers and the loose sheep-skin jacket of his easy-going home-life.

He chafed, too, under the rigid rules of church-discipline, — that is, if he submitted to it at all. His household was no model of manners or morals ; he was at best an easy, fond, indulgent father, with a heart more large than wise ; and he never quite gave up the quasi-polygamy which had made the old scandal of Frankish chiefs. His broad, bluff, generous humor, too, no doubt scandalized and perplexed his spiritual instructors ; though there was nothing that kept him nearer the heart of his own people, or that we find it easier to pardon : no precisian or martinet, but a large-souled and whole-souled man.

To these traits we should add the immense external activity of his long reign :* relief of Rome from Lombard pressure, till that kingdom was extinguished in 774 ; war against the Saracens in Spain, where the

* Of forty-six years, extending in all from 768 to 814.

hero Roland, favorite of romance, fell in the retreat at Roncesvalles; thirty-three campaigns across the Rhine, mainly against the pagan Saxons, who were not reduced till after forty-five hundred prisoners had been slaughtered in one bloody act of reprisal, and ten thousand families, a third of the population, dispersed in colonies in the heart of France. So the conqueror finished what the monk began.

The toils of war are even outdone by the restless industry of his administration. This shows the minute organizing of a civilized state, just emerging from rude disorder. He orders tithes to be given to the churches; standard weights and measures to be kept; vines to be especially attended to; shelter for cattle, sheep, swine, and goats to be prepared in every village. He gives special directions for the care of stables, the curing of provisions, and the furnishing of houses, not neglecting the condition of stock and crops, or the price of eggs and poultry. He attends to the keeping and training of hawks and hounds; directs the great wolf-hunts, when and how they shall be carried on, the skins to be exhibited to him; and the housekeepers on his estates must understand making cider, beer, and perry. I have counted a list of more than a hundred herbs and fruit-trees which he desires always to have kept in the imperial gardens.* Some of the largest stones used in building his own cathedral at Aachen, it is said, he bent his sturdy frame to bear. Messengers in his name must visit every district four times a year, to correct or at least report all irregularity. Every estate of a given size

* See the Capitulary *De Villis Imperialibus*, A. D. 812, § 70.

must send one man to serve in the public defence. Rules equally vigilant and precise lay down the duty of the local clergy, or order periodical visits of the bishop. He is as prompt to supersede a churchman as an army officer, when found guilty of gross neglect.*

It is necessary to speak of these personal cares of office, because the government had to be personal in the strictest sense. Most likely, there was no other mind clear enough to see the need, or conscience to feel the burden, any more than there was another hand strong enough to do the task. The weight of that great personality is felt all the more, that his empire fell to pieces so soon after his death. In one sense it was premature, an experiment that had to fail. The mere fact that he carried all that weight would help to keep any other from growing up fit to bear it after him. The real organization of European society, which he attempted so heroically, had to come about at a later age. The unwieldy empire had to be broken up in fragments, so that a new

---

* Thus in the first of his Capitularies, §§ 6, 7 : " We ordain that, according to the canons, every bishop shall give heed within his own charge, that the people of God do no pagan rites; but that they reject and put away all defilement of the gentiles, — profane sacrifices for the dead, or fortune-tellers or diviners, or amulets and charms, or incantations, or immolating of victims, which fool-ish people do near churches with pagan rite in the name of holy martyrs or confessors of the Lord; who invite their saints rather to wrath than mercy. We advise that each year every bishop shall carefully visit his charge in circuit, and endeavor to confirm, instruct, and watch the people, and forbid pagan rites, diviners, fortune-tellers, auguries, amulets, incantations, and all defilements of the gentiles." Churchmen are forbidden (Capit. Ann. 781) to keep hawks or hounds, — the latter, lest those who appeal for char-ity should be " torn by the bite of dogs."

structure might strike innumerable roots into the soil, and grow up in innumerable independent shoots. The great need then was that the ideal of an orderly and Christian State should be conceived in one powerful mind, and its foundations should be laid by one strong hand. The events of Charles's reign, and its inordinate activities, are the mere incidents and surroundings of the great work he really did, in creating such an ideal of Christian sovereignty.

That this ideal lay very close to his heart, and was always present to his thought, — whatever the defects of its carrying-out, — appears in one very interesting trait recorded by Eginhard. " He took delight," he says, " in the books of St. Augustine, and especially in those which are entitled *Of the City of God*," which were read to him at meal-time. Those books, it is true, do not give any plan or pattern of a Christian State to be realized on earth, such as we might possibly expect. But they set forth with great emphasis the contrast of right and wrong, of the state sacred and profane. They put in strong light the corruption and violence that had destroyed the Pagan Empire ; they bring into equal relief the virtues of the Divine Kingdom, and the peace that grows out of them. They set forth vividly the warning given in the fall of Rome, crushed under its own vices and feuds long before the assault of barbarian arms. And, from the hint just given, as well as from the incessant coupling of religious things with secular in his laws, it is likely that these lessons and these warnings had been taken very much to heart by Charles, in his reflections on the duties of empire.

We may see the same thing, perhaps, in his shrinking from those duties and from the name of Emperor. His coronation took him by surprise. He protested, says his biographer, that he would not have gone to the church that day, if he had known what Leo had in store for him. Possibly his sagacity foresaw the use that would be made of that act by Leo's successors, to bolster up their enormous claim that the Empire itself was in their gift, to bestow or revoke as their policy might demand. It has been noticed that an interval of more than a year passed, before he claimed allegiance as Emperor; and then he stays to explain "how many and how great things are comprehended in that vow: not merely, as many even now suppose, to the lord Emperor in his own lifetime, and not to bring any enemy for hostility within his realm, and not take part in or conceal any one's infidelity towards him; but that every man may know that this vow has bearing direct upon himself"; and so he goes on, in forty chapters, to recite a whole code of civil and religious duty.*

That rude time could not show any very flattering fulfilment of such an ideal. But there is no question that the reign of Charlemagne did very much to stamp that conception on the general mind; to make it part of the notion of what a state should be, as well as to enshrine him in memory as a sort of model sovereign. There have been many emperors and kings who have come nearer the commonly received pattern of Christian living; but not one so dignified or idealized in the imagination of the world. The Church

* See the 24 Sections of the Capitulary dated at Aachen, 802.

puts him in the next rank to saintship, and in some countries he has been frankly reverenced as a saint. Miracles are recorded to have been wrought at his tomb. Within a century of his death he is made the hero of legend and marvel, and volumes of popular romance already gather about his name. His military adventures are transfigured to make him the ideal Champion of Christendom, carrying his conquests as far as Jerusalem, as the great typical Crusader. And he is so appealed to in the oration by which Urban II. stirred the multitude at Clermont to the first Crusade (1094).

The real man, in his hearty humor, his rude sports, his cordial loves and enmities, and his serious wish to do his work, is a much more interesting person than this fabulous ideal. His traits are known to us, as few men's are of a former age, by personal description and admiring anecdote. I copy here a few sentences from his friend, favorite secretary, and biographer, Eginhard, — the hero of the romantic tale which tells how he won the love of his sovereign's stalwart daughter, and how she once carried him on her shoulder from a stolen visit, lest his footsteps should betray him in the new-fallen snow : —

" In eloquence he was copious and ample, well able to express plainly whatever he would. Not content with his native speech, he bestowed pains in learning foreign tongues. Latin he could speak as well as his mother tongue ; Greek he could understand better than pronounce. He was so ready of speech that one might think him a schoolmaster. He studiously cherished liberal arts, and bestowed the highest honors on the teachers of them. A great deal of time and labor he spent in learning rhetoric and logic, and particularly astronomy. He learned the art of reckoning, and with eager curiosity would trace the path of the stars. He made attempts to write, and used to carry tablets or bits of bark, or keep them under his pillow, that he might practise his hand at odd times in shaping out the letters; but this late and unseasonable effort had poor success. As long as health permitted, he promptly attended church, morning and evening, even in the night at time of service, and took great care that all should be done decently and in order; and with great diligence he improved the style of reading and chanting. He was well skilled in both; though he never read in public himself, and only sang softly, and in concert with others."

Some copies add that he furnished eight hundred and eighty-six churches at his own expense, and restored in all three thousand seven hundred. He gathered about him learned men and artists, tiring them out with his incessant activity (says Guizot), and through them giving strong impulse to every form of culture. His imperial title challenged the regard of other powers. Irene, reigning Empress of Constantinople, proposed to unite East and West by marriage, having already been the death of her husband and son; an alliance which Charles discreetly but firmly declined. From Haroun-al-Raschid, Caliph of Bagdad, he received an embassy, bringing, along with command of the Holy Places, rich Oriental gifts, — the first elephant ever seen in France,* with a Moorish lion, a Numidian bear, eastern spiceries and drugs, "so

* It arrived at Aachen, July 16, 812.

that the East might be thought to be stripped to furnish out the West"; a set of chessmen, said to be still preserved, and a clock of curious skill.* These embassies marked a period of almost universal peace. Free passage for western pilgrims was given to the Holy Land. A fair was held yearly at Jerusalem for a fortnight, and arts of peace flourished from India to the farthest West.

From the Ebro to the Danube, the limits of Charles's empire, the local names, it is said, incessantly recall his memory; while to write his history one should know at once the mountain-passes of Spain and the Alps, the Lombard towns, the old monuments of France, and the legends of the Rhine. His traditional beard and sceptre are travestied in the popular figure of the King at cards.† Or, to see the same figure on a larger canvas, barbarian tribes (it is said) in their rude traditions keep the memory of three great conquerors — Timour the Tartar, Alexander, and Charlemagne.

But the interesting and instructive thing to us is to see how far we have got in the development of the Christian idea. And we find that we have got so far as this. Organized Christianity has completed its period of struggle and conquest. It has definitely

---

* At the twelve figures were twelve little doors, which opened successively, letting drop so many balls to strike the hour; and when the circle was finished, a row of little knights in ivory passed round and closed them all. The last two are not included in the documents of the *Monumenta Carolina.*

† The game was invented to cheer the moody insanity of Charles VI. of France; and this unhappy prince, it is said, always crossed himself when he touched the picture of the emperor-saint.

superseded those old forms of Pagan society which had tried so hard to destroy it. What was worth saving in those old forms it has adopted into itself : something of the old art and culture, all the old executive and organizing skill. It has persevered, with incredible energy and patience, till the intelligence and heart of pagan barbarism have been brought distinctly to accept the Christian ideal and the Christian law. That law and that ideal it has now succeeded in implanting in the thought and embodying in the institutions of an Empire which distinctly adopts them as its own. This one moment has been achieved of absolute coincidence and harmony between the two great powers, spiritual and temporal, that together rule the world. It is but for a moment; but it marks the passage to the next great era, when the task is no longer conquest, but administration; when it is not an army or a campaign we have to do with, but a government and a constitution.

A word remains to be said of the fortunes of the Christian Empire founded by Charlemagne. That perfect harmony of interest and motive between Church and State which made its ideal* could be at best but for a moment of unstable equilibrium. On one side violences and passions thinly covered, on the other natural jealousies and honest fears, were enough to dissolve an alliance which was the harder to keep the closer it had been knit. These are fatal dissolving forces in all human things. But, besides these, a

---

* This ideal theory of sovereignty makes the argument of Dante's *De Monarchiâ*. It is amply stated and illustrated in Bryce's " Holy Roman Empire," pp. 102–108 (7th ed.).

great political revolution was impending, which the Church must have seen with terror; which it met, at any rate, with masterly determination and craft. The constitution that made its political scheme through seven centuries was founded on forged decretal and canon law. Its theory was Sacerdotalism, the absolute sanctity, immunity, and authority of the priestly Order. True to that theory, it would have overridden and absorbed all other power whatsoever. It would have established a universal Empire, supreme to men's thought in heaven, earth, and hell, and so laid mankind helpless at the feet of ecclesiastical absolutism.

When the political fabric that Charles had painfully built together was broken up, in the great change we call the rise of Feudalism, the Church held to its theory; and, after an age of incredible corruption and disorder, declared open war upon the State. The Empire, which was in theory one, holy, and indissoluble, ally and partner with the Church in the great work of civilization, was matched against it in an obstinate and bitter struggle of near two hundred years. Its title of "Holy Roman Empire," and its claim to dominion over Italy, were maintained by a long line of German kings. The proudest-tempered of them all, Henry IV., wore himself out to beggary and death (1073–1106) in a struggle with Hildebrand and the successors trained in the school of Hildebrand. The greatest of them all, Frederick Barbarossa, bent his stubborn will to beg peace of Alexander III., and his terrible Italian campaigns closed in the dramatic scene of his humiliation before the Pope at

Venice (1177).  The most brilliant and accomplished of them all, Frederick II., found himself thwarted and foiled at every hand by that stern old man, of nearly ninety, who ruled as Gregory IX. (1227–1241), and held him under the invisible spell of excommunication.

That close alliance of Church and Empire was a dream, out of which both awoke, to find themselves deadly enemies.  It need not have been so, perhaps, if the boundaries of secular and spiritual power had been more clearly drawn and honestly kept.  Unquestionably, the Empire observed those bounds better than its ghostly rival.  There was a political order, a secular justice, a national independence, which in good faith it made many efforts to establish.  Temporal sovereignty, dealing with secular conditions only, may be fairly just ; spiritual sovereignty, in human hands, is necessarily tyrannical.  A theory of supremacy was growing up within the Church, assiduously developed, incessantly urged and pressed, resting on the deep foundations of imagination and religious fear, which held that all human government·existed only by its sufferance ; which would have made any independence in the State, nay, any decent secular government at all, impossible.

Such as it was, however, after the fall of the great imperial houses, the Holy Roman Empire retained almost to our own day something of its sanctity and prestige.  A few great names — the names of Rodolph and Sigismund, of Maximilian and Charles the Fifth — illustrate its later fortunes.  But in the great dynastic wars and political revolutions its splendor steadily faded out. Other forces held the field. Dignity was left it when its strength decayed. A phantom of authority long survived the substance of power. And no shock was felt in the political system when Napoleon, who had seized the imperial name as the symbol of his conquests, compelled the last heir of Augustus, of Constantine, of Charlemagne, to abdicate the title in 1806, and the Holy Roman Empire was no more.

# XII.

## THE CHRISTIAN SCHOOLS.

IN a poetical "Lament" on the division of the Empire after the death of Louis the Pious, the writer speaks of the good time past, when "a noble realm wore its bright diadem as a wreath ; when there was one Prince, and one subject people ; when all cities flourished under one law and judgment; citizens were bound in peace, the enemy repelled by their valor"; when "the cherishing care of the priesthood was emulous in its task; in frequent councils insuring righteous laws to the people; and the word of salvation sounded from far to a holy clergy, to noble princes, and to common men"; when "everywhere young men learned the book of God, and children's hearts drank in the art of letters."*

* Florus Diaconus, *Querela de Divisione Imperii post mortem Ludovici Pii :* —

> Floruit egregio claro diademate regnum ;
> Princeps unus erat, populus quoque subditus unus.
> Lex simul et judex totas ornaverat urbes ;
> Pax cives tenuit, virtus exterruit hostes.
> Alma sacerdotum certatim cura vigebat,
> Conciliis crebris, populis pia jura ministrans.
> Hinc sacris cleris, hinc plebibus eximiisque
> Principibus late resonabat sermo salutis.
> Discebant juvenes divina volumina passim ;
> Littereas artes puerorum corda bibebant.

11*

Nothing so softens our notion of that rude time as to be reminded in this way that there were tender thoughts and vigilant care, then as now, concerning the education of the young. The time which this Christian poet looks back on regretfully was when the schools flourished under the vigorous impulse of Charlemagne himself, or were continued by his son; when they made, in one sense, the crowning work of that Christian Empire which stood in men's minds as the ideal of sovereignty.

The great Emperor had, in fact, not only made his court the head-quarters of learning at that day, sparing no cost to bring together eminent scholars like Alcuin and Eginhard; but he took delight in directing himself the instruction of children, examined their classes, heard their essays, promised rewards to the diligent, or menaced the idle with the loss of all his favor; and even undertook the task of superintending or (it is said) practising with his own hand the copying and elaborate ornamentation of manuscripts. Under the same powerful impulse, a great work of editing went on; and famous writings were cleared of the blots and blunders that had grown upon them in the ruder times that went before. So that we have to look upon this period as an early revival of letters. It gathered up on one hand whatever could be gathered from the past; and, on the other, it planted the seeds of a new, vigorous, and remarkable growth of independent thought.

These two views, then, remain to be taken of the Christian Schools of the ninth century: first, looking to the past, as they represented the learning and culture of the barbaric age; next, looking to the future, as they opened the way to a new development of thought. The first must be treated very briefly; the second, in a little more detail.

The first thing we have to conceive, then, as distinctly as we can, is the course of that unbroken stream of tradition, which had floated down the germs of ancient culture through what we call the Dark Ages. So far as this term is a fit one to use at all, it belongs to the period from the latter part of the fifth century to near the end of the eighth; that is, from the time of Leo the Great to that of Charlemagne.* In Leo's time, we saw the great vigor of the pagan reaction in art and letters; and we know the obstinacy of the pagan tradition in the world of imagination and poetry, down to a very late day. In fact, what we call the classical school, as distinct from the romantic, holds avowedly to that tradition, even now.

The reasons of this immense vitality of the pagan classic thought lie deeper than we are apt to think. It may perhaps be more accurate to say that they are strown thicker upon the surface, and are more carefully worked into the soil, than we are apt to think. If we subtract from the school system of the present day what belongs properly to our own time, — as modern history, science, and literature, — we still see how great a space is left, in what most strongly affects the habit of mind, to the purely traditional culture of

* The tenth century, it is true, is in a sort of eclipse, deeper perhaps than the darkness of either of the preceding; but this appears to be from moral or social causes rather than intellectual. What we may call the Catholic philosophy had, at all events, been well established in the ninth.

ancient languages and formal grammar. We may even doubt whether the most powerful educational influences, even now, do not run in the old channel, in our own best schools and colleges. Every educational reformer has been astonished, if not staggered, at the dead-weight of resistance he has encountered from classic prejudice.

It is, really, the momentum of more than two thousand years' unbroken tradition that we are dealing with. The methods we use to-day, if not the same with, were at least developed step by step from, the methods of children's schools in Athens and in Rome. Our best instruction in morals is exactly what we find in Plato's *Lysis;* the forms of words, the logic of structure, that we teach now, are the same that children were drilled in, conscientiously, in the Roman imperial schools. The same rules and forms were carefully instilled as school-rudiments, the same literary tradition was sacredly held fast, in all the ages that followed. They were retained with a clinging and (as it were) desperate tenacity through the barbarian times, as if there were some peculiar sanctity in this one living link of connection with the ancient splendor. When Rome was almost famished, beggared, and depopulated, there was still heart left to celebrate a literary holiday. On one occasion a new poem — a versifying of the Book of Acts — had to be recited in public seven times over, occupying many days in all, to satisfy crowds that could not all hear at once, and that insisted on the repeating of favorite passages. And, as Rome impressed the barbarian imagination in other ways, so it imposed respect for ancient letters, mixed possibly with a little awe. When the Goths were masters of Italy, it was publicly ordered (about 530) that the revenues of the public schools should be untouched. All else was fair plunder in the rage of conquest; but the generous barbarian would not take away what was to feed the life of coming generations.[*]

It would not be hard, though it might be pedantic, to trace the series of names that make an unbroken chain through the centuries of barbarism. I shall mention only two or three.

Cassiodorus, who lived, according to some accounts, to the great age of a hundred (463–563),[†] has been called the chief instructor of the barbarian world. He more than any other is the visible link between the old world of culture and the new. Till the age of seventy he was the confidential minister of Theodoric and his successor, Gothic kings of Italy; and his correspondence, under their names, is the best picture we have of that period of change. In particular, there are two letters addressed to Boëthius,[‡] the honored counsellor and afterwards the victim of Theodoric, which give a lively notion of the skill and intelligence of the age. One is in praise of music; one commissions him to send gifts to a Burgundian prince, a sun-dial and a water-clock; and he takes occasion to enlarge on these marvels of science, as we might on the electric light or the telephone. Evidently the argument is addressed not to Boëthius, the most cul-

---

[*] Cassiodorus, Epist., ix. 21.　Compare Ozanam, *Civilisation des Francs.*

[†] More probably 468–563.　　　　[‡] Lib. i. 45; ii. 40.

tivated man of his age, but to the imagination of rude, eager, curious men, such as made up these nations of invaders. In the tumult and ruin of the time, it is pathetic to see this eager clinging to the wealth of intelligence and art that seemed drifting to hopeless wreck. It was carrying on the same task in another way, when in his old age Cassiodorus withdrew to a monastery of Southern Italy, and spent his thirty remaining years in arranging, copying, correcting, restoring the treasures of classic learning, and in preparing the manuals of instruction that were of chief authority in the schools for the next few centuries.

I have already spoken of the Christian poets of this dark period — such as Prudentius, Sidonius, and Fortunatus; and of the pains they took to copy the form and preserve the diction of the Roman writers. We are apt, perhaps, to think of the Latin hymns, from Ambrose down, in very simple measures, accented and sometimes rhymed, as if they were the only poetry of the time; as if the classical model had quite perished. Nothing, on the contrary, strikes us oftener or sooner in looking through the body of the Christian literature, than the fond, abundant, often skilful handling of the metres of Virgil and Horace: in simple hymns, in narrative, in elegy, in familiar playful or occasional address, — sometimes a little awkward in phrase, with false quantities now and then that rasp the ear; but with serious painstaking that the literary art should not be lost. These poetic essays belong to every century, coming below the time and including the name of Charlemagne himself, who was a diligent learner in all arts of refinement, and whose epitaph on his personal and dear friend, Pope Adrian I. (to whom he had renewed and extended his father's grant in 774), is but a specimen of his very creditable skill.*

Doubtless, the value of this large body of Christian verse is not chiefly what it is in itself as poetry. It is rather a testimony to the faithful, patient, skilful school-instruction that went on from age to age. There was no contempt of pagan letters. The grave tone of Cicero's moral dialogues, and especially the prophetic strain of Virgil's fourth eclogue, in which he predicts a golden age of righteousness and peace, wholly won the Christian heart. Virgil's, it was said, was the golden key that opened to all classic antiquity the door of the Mediæval Church.†

Another thing is very noticeable in the large body of early Christian literature, — that is, from the fifth century to the ninth. It is the vast amount of com-

---

* If we were to set any date for the dying out of the classic literary tradition, it would be that assigned in the "Lament" already quoted. It is not until now that letters are quite overlaid by theology; it is not till about five centuries later that that heavy atmosphere has rolled quite away.

† This fondness for the name and memory of Virgil is illustrated in a legend which tells how St. Paul, on landing at Puteoli, went to pay his homage at the poet's tomb. The following verses are said at one time to have been chanted in the cathedral of Mantua : —

> Ad Maronis mausoleum
> Ductus, fudit super eum
>    Piæ rorem lacrimæ :
> " Quem te " inquit " reddidissem,
> Si te vivum invenissem,
>    Poëtarum maxime !"

And the chapel above the tomb used to be pointed out as the spot where Virgil went to hear mass.

ment and homily on the books of Scripture, the only recognized authority in religion, history, or morals; and especially dwelling on the historical record of Scripture, all the way down from the Creation. In itself this is not surprising in an age ignorant of almost everything else. Still, one is led to think there was a motive in thus incessantly directing the mind of barbarian converts to the detail of Hebrew annals, often far from edifying.* This motive we shall find, if we reflect that those barbarians were men, so to speak, *without a past*,— except it might be a very near and bloody one. To the barbarian mind the past closes up behind, like a bank of mist, hiding all but a few distorted and exaggerated forms. Thus —to take historic examples— the same Theodoric whom Cassiodorus served, and the Brunehild who figures in the recital of Gregory of Tours, became mythologic hero and heroine in the Nibelungen; or, to go farther back, the same Odin who ranks chief among the immortals in Scandinavian fable is held by some writers to have been the purely human leader of a migration out of Asia not many generations before.

This great void in the barbaric mind must be filled, or this wild phantasmagory displaced, by the Christian tradition. The rude tribe-life must be bound by religious association to the remotest past that could be conceived then, and widened to the broadest fellowship that might be consecrated by a common origin. Such crude ethnology as their teachers could

---

* Ulfilas, in translating the Bible for his Gothic converts, omitted "Samuel" and "Kings," since the barbarian passion for fighting had no need of such stimulus or sanction.

explain thus entered as an element in that long task of education.

This is as convenient a place as any to state an impression which flatly contradicts the notion some of us have got from other sources, as to the spirit of religious teaching in this period. The many volumes — some scores of thousands of pages — of early Catholic theology leave upon my mind a strong feeling of surprise at finding so little appeal to the vulgar terrors of the future world. I do not mean by this that the doctrine implied all along was not as grim and terrible as it has ever been. It is assumed, we may say, as a matter of course, that there is no salvation out of the true Church. It is taken for granted that the penalty of sin or unbelief is everlasting death, — or, a good deal worse, everlasting torment. But this lurid background *is a background* merely. It is not forced, as we might expect, upon the imagination of the believer. Rather, it is made simply an appeal to his conscience, and is, on the whole, greatly obscured by the emphasis laid on other things. No doubt cases might be quoted to qualify this statement. A few are readily recalled: a rhetorical flourish of Tertullian; an appeal or two of the somewhat harsh and gloomy Ambrose; a chapter in Augustine's "City of God"; and a paragraph of some twenty lines from a homily of Boniface to the barbarians, — hardly a faint echo, all told, of the terrors of the Apocalypse. But I should say (not as a fact, but as an impression) that there is more "blood-theology" and "hell-fire" — that is, the vivid setting forth of everlasting torment to terrify the soul — in one sermon of Jonathan Edwards, or one harangue at a modern "revival," than can be found in the whole body of homilies and epistles through all the Dark Ages put together. Purely speculative doctrine, such as the Trinity or the Sacrament, is abundantly urged. No emphasis can be strong enough to state the need of strict accuracy of one's belief as to the most abstract, mystic, unprovable, unintelligible points of faith, with an implied menace of dreadful consequences to the lack of faith. And the moral doctrine taught we may often censure as overstrained and unwholesome, or else coarse and low. But, set beside more modern dispensations, the Catholic exposition of this period is surprisingly merciful and mild. The Church had other and better business in hand, than to add the terrors of eternity to those of time, which were black enough already.

The sacred task of education, with its strong impelling motive, is brought even more vividly before us in the next name on the list, that of "the Venerable Bede" (673–735). I wish there were time to go a little into the detail of the sweet and patient labor of his life, or at least to repeat the gentle and pathetic story of his death.* Bede, or Baeda, with whom the title "venerable" has grown to be almost part of his name, is best known to us as the historian of the Saxon Church, from Augustine of Canterbury to within three years of his own death. That, however, is only a chapter of his very voluminous works. These include extended homilies and comments on

* It is well told in Green's " History of the English People "— with some slight affectations of speech, as Mr. Green's manner is.

almost all the Bible, and — more to our point — a
.considerable treatise on the learning of the day. It
begins with an essay on Orthography, the essential
basis of true learning then, when trained proof-readers
there were none, and all accuracy of speech was in
danger of being lost by unskilful copyists. Then come
the rules of Metre ; and then a series of treatises on
the Reckoning of Time, — a very perplexed thing
when there was no true astronomy, and when so
many festivals turned on arbitrary reckoning. Thus
the topic includes the whole science of arithmetic as
then known, and such knowledge of the sun and
moon as could be given, and the cause of eclipses,
and expositions of the calendar ; and these lead,
again, to some simple lore of meteorology, and the
cause of thunder, and how tides are affected by the
moon. Certainly we have not much to learn of natural science from these crude essays of near twelve
centuries ago. But we see, at least, that there were
leisure and intelligence to observe such things ; and
again we honor the high aim and motive of these
pious teachers.

The next name brings us down to the time we
have been looking back from. Alcuin, most famous
of all these teachers and men of learning, was born
in the year of Bede's death, and died ten years before
his friend and pupil Charlemagne (735–804). He
also was an Englishman, caught on his return from
Italy by the all-embracing Empire, and detained for
his life-work at Charles's court, or at his monastery-
school in Tours. He is the author of a great many
of the pious and occasional verses I have mentioned ;

and it is a little odd to hear him address the king as " my David," speak of himself as " Flaccus," and call his other friends by such names as " Homer " and the rest. Some of his letters and one or two dialogues turn on " enigmas," or plays upon words, riddles, and quaint forms of speech. These sportive efforts do not much disturb his gravity : the wit we may call ponderous and slow, the gravity genuine and sincere. His correspondence is a very long one, and includes some of our most curious pictures of the time. But you are more struck with the great share it gives to serious counsel : at least a third are letters of advice ; at least half, if we include all the appeals to religious and moral motive. Cheerful in the main, and always showing how close to his heart is the thought of friendship, he never forgets, or lets you forget, that he is first of all a teacher. His longest dialogue, and most vivacious,* is a compēnd of Latin grammar.

The above names do not give us the history, but they will serve to illustrate the course, of the Christian Schools down to the time of Charlemagne. One thing in particular should be noticed in regard to them. They are strictly schools of instruction, not of investigation or of philosophic thought. Their foundation is wholly on precedent, or else on dogma. Their task is simply to co-operate with the Church in its great work of civilization. Their instructions they take unquestioning from the Church, when not given outright in the literary tradition. A little they may

* Except an entertaining chapter of quirks and repartees in a conversation between Alcuin and the boy Pepin, son of Charlemagne

have done in the development of doctrine : as when
Bede comments on the texts of Paul, or Alcuin dis-
cusses the Adoptian heresy.*  Aside from such instances as these, we do not find a ray of original
thought or independent speculation in what has
proceeded from any of these schools.  Their great
teachers were content to be learners.†  Their work was
to instruct the childhood of a powerful race, and thus
prepare the way for what it should do in its maturity.

This task of preparation may be said to have come
to a natural term with the formation of the Christian
Empire.  That event marks, in a sense, the political
manhood of the race ; and, in a sense still more qualified, its mental emancipation.  It will be found, in
the history of literature, that the chief productive
periods of the human mind have generally come a
little after some great political event, or series of
events, that powerfully appealed to men's imagination ; that shifted their mental bearings, so to speak,
and compelled them to see all things in a new light.
So it was with the age of Pericles, in the generation
next after the great Persian war.  So it was with
the Augustan age, following the collapse of parties in
Rome.  So it was with the Elizabethan age, following
the violent shocks of the Reformation.  The ninth
century was no such brilliant period of literature and

---

* See below, page 262.

† Their modest course of preparatory instruction was the
*Trivium:* Grammar, Rhetoric, and Logic ; their narrow circle of
the sciences was the *Quadrivium:* Arithmetic, Geometry, Astronomy and Music ; as in the memorial verses : —

*Gram.* loquitur ; *Dia.* vera docet ; *Rhet.* verba colorat ;
*Mus.* canit ; *Ar.* numerat ; *G.* ponderat ; *As.* colit astra.

art as those ; yet its great fertility and comparative independence of intellect are naturally and justly to be associated with the momentous revolution in the State before described.

An occasion as well as a cause, however, is to be sought for any marked phase of mental activity ; and the nature of the occasion will determine the character of the phase. In this case, what we notice is a remarkable and sudden development of speculative philosophy, running in the old channels of theology, but widely overflowing its banks, and forming the head-water of streams that continued a great way farther down.

And for this we find not one occasion only, but two. The controversy with the Adoptionists, which was carried on at Frankfort in 794, and determined five years later at Aachen, had served to launch the Western mind upon the shoreless sea of transcendental metaphysics. In itself, the Adoptian heresy * was a form of Nestorianism which need not detain us here. It was developed in Spain by contact with the rigid and unimaginative monotheism of the Arabs, intolerant of mystic speculation ;† and had been car-

---

* Making Christ son of God *by adoption*.

† Another view, given by Peyrat (*Les Réformateurs au 12me Siècle*), is, that the view of Christ called " Adoptian " — and, in general, the " Arianism " of the German tribes — was derived from no Oriental source, but was native to the Gothic races which now occupied the country near the Pyrenees. It was a view which might naturally take the place of their belief in Balder, son of Odin, who had suffered death from the machinations of the Adversary, but was to return as Prince of a coming reign of peace. In this view, Christ was not *made out of nothing* (as held by Arius), but was Son of God, so to speak, in the ordinary sense.

ried over into France, to the perplexity of the priest-hood and the confusion of unsophisticated faith. It was easily vanquished in the church councils of that pious time ; but left a mental unrest that would be sure to show itself in some other way.

That other way was soon found. In the course of the Greek metaphysical discussions of the Trinity, some three or four hundred years before, certain writings had turned up, said to be by Dionysius the Are-·opagite, the one educated man at Athens that had been converted by Paul's address on Mars' Hill. Copies of them had found their way into France, where, tradition would have it, the same Dionysius had been one of the first teachers of Christianity, and was, in fact, the St. Denys whose name has rung since on so many a French battle-field. Very little was known of the contents, for these were in Greek ; and this, especially metaphysical Greek, few scholars of that day were competent to understand.

Among the rest, a copy beautifully written and adorned had been sent as a complimentary gift from the Eastern Emperor Michael to Louis, son of Charlemagne. It lay a good while in the imperial library, unread, — as presentation copies sometimes will ; and was overlooked in the disorders of Louis's unhappy reign. But his son Charles, who goes in history by the name of Bald, had inherited some of his mother's * brilliant gifts and his grandfather's love of letters ; and his court was the home of the most famous scholar of his age, John the Scot, known in the history of phi-

* The Empress Judith. His medallion shows something too of her beauty.

losophy as Scotus Erigena, that is, Irish-born.* For the British schools of learning, and especially the Irish schools, had been out of the reach of storms that blew upon the Continent; and we have already seen how the English Bede, Wilfried, and Alcuin had had a large share in keeping up the tradition of letters in Europe.

Of all the Christian Latin writers, Scotus Erigena was perhaps ablest up to this time, at any rate since Augustine, and certainly the most independent in his speculative temper. The poet, whose Lament I began by quoting, calls him "a man vain of speech, and garrulous, who has dared, forsooth, to define presumptuously of the Divine foreknowledge and decree; disputing by arguments of philosophy, without reason rendered, or alleging any authority of the Scriptures or holy Fathers; held in admiration, I hear, as a scholar and man of learning; who possesses all his hearers and admirers with his empty wordiness and windy talk, so that they no longer obey the authority of holy Scripture or the Fathers, but follow rather his fantastic babblings." This language sounds quite familiar: the bigotry of ignorance, or theologic terror of free thought, could not be more neatly expressed.

This famous scholar was set by Charles the Bald (about 850) to interpret the obscure writings of the

---

* His was the famous repartee which illustrates the court manners of those days. As he sat opposite Charles at dinner, he offended the nicer code of French manners, — possibly, passing his cup once too often, — which led the king to say, "What is the difference between a Scot and a Sot?" "Just a board's width," he instantly replied. [*Quid distat inter Scotum et Sottum? — Tabula tantum*]. At which the good-natured monarch laughed with the rest.

Alexandrian mystic who passed under the name of Dionysius the Areopagite; and it is not, perhaps, unfair to ascribe the extraordinary freedom of his own speculations to the intoxication of that contact.

Of the false Dionysius little need be said. He represents a line of independent tradition, that had come down, parallel with the orthodox dogma, from the early time of Gnosticism. It cropped out in many an Eastern heresy. It had blended more or less in the theology of many who did not forfeit their place of honor in the Church. Origen was not held free from the taint of it. Synesius, the famous "squire-bishop" of Ptolemais, held his Platonism as dear as his orthodoxy, and in his letters to Hypatia he addresses her as his teacher, his sister, his mother in philosophy. Particularly it throve in those schools of New-Platonists who tried to build up a spiritualized and diluted Paganism. Their hazy speculations, their incessant allegorizing, liken them to the Swedenborgians; their ecstasies and trances, giving them direct visions of divine things, their animal magnetism and natural magic, are the express counterpart of modern Spiritism. These acts, or nervous states, they had cultivated as part of their philosophic piety; and they make a curious double, reflex, or travesty of those high forms of Christian mysticism that have appeared from age to age.

In form, the Dionysian writings are fervently, we might say emulously, Christian. Jesus is "a most divine and super-essential soul"; the theosophic system they teach is the revelation of the Eternal Word. As we might anticipate, the Latin language reels and staggers in its effort to carry the weight of transcendental speculation, to find its way in the mazes of incessant allegory.*

Of the four Books, the first is on the "Celestial Hierarchy,"— one vast field of allegorizing on the scripture symbols of angels and archangels, cherubim, seraphim, thrones, powers, and dominions, that answer to the Gnostic genealogies. The second gives the "Ecclesiastical Hierarchy": that is, not of ranks and orders in the Church, but (as I understand it) the reflex or parallel, as it were, of the celestial order in variously gifted souls. The third, "on Divine Names," deals with such topics as being, life, likeness, unlikeness, motion, rest, and similar abstractions, setting forth, in particular, that Evil is nothing in itself, nor produced from anything that is, but is pure negation, — a doctrine which seems to have had a profounder effect than any other on the views of the translator. A very brief book follows "On Mystical Theology," closing with an astonishing period, in which all imaginable attributes are denied of the Universal Being, which is above all possible conceptions of human thought, as it is itself the crown of all things.†

---

* For example: "Ut ascendamus in deiformosissimam eorum simplicitatem per mysticas reformationes, et simul omnis ierarchicæ scientiæ principium laudabimus in divinitus præfatâ religiositate et teletarchicis gratiarum actionibus. . . . . Omnia igitur, quæ sunt, participant providentiam, ex superessentiali et causalissimâ divinitate manantem." — Lib. i. cap. 4.

† "Neque anima est, neque intellectus, neque phantasiam aut opinionem aut verbum aut intelligentiam habet. . . . . quoniam et super omnem positionem est perfecta et singularis omnium causa, super omnem ablationem excellentia omnium simpliciter perfectione, et summitas omnium." — Lib. iv. cap. 5.

I do not give this as a summary of that famous scheme of transcendental theology ; only to hint what ranges of speculation were thrown open by it. The writings of the false Dionysius have been held to be the real fountain-head of the vast flood of Scholastic theology ; and Scotus Erigena has been called first and greatest of the Schoolmen. I have not, however, to deal here with this line of speculation as a system of opinion. Of that we shall have more to say, when we come to the great age of Scholasticism. All we have to do now is to see its effect on the mind of the time we are dealing with, — the reality of its influence, and the nature of it.*

That influence is seen not so much in the questions that come up for discussion as in the treatment of those questions, and the nature of the arguments employed. As a system of doctrine, Scotus set his opinions forth in his most labored work, a long philosophic dialogue "On the Division of Things," — a treatise of mixed logic and metaphysics. The exposition of this belongs to a history of philosophy. In

* An interesting example of the speculative temper of the day is found in the correspondence of Servatus Lupus, Abbot of Fulda, who writes to Gottschalk of the beatific vision, doubting whether we can see the Divine glory in the resurrection with our fleshly eyes. "In this vision will consist at once our secure blessedness and our blessed security ; and for beholding it, the Truth admonishes that the eyes not of the body but of heart and mind be made clear." These words are the very echo of the Dionysian writings, or of St. Augustine. A little before, he has been discussing the quantity of Latin syllables ; a little after, he sets pitifully forth to Hincmar the desolate condition of his estate. "We have," he says, "to wear patched and worn-out clothes, and stay our hunger almost always with garden-stuff and market vegetables." See also his urgent letters on the same subject to Charles the Bald.

the history of theology his place is known as the antagonist of Gottschalk in the famous controversy on Predestination; and a few words on this become necessary, as part of the general history of the time.

Gottschalk was a Saxon monk, who had long brooded in his solitude over the works of Augustine, then of unquestioned authority; until he startled the theological mind of the day by the fervor, almost the fanaticism, of his assertion of a "double predestination," of the elect to life eternal, of the reprobate to everlasting death. This doctrine is, in moral tone, like that form of Calvinism which we should call Hopkinsian, — a doctrine of unspeakable horror to those who do not hold it, but of fervid and obstinate conviction to those who do; a doctrine which is the necessary logical result to all who hold consistently the view at once of absolute Divine foreknowledge and of an endless hell.

Of Gottschalk himself hardly anything remains except his two Confessions, which consist of little else than a very positive statement of that one thing. He is spoken of in a letter from Hincmar to Pope Nicholas, as "a man of high-strung temper (*animo elatus*), impatient of repose, fond of new phrases, burning with quenchless thirst of reputation, vehement and fractious." We should have called him rather moody, gloomy, and intractable. "He was condemned in a council at Mentz," Hincmar goes on to say, and "by their order severely beaten with rods." To that rude and secular clergy this was easier than a contest of logic. They would rather fight in battle (and very likely did), or hunt with hawks and hounds.

Gottschalk, in fact, was far too confident of his opinion to trust it to the mercy of any logic. The judgment of God, to the mind of that age, was best to be known by ordeal. "Set me here," said he, "four vessels in a row; fill one with boiling water, one with heated oil, one with hot pitch, and one with blazing fire; and let me, to prove this faith of mine, which indeed is the Catholic faith, go into and pass through each one of them." This grim fatalism had its natural effect, in wild despair with some, in reckless antinomianism with others.

Hincmar himself, the great domineering prelate, tried his hand at the sad, impracticable dogmatist, and thought to bring him over by a compromise which taught God's foreknowledge and predestination of the good, his foreknowledge and permission only of the evil. But such weakness was not for Gottschalk, who chose rather to be shut up in prison, and in fact ended his days there, deluded by visions, his morbid temper made really insane, but sturdily holding his rigid creed. As with Calvin, he saw nothing in all the world, evil or good, salvation or damnation, that was not the express act of God.

So, as the ablest philosopher of the day, Scotus Erigena was drawn into the debate. But, in opposing Gottschalk's doctrine of arbitrary destiny, he opposed just as much the church doctrine of creation and the fall, of sin and judgment. His language was as devout, and his claim of authority as sincere; but the whole dogmatic scheme melted away in the mist of his abstractions. True philosophy, said he, is true religion; true religion is true philosophy. To him, there is nothing arbitrary anywhere; no room seems left for what we should call freedom, human or divine, only one broad " Stream of Tendency." Harmony with that is apparently the real freedom he asserts. That universal life, that flood of eternal light, pours with absolute impartiality upon all; it falls on men, according to their nature, whether for blessing or curse. As a blind eye cannot see the light, as an inflamed eye is only pained by the light which yet is meant for blessing to all, so with the ignorant or sinful soul. "There is no misery," he said, "except eternal death; eternal death is ignorance of the truth, and there is no misery but ignorance of the truth; and where the truth is unknown there is no life."

There is, again, no beginning of creation with God, and no end of things except that all shall be received back into the one source of life. In his own essence God cannot be known : his personality is simply "an act of man's imagination"; the revelation of Scripture is only figurative and symbolic. Existence itself is more and more abstract as it becomes more real; in its highest form it cannot even be conceived. The divine trinity is Being, Wisdom, Life; and to this answers the trinity in man's nature, — to be, to know, to will. The "division of nature" is fourfold : — 1. That which creates and is uncreated, — the First Cause ; 2. That which is created and creates, — second causes ; 3. That which is created and does not create, — things as known in time and space ; 4. That which neither creates nor is created, — under which head will come the world of Evil. This logical formality is the groundwork of an immense amount of allegorical interpretation ; it is also the formal pattern, or type, of the ponderous discussions known as the Scholastic philosophy of the Middle Age.

Much of the language I have quoted is familiar to us now ; but it was strange and alarming then, particularly in the inference which Scotus seems to draw. His theory denies the possibility of Evil, which to the common mind is the most real of existences. His logic leads us straight to a pantheistic Fatalism, as that he opposed declares an arbitrary Destiny. Everything is swallowed up in the vague impersonality of Pantheism. All life is one. Human freedom is lost in the Divine necessity. Guilt itself is the only penalty of guilt. Nay, evil itself, of any sort, is only the negation of good : it is nothing of itself ; and, being nothing, of course it could neither be predestined nor foreknown. To which we may add, that it could not be committed, either.

But our business is not with his philosophical system, or with the events of his life, which are very obscure ; only with his place in history. It is probable that he took part in the discussion raised by Radbert's doctrine, that the bread and wine of the Eucharist are literally the body and blood of Christ ; *

* This discussion (of which an eminently satisfactory account is given by Neander) opens in the period we have been reviewing, and embraces several names hardly less eminent than those already cited, particularly the great encyclopedist of the age, Rabanus Maurus, and the keen theologian Ratramnus (or Bertram). The doctrine, however, belongs strictly to the mediæval system of thought, and will be more appropriately considered elsewhere. The same may be said of the discussion respecting the Forged Decretals, — associated with the names of Radbert and Hincmar, — which first appeared during this century (about 850).

and one may imagine the cheerfulness with which he would bring allegory to bear on that great mystery. To him, the Real Presence is not in the bread and wine only, but in all things. The striking thing to notice is the positive and (as it were) unconscious tone in which he sets aside all authority except that of reason. "Authority," he says, "proceeds from right reason; reason by no means from authority. All authority not approved by right reason is invalid. Right reason needs to be strengthened by no agreement with authority."

These are brave nineteenth-century words. It is likely that their reach and force were not felt then, whatever uneasy jealousy they may have stirred. It does not appear that Scotus lost favor in court or school; or that the death he was said to have suffered — stabbed with styles (pricked to death, as we should say, with steel pens) by a mob of students — had any other motive than the sharpness of his discipline. Some have called him "a saintly man through and through"; others have carped at his fame, as "a liar, a fool, a madman, and a heretic." A glance through his writings shows a wide contrast between his purely intellectual method — whether we call it religious mysticism or speculative pantheism — and all the church theologians from Augustine down. So that to us the interest in him is not merely as a scholar or a philosopher, the father of mediæval speculation, but, still more, as the forerunner, by nearly a thousand years, of the newest forms of transcendental free thought.

I have spoken of the time of Charlemagne and his

successors of the next half-century as an age of early revival; and have indicated some of the causes and results that seem to justify this view. In one sense, the revival was not only early, but premature, and it faded quickly. Hardly anything seems left, a century later, of what had such vigor and promise. As when wheat is sown in autumn, the fields were green a little while, and then buried under a sudden change of season. The real growth, and the real harvest, came after the winter that followed. The change that passed over the face of society with the breaking-up of the short-lived Empire, and that seemed to undo the whole fabric so painfully built together, — nay, to overwhelm learning, religion, and morality in a common wreck, — we call by the general name of Feudalism, whose relations with the Church make the plot of the vast drama which we know as the history of the Middle Age.

# CHRONOLOGICAL OUTLINE.

[Many of the earlier dates are uncertain.  The mark † denotes the year of death; ✠ indicates the name of a Pope.]

|  |  |  |
|---|---|---|
|  | EMPERORS. |  |
| B. C. 30. | AUGUSTUS. |  |
| A. D. 14. | TIBERIUS. | 25. Pilate in Judæa. |
|  |  | 30. THE CRUCIFIXION. |
| 37. | CALIGULA. | Conversion of Paul. |
| 41. | CLAUDIUS. | Simon Magus. |
|  |  | 50. Council at Jerusalem. |
| 54. | NERO. |  |

64. Conflagration of Rome.  First Persecution. Death of Paul.

| 69. | VESPASIAN. | 70. Destruction of Jerusalem. |
| 79. | TITUS. |  |
| 81. | DOMITIAN. | Cerinthus. |

95. Persecution; death of Clement.

| 96. | NERVA. |  |
| 98. | TRAJAN.  Edict against Secret Societies. |  |
| **100.** | Pliny in Bithynia : Correspondence with Trajan. |  |

*Apostolic Fathers :* Ignatius † 115.

| 117. | HADRIAN. | Polycarp † 165. |

*Gnostics :* Basilides (c. 130).

Valentinus (c. 150).

| 138. | ANTONINUS PIUS. | Marcion (c. 150). |

*Apologists :* Justin † 168.

Athenagoras † 180.

| 161. | MARCUS AURELIUS. |

*Montanism* (chiefly in Asia Minor).

177. Martyrs of Lyons (Pothinus, Blandina).

*Alexandrian School :* Pantænus † 202.

| 180. | COMMODUS. | Clement † 220. |

*Western Church :* Irenæus (Gaul) † 202.

| 193. | SEPTIMIUS SEVERUS. | Tertullian (Africa) † 220. |

**200.** 202. Martyrs of Carthage (Perpetua, Felicitas.)
211. CARACALLA.
218. ELAGABALUS. *Christian Writers.*
222. ALEXANDER SEVERUS. Hippolytus † 236.
    238. Invasion of Franks. Origen † 254.
    241. " of Burgundians. Cyprian † 258.
249–251. DECIUS. Persecution.
    ·NOVATIAN SCHISM. Sabellius † 260.
    PAUL the Hermit † 351. Paul of Samosata † 275.
260. GALLIENUS. Edict of Toleration.
270. AURELIAN. Captivity of Zenobia.
    272. *Goths settled in Dacia.*
284. DIOCLETIAN (to 305): two Augusti and two Cæsars.
**300.** GENERAL PERSECUTION.
306. CONSTANTINE. 312. Defeats Maxentius.
    Lactantius † 330.
    313. *Edict of Milan.* DONATIST SCHISM.
314–336. ✠ SYLVESTER I.
    ARIAN CONTROVERSY. 325. *Council of Nicæa.*
    Eusebius † 340.
337. CONSTANTIUS. *Eastern Monasticism.*
    Athanasius † 373.
    St. Anthony (251–356). Basil, 329–379.
361. JULIAN (the Apostate). Gregory Naz., 330–391.
364. VALENTINIAN, VALENS.
    375. *Goths in Mœsia.* Gregory Nyss., 331–395.
    378. Battle of Adrianople. Chrysostom, 347–407.
379. THEODOSIUS. 381. *Council of Constantinople.*
Suppression of Pagan Worship. St. Martin in Gaul.
    Ambrose, 340–397.
395. ARCADIUS (East) and HONORIUS (West).
    Jerome, 340–420.
**400.** 410. Sack of Rome by **Alaric.** Augustine, 354–430. )
    PELAGIAN CONTROVERSY.
408–450. THEODOSIUS II. 423–455. VALENTINIAN III.
    429. **Vandals in Africa.** 431. *Council of Ephesus.*
440–461. ✠ LEO I. (the Great). 445. Edict of **Valentinian.**
    451. **Huns:** Defeat of **Attila.** *Council of Chalcedon.*
    MONOPHYSITE CONTROVERSY.
    St. Severinus in Germany.
476. **Odoacer.** Fall of Western Empire.
    482. *Henoticon* of Zeno. 484. Schism of East and West.
493–526. **Theodoric:** Gothic Kingdom of Italy (to 554).
    496. Conversion of **Clovis.**
    *Merovingian Kingdom in France.*

**500.**    493. *Gothic Kingdom of Italy.*

Cassiodorus, 468–563.

518–527. JUSTIN, Emperor of the East.

519. Reconciliation of East and West.

Benedict at Monte Casino, 529–543.

527–565. JUSTINIAN.   Reform of Roman Law.

533–548. Conquests of Belisarius.

554. Gothic kingdom destroyed by Narses.

568. *Lombard Kingdom in Italy.*

St. Columba at Iona † 600.

Gregory of Tours, 540–595.

590–604. ✠ GREGORY I. (the Great); Augustine in England, 597.

**600.**    St. Columban in Gaul † 615.

St. Gall in Switzerland † 627.

622.  **Mahomet** (Hegira).    Isidore of Seville † 630.

632–732. *Conquests of Mahometanism.*

MONOTHELETE CONTROVERSY.

668, 716. Constantinople besieged by Arabs.

687. **Pepin** (d'Heristal) founds the Carolingian House.

**700.**    Bede (the Venerable), 672–735.

711.  *Saracen Conquest of Spain.*

718–741.  LEO III. (*Isauricus*), Emperor.

IMAGE CONTROVERSY.

732.  Battle of Tours: Saracens defeated by **Charles Martel.**

St. Boniface in Germany † 755.

741–752.  ✠ ZACHARY.   752. Coronation of **Pepin.**

755. Donation of Pepin (extended, 774).

771.  **Charles** (*Charlemagne*), king of Franks.

772–795.  ✠ ADRIAN I.    774. Conquest of Lombards.

ADOPTIAN CONTROVERSY.

787. *2d Council of Nicæa.*    794. *Council of Frankfort.*

795–816.  ✠ LEO III.    .    Alcuin, 735–804.

**800.**  CHARLEMAGNE, Emperor of the West.

THE HOLY ROMAN EMPIRE.

814.  LOUIS I. (the Pious). Anschar, Apostle of the North, † 865.

843. Partition of the Empire.  FEUDALISM.

843–877.  CHARLES II. (the Bald).    Scotus Erigena † 877.

858–867.  ✠ NICHOLAS I.    *Forged Decretals.*

# INDEX.


I. The Messiah and the Christ, 1-20. — The Messianic hope, 2. Chronological outlook, 3. Sources of the Messianic hope, 6; its character, 8. A national passion (parallels), 9. The Messianic period, 12. Sermon on the Mount, 14. Messianic consciousness of Jesus, 16. The entrance into Jerusalem, 17. The hope transfigured by his death, 19.

II. Saint Paul, 21-46. — The primitive Church, 23; power of the communistic sentiment, 25. Conversion of Paul, 28. His personal characteristics, 29; his trials and contentions, 30; jealousies towards him, 32; his death, 34. Writings of Paul, 35; his Christology, 36; his doctrine of sin and justification, 40; his conviction of sin and assurance of salvation, 44.

III. Christian Thought of the Second Century, 47-70. — A gulf of eighty years, 48; development of doctrine during this period: the Logos, 50. A longing for Redemption, 51; how conceived, 52. The Gnostics, 54; the problem of Gnosticism, 57; scheme of Valentinus, 58; failure of Gnosticism, and why, 60. The Apologists, 61; character of their Defence, 62; seriousness of the Christian mind at this period, 63. Relations to the Roman world, 65; calumnies against the Christians, 66; Montanism; results of this period, 69.

IV. The Mind of Paganism, 71-99. — A Pagan Revival, 72; Cicero, 73; a religion of the Empire, 74. Doctrine of the Stoics, 75; cosmogony, 75; ethics, 76. Law Reform, 78. Persecution of Christianity, 80. The old Italian religion, 81; gods of the Nursery, 83; the great gods, 84; Rome as an object of worship, 86; her tyranny, 87. Peace of the Empire, 88; the Emperor deified, 89; formal worship of the Emperor, 91; collision with Christianity, 92; Marcus Aurelius, 93; degradation and decline of this worship, 95. Oriental superstitions, 96; sacrifices, 97; the *taurobolium*, 98. Ideas of Incarnation and Sacrifice, 99.

V. The Arian Controversy, 100-121. — Accession of Constantine, 100. Doctrinal development meanwhile, 101; analysis of the Logos-idea, 102. Sabellius and Arius, 105. Christianity and Paganism, 107. The method of Faith, 109. Character of Arianism, 110. Constantine, his character and circumstances, 112; at the Council of Nicæa, 115; the Nicene Creed, 116. Athanasius, his adventures and character, 117. Results of the Controversy, 119; the triumph of Orthodoxy, 120.

VI. SAINT AUGUSTINE, 122–145. — His doctrine and character, 122; his place in history, 125. Circumstances of his life, 126; terror of the time, 127. His Conversion, 129; a reaction against Manichæism, 130; the Manichæan dualism, 131; a system of fatalism, 133; nature of the crisis, 135; source of Evil, 136. The Pelagian Controversy; destiny and moral freedom, 137; Augustine and Pelagius, 138; issue of the controversy, 139. The *City of God*, 141; time of its completion, 142; the ancient city, 143; moral effect of the work, 144.

VII. LEO THE GREAT, 146–164. —Character of the period; a Pagan reaction, 147. Controversies of the Fifth Century, 150; Nestorius and Eutyches; the "robber-synod," 151. Character of Leo, 152; the saviour of Rome, 153; conception of his work, 154; the Council of Chalcedon, 156; faith in the destinies of Rome, 157; his ecclesiastical policy, 159; Hilary of Arles, 161. Creation of the Papal Power, 163.

VIII. MONASTICISM AS A MORAL FORCE, 165–184. — Christianity as a conflict, 165; need of a reserve force, 166; enormous evils of Pagan society, 168; horrors of the Roman spectacles, 169. The martyr-spirit: Perpetua, 171. The ascetic motive, 173; Simeon Stylites, 174; the moral craving and habit of sacrifice; examples of Eastern asceticism, 175. The monk Telemachus, 178. The monk and the barbarian, 180; Benedict (of Nursia) at Monte Casino, 181; the monastic vow, 183.

IX. CHRISTIANITY IN THE EAST, 185–203. — Contrast of East and West, 185; in language, 186; in political life, 187. Qualities of Eastern religious life, 188; illustrated by four great divines, 190; effect on the vitality of the Greek language, 192. Reign of Justinian, 193; his conquests and public works, 194; Monophysite and Monothelete controversies, 195. Image-Controversy, 196; forms of image-worship, 197. Mahomet, 198; spread and conquests of Islamism, 199; its strength and weakness, 201.

X. CONVERSION OF THE BARBARIANS, 204–226. — A larger conception of the Christian work, 205; a three centuries' campaign, 206; comparison of Imperial and Papal Rome, 207; spirit of the enterprise, 208. The Barbarian as he appeared: testimonies, 209. Clovis and his House, 211; the "Merovingian times," 212. The Conversions: examples; what were they worth? 214. Gregory the Great, 217; conversion of the Saxons, 218. Boniface, the Apostle of Germany, 219. Anschar, the Apostle of the North, 224.

XI. THE HOLY ROMAN EMPIRE, 227–248. — The imperial idea, 228; Rome as it impressed the barbarian mind, 231; the barbarian conquerors, 233; Clovis as Patrician, 234. Donation of Pepin, 235. Coronation of Charlemagne, 236; his conquests and administration: details, 237; his ídeal of sovereignty, 240; reverence for his memory, 244. The period of organization, 244; ultimate divorce and rivalry of Church and Empire, 245; the mediæval conflict, 246; later fortunes of the Empire, 247.

XII. THE CHRISTIAN SCHOOLS, 249–273. — Partition of the Empire, — the loss to civilization, 249; its care for learning, 250; the classic tradition, 251; the imperial Schools, 252. Cassiodorus as minister of Theodoric, 253; as a monastic recluse, 254. The barbarian mind; how instructed, 256; mild doctrine of the Church, 257. The Venerable Bede, 258. Alcuin: his writings, 260; the Adoptian controversy, 262. Writings of Dionysius (the Areopagite), 263; Scotus Erigena, 264. Gottschalk: controversy on Predestination, 268; doctrine of the non-existence of Evil, 271. The intellectual development is checked by the invasion of Feudalism, 273.


Adoptian Controversy, 262.

Adrianople, battle of, 114, 120, 148.

Æons of the Gnostics, 58, 59.

Alaric, 129, 148, 232.

Alcuin, 260.

Alexandrian Jews, 5; theology, 50.

Ambrose, 120.

Anschar, Apostle of the North, 224.

Apollinaris, 150.

Apologists, character of their defence, 62, 68.

Apostolic Fathers, 48. .

Arabia, 200.

ARIAN CONTROVERSY, 100–121; civilization of Goths and Burgundians, 211, n.

Arianism. 110; its drift, 111.

Arius, 105.

Asceticism, its motive, 175.

Athanasius, 117; his adventures and character, 118.

AUGUSTINE, 122–145; his character, 123, 125; circumstances of his time, 126; his conversion, 130; controversy with Manichæism, 132; with Pelagius, 137; the City of God, 141.

Attila and Leo, 152, 233.

Babylon, Jews in, 5.

Barbarians, their aspect, 209; the barbarian mind, 256.

Bar-cochab, 12.

Basil (the Great), 190.

Basilides (the Gnostic), 61.

Bede (the Venerable), 258.

Belisarius, his conquests, 193.

Benedict, St., founder of monastic rule, 181.

Boniface, Apostle of the Germans, 219; his catechism, 221; his death, 223.

Byzantine Empire, 189.

Cæsar, 82, 88.

Calvin and Augustine, 140.

Cassiodorus, 181, 253.

Chalcedon, Council of, 147, 194.

Charges against Christians, 66, 67.

Charity, what it means, 124.

Charles Martel, 202, 234; relations with Boniface, 223.

Charles (Charlemagne), 235; his coronation, 236; conquests and administration, 237; effects of his reign. 240; character and memory, 244.

Charles the Bald, 263.

Church, causes of its early growth, 25; its relations to the Roman world, 65, 92.

Cicero, as representing Pagan thought, 73.
Circumcellions, 173.
City of God, 141; the ancient city, 143.
Classic tradition, 251.
Clement of Alexandria, 63.
Clovis, his conversion, 211; his descendants, 212; as Patrician, 234.
Columban, his monastic rule, 215.
Commodus, 95.
Communistic spirit of early Church, 26.
Confessors, 61.
Constantine, 100, 227; his character, 112; legislation, 113; at the Council of Nicæa, 115.
Council of Nicæa, 106, 115; of Ephesus, 151; of Chalcedon, 116, 156; later councils, 195, 196.
Creed, Nicene, 116.
Daniel, 4; date, 6; predictions, 7.
Destiny and moral freedom, 139; Mahometan doctrine of, 201.
Diocletian, 80, 114.
Dionysius the Areopagite, 263, 265.
Divinities of Rome, 84.
Donatist Schism, 125, 173.
Dualism (Manichæan), 131.
EAST (Christianity in), 185–203; separation from the West, 186.
Education a care of the State, 250
Eginhard (Einhard), biographer of Charlemagne, 240, 242.
Emanation or Evolution, 58.
Emperor (Roman), as a Divinity, 89.
Empire, Peace of the, 88; ideal of, 227; restored under Charlemagne, 236; mediæval, 247.
EMPIRE (Holy Roman), 227–248.
Ephesus, Council of, 151; robber-synod, 156.
Ethics of New Testament, 43.
Eutyches, 151, 156.

Evil, Pauline doctrine of, 42; Gnostic doctrine, 66; Manichæan, 133.
Faith, the method of, 109.
*Filioque*, 120, 186.
Formalism of Roman religion, 81.
Fulda, foundation of, 222.
Gnosticism, its early appearance, 54; its character, 55; its problem, 57; its doctrine, 59; its failure (cause of), 60.
Goths, their victory over Valens, 114, 120; their Arian civilization, 211, *n.*
Gottschalk, 268.
Gracchi, the, 88.
Greek language, its subtilty, 186; its vitality, 192.
Gregory of Nazianzus, 190; of Nyssa, *id*; of Tours, 211; the Great, 205, 217.
Henoticon of Zeno, 194.
Herod, 4.
Hilary of Arles, 161.
Hincmar, 268.
Huns, as described by Jornandes, 210; their defeat at Troyes, 157.
Hypatia, 148.
Hypostasis, 102, 116.
Image-worship, 197; controversy, 196–198.
Interval after the Pauline period, its importance in history, 47.
Islamism, 201. [84.
Italian worship, 81; the great gods, Jerome, 209.
Jesus of Nazareth, his messianic consciousness, 13, 16; his moral teaching, 14; the entrance into Jerusalem, 17.
Justification by faith, 45, 137.
Justin Martyr, 63, 64, 68.
Justinian, reign of, 193, 194.
Law, Roman, reform of, 78.

LEO THE GREAT, 146–164; his character, 152; deliverance of Rome, 153; faith in the destiny of Rome, 157, 206; assertion of papal claims, 160.

Leo, the Isaurian, 197.

Logos, doctrine of, 40, 51, 76, 101; how interpreted, 106.

Maccabæan period, 3.

Mahomet, 196.

Malachi, 3.

Mani (or Manes), founder of Manichæism, 132.

Manichæism, 131; a system of fatalism, 133.

Marcion, 68.

Mariolatry, 151, 195.

Martyrs, 171.

MESSIAH AND CHRIST, 1–20.

Messianic predictions, 6; hope, its character, 8, 11; period, 12; how transformed, 19, 37, 142.

Miracles in the early Church, 23.

MONASTICISM, 165–184; in the West, 166; its root in the moral nature, 175; monastic vows, 182.

Monks as missionaries, 180.

Monophysite (single-nature), and

Monothelete (single-will), 195.

Montanism, 69.

Mythology: Roman compared with Greek, 85.

Nestorius, 151.

New Paganism, 74.

New Platonism, 148, 265.

Nicæa. Council of, 106, 115.

Nicene Creed, 112, 116.

Numina (functions of divinity), 84.

Nursery-gods of Rome, 83.

Odoacer (or Odovaker), 233.

Ovid, myth of Numa, 81.

PAUL (the Apostle), 21–46; his character, 22, 30; person, 29; trials, 32; death, 34; writings, 35;

doctrine of Christ, 36; of sin and justification, 40.

Pagan virtues, 41; worship, destruction of, 127.

PAGANISM, MIND OF, 71–99; revival of, 74; its weakness, compared with Christianity, 107; suppressed by Theodosius, 127; reaction, 147; its hold on the imagination, 149.

Papal power, its growth, 163; its extent, 206.

Paschasius Radbert, 224, 271.

Pelagius, 137.

Persecution of Christianity, 66, 80.

Philo, 5, 50.

Radegonda, 212.

Redemption, the gospel of, 51.

Religion of Rome, 86; it discourages emotion, 96; of the humbler classes, 95.

Resurrection, 24; doctrine of, 64.

Rome as a divinity, 87; taken by Alaric, 129; its spiritual and military empire, 206; how viewed by the barbarians, 231.

Sabellius, 105.

Sacrifice of Christ, 19; in Antiquity, 81, 97, 99.

Saints of the ascetic period, 175; of the missionary period, 216.

Salvation, how taught by Paul, 45; the aim of the gospel, 52.

Saracen conquests, 202.

Scandinavia, how converted, 225.

Schools, imperial, 252; of the ninth century, 261.

Scotus Erigena, 264, 267–271.

SECOND CENTURY, Christian Thought of, 47–70.

Second coming of Christ, 19, 25, 37.

Simeon Stylites, 174.

Simon Magus, 32.

Son of God, interpretation of the phrase, 102.

Spectacles at Rome, 148, 169.
Stephen, martyrdom of, 28, 44.
Stoic doctrines, 75; cosmogony, 76; morals, 77; failure of, 78.
Symbol, value of, 104.
Tatian, 64.
Taurobolium, 98.
Telemachus, the monk, 178.
Tertullian, 60, 68; his testimony, 79, 168.

Thekla, St. 172.
Theodosius, 120, 127.
Tours, battle of, 202.
Trajan, 66, 93, 128.
Valentinus, the Gnostic, 55, 60.
Vandals, 160, 194.
Virgil, his anticipation of a golden age, 74; regard of him in Christian tradition, 255.

THE END.

University Press: John Wilson & Son, Cambridge.